The Explosive World of Tatyana N. Tolstaya's Fiction

Writers'
WORLDS

The series publishes interdisciplinary studies of the fictional universes created by authors of international stature.

Series Editor:
Vladimir Padunov, University of Pittsburgh

The Explosive World of Tatyana N. Tolstaya's Fiction
Helena Goscilo

Also from M. E. Sharpe

The Marginal World of Ōe Kenzaburo
Michiko Niikuni Wilson

Fruits of Her Plume: Essays on Contemporary Russian Women's Culture
Edited by Helena Goscilo

Writers'
WORLDS

The Explosive World of Tatyana N. Tolstaya's Fiction

Helena Goscilo

M.E. Sharpe
Armonk, New York
London, England

Library of Congress Cataloging-in-Publication Data

Goscilo, Helena, 1945–
The explosive world of Tatyana N. Tolstaya's fiction / by Helena Goscilo.
p.   cm.—(Writers' worlds)
Includes bibliographical references and index.
ISBN 1-56324-858-1 (c : alk. paper)
ISBN 1-56324-859-x (p: alk. paper)
1. Tolstaia, Tat′iana, 1951–   —Criticism and interpretation.
I. Title.
II. Series.
PG3476.T58Z67   1996
891.73′44—dc20
96-14577
CIP

Printed in the United States of America

The paper used in this publication meets the minimum requirements of the
American National Standard for Information Sciences—
Permanence of Paper for Printed Library Materials,
ANSI Z 39.48-1984.

♾

BM (c)   10   9   8   7   6   5   4   3   2   1
BM (p)   10   9   8   7   6   5   4   3   2   1

To Bożenka,
with love and lasting gratitude
for those "mira" and "mini" moments
and for a fully shared life

Contents

Born in Leningrad in 1951, Tatyana Tolstaya majored in philology and classics at Leningrad State University, from which she graduated in 1974. Upon moving to Moscow, she worked for eight years as an editor at the Nauka Publishing House. She made her literary debut in 1983 and four years later published a slim collection of her short stories, titled *On the Golden Porch*. Her first stint as writer in residence at the University of Richmond (in Virginia) during 1988 was followed by stays at a variety of universities and centers in the capacity of visiting writer, lecturer, and fellow. Now a permanent resident of the United States, since 1994 Tolstaya has held the post of Associate Professor in the English Department at Skidmore College, where she teaches creative writing and Russian literature.

Annotated Bibliography
of Tolstaya's Works

True to long-standing Russian and Soviet traditions, all of Tolstaya's twenty-one short stories were first published in literary journals or magazines. Her twenty-second "story" appeared in the émigré journal *Sintaksis*. *"Na zolotom kryl'tse sideli . . ." (On the Golden Porch)*, the only collection of her prose issued in Russia, contains thirteen of her stories (identified below by an asterisk [*]). An anthology of her other narratives slated for publication never materialized, for at the galley-proof stage insuperable financial difficulties caused the publishing house to close down.

The bibliographical items that follow are listed alphabetically and confine themselves to Tolstaya's fiction in Russian, omitting her many interviews, reviews, critical commentary, and satire:

*"Chistyi list." *Neva* 12 (1984): 116–26.
*"Fakir." *Novyi mir* 12 (1986): 119–30.
*"Krug." *Oktiabr'* 4 (1987): 99–104.
"Limpopo." *Sintaksis* 27 (1990): 75–121 and *Znamia* 11 (1991): 45–70.
*"Liubish'—ne liubish'." *Oktiabr'* 4 (1987): 89–95.
*"Milaia Shura." *Oktiabr'* 12 (1985): 113–17.
*" 'Na zolotom kryl'tse sideli. . . .' " *Avrora* 8 (1983):94–101.
*"Na zolotom kryl'tse sideli . . .". Moscow: Molodaia gvardiia, 1987.
"Noch'." *Oktiabr'* 4 (1987): 95–99.
*"Ogon' i pyl'." *Avrora* 10 (1986): 82–91.
*"Okhota na mamonta." *Oktiabr'* 12 (1985): 117–21.
*"Peters." *Novyi mir* 1 (1986): 123–31.
"Plamen' nebesnyi." *Avrova* 11 (1987): 130–39.
"Poet i muza." *Novyi mir* 12 (1986): 113–19.
*"Reka Okkervil'." *Avrora* 3 (1985): 137–46.
"Samaia liubimaia." *Avrora* 10 (1986): 92–110.
"Serafim." *Novyi mir* 12 (1986): 130–33.
"Siuzhet." *Sintaksis* 31 (1991): 100–9.
"Somnambula v tumane." *Novyi mir* 7 (1988): 8–26.
*"Sonia." *Avrora* 10 (1984): 76–83.

*"Spi spokoino, synok." *Avrora* 4 (1986): 94–101.
*"Svidanie s ptitsei." *Oktiabr'* 12 (1983): 52–57.
"Vyshel mesiats iz tumana." *Krest'ianka* 4 (1987): 32–35.

Only one narrative by Tolstaya, the idiosyncratic "Plot" ("Siuzhet"), has not been rendered into English. The rest are contained in two anthologies:

- Tatyana Tolstaya, *On the Golden Porch*. Trans. Antonina W. Bouis. New York: Alfred A. Knopf, 1989.

   Riddled with inaccuracies, though adept at intimating the energy and richness of Tolstaya's prose, Bouis's renditions were enthusiastically reviewed. The contents are as follows:

   "Loves Me, Loves Me Not"
   "Okkervil River"
   "Sweet Shura"
   " 'On the Golden Porch' "
   "Hunting the Wooly Mammoth"
   "The Circle"
   "A Clean Sheet"
   "Fire and Dust"
   "Date with a Bird"
   "Sweet Dreams, Son"
   "Sonya"
   "The Fakir"
   "Peters"

- Tatyana Tolstaya, *Sleepwalker in a Fog*. Trans. Jamey Gambrell. New York: Alfred A. Knopf, 1992.

   Scrupulous accuracy to the original marks Gambrell's English versions, which consist of the following:

   "Sleepwalker in a Fog"
   "Serafim"
   "The Moon Came Out"
   "Night"
   "Heavenly Flame"
   "Most Beloved"
   "The Poet and the Muse"
   "Limpopo"

Other translations of individual stories or earlier, separate publications of Gambrell's renditions are listed below in alphabetical order:

"Heavenly Flame." Trans. Jamey Gambrell. *The New Yorker*. October 15, 1990: 43–48.

"Night." Trans. Mary F. Zirin. *Glasnost: An Anthology of Literature under Gorbachev*, ed. Helena Goscilo and Byron Lindsey. Ann Arbor: Ardis, 1990, 187–94.

"Peters." Trans. Mary F. Zirin. *Balancing Acts*, ed. Helena Goscilo. Bloomington: Indiana University Press, 1989, 6–18. Repr. Dell, 1991, 8–27.

"The Poet and the Muse." Trans. Jamey Gambrell. *The New Yorker*. January 15, 1990: 36–42.

"Sleepwalker in a Fog." Trans. Jamey Gambrell. *Soviet Women Writing*, ed. Jacqueline Decter. New York: Abbeville Press, 1990, 51–84.

"Sonia." Trans. Nancy Condee. *Newsletter*, Institute of Current World Affairs, No. 17.

The Explosive World of Tatyana N. Tolstaya's Fiction

Introduction

Of all contemporary Russian women writers, none catapulted onto the Western cultural scene more dramatically than Tatyana Tolstaya. A comparison with Liudmila Petrushevskaia's case offers an instructive insight into the rapidity with which Tolstaya became a luxury product suitable for export and elaborate foreign marketing. Just four years after her literary debut in 1983, Tolstaya published a volume of her stories in a print run of 65,000 copies. It instantly sold out in Russia and abroad, and a scant two years later was rendered into English as *On the Golden Porch* (trans. Antonina Bouis, 1989), thanks to Alfred A. Knopf, which in 1991 brought out a second volume of her prose, *Sleepwalker in a Fog* (trans. Jamey Gambrell). Although Petrushevskaia has been writing for more than a quarter century, no sizable collection of her drama or fiction saw publication in Russia until 1988, and American publishers have yet to assemble a comparable anthology of prose or plays gleaned from the substantial corpus of her works.[1] No American journalist has solicited Petrushevskaia's opinions on topics ranging from Pirandello to pelmeni, as has happened with Tolstaya.

Made accessible to an anglophone readership through translation, Tolstaya exudes panache and self-confidence, has an excellent command of English, and relishes speaking her mind—all factors that partly account for continued American and British interest in her observations about Russian and American life, academia, the literary scene, glasnost, and, above all, women and feminism. These opinions, couched in colorful and self-conscious hyperbole, have been publicized through interviews and articles printed in magazines and newspapers ranging from *The New York Review of Books* and *The New Republic* to local and university papers.

Much of Tolstaya's notoriety in the United States, at least among liberal academics and journalists, springs from her vociferous, selective, and largely unreasoned attacks against feminism, American life, and what she scorns as a crudely ideological cast to current academic trends. Given Tolstaya's background and the society in which her values evolved, her views are not only unsurprising, but quite typical of the middle-aged Russian intelligentsia. If those views frequently appear self-contradictory and, moreover, puzzling in light of Tolstaya's attendance at conferences on feminism, her continued residence in America, and her employment at American universities, they merely attest that Tolstaya, like most people, is inconsistent and sometimes driven by considerations other than deeply held convictions.

Indeed, the very expectation of a unitary self, all of whose statements, creativity, and daily actions neatly coincide, seems rather naive on the part of readers and critics in a poststructuralist age. Rather than relying on Tolstaya's personality as a clue to her fiction, it might prove more enlightening to work from text to author, for the perspectivism that marks Tolstaya's oeuvre prepares one for, and to an extent parallels, the diverse and often clashing viewpoints articulated by Tolstaya in her journalism and interviews. Furthermore, that journalism is never completely divorced from her fiction, from her irrepressible impulse to narrativize, even if seemingly in the style of impromptus. Such a blurring of genre boundaries manifests itself with particular vividness in Tolstaya's reviews of works ranging from Elena Molokhovets's cookbook titled *A Gift for Young Housewives* (trans. Joyce Toomre, 1992) to Aleksandr Solzhenitsyn's querulous "essay" *"The Russian Question" at the End of the Twentieth Century* (trans. Yermolai Solzhenitsyn, 1995). Although numerous aspects of American and Russian society and cultural life have provoked Tolstaya's derision, the most frequent target of her impassioned dismissal at conferences or lectures, as well as in print, remains Western feminism.

Any discussion of feminism in literature, of course, is well advised to take into account an elementary critical distinction between intention and reception formulated by Nelly Furman many years ago in "The Politics of Language": "From a feminist viewpoint the question is not whether a literary work has been written by a woman and reflects her experience in life, or how it compares to other works by women, but rather how it lends itself to be read from a feminist position" (69). Although Furman's statement, in nakedly deconstructionist terms, slights those avowed feminists who programmatically commit the intentional fallacy and tether it to an immanent approach, her notion nevertheless discriminates usefully between two possible options bracketing the feminist spectrum. Within this distinction, Tolstaya's prose falls outside of the first category, for it does not manifestly and directly reflect the author's own experiences, as I. Grekova's fiction, for instance, does hers. Nor do endeavors to wedge Tolstaya into the general picture of 1980s' women's prose yield rewarding insights, for what emerges is the bland conclusion that her writing has virtually nothing in common with that of, say, Natal'ia Baranskaia, Maiia Ganina, Nina Katerli, and others, but even a cursory glance at one of Tolstaya's paragraphs suffices to bring that rather trivial point home.

Whether Tolstaya's fiction can sustain a reading from a feminist stance, however, is a more fruitful question, and one that may be answered in the affirmative, as I contend in Chapter 5 of this study.

One of the litmus-paper tests feminists administer to texts so as to determine their misogynist/feminist orientation or implications is to assess authorial handling of female characters and gender-marked issues. Characterologically inclined readers who subject all of Tolstaya's twenty-one stories to a quick perusal will probably best remember her imaginative, impressionable children ("Rendezvous with a Bird," "Loves Me—Loves Me Not"); her powerful, henpecking beauties (" 'On the Golden Porch,' " "The Poet and the Muse"); and her ostensibly pathetic old women ("Dear Shura," "Most Beloved"). Since the literary portrayal of predatory lovelies, solitary decrepit old ladies, and vulnerable children hardly challenges canonical masculine stereotypes of womanhood or women's supposedly quintessential concerns, the rapid reader might conclude that Tolstaya's fiction confirms, instead of transgressing, patriarchal premises and paradigms.

A more attentive examination, however, soon reveals (1) the diversity of Tolstaya's fictional women: what unites them is Tolstaya's style, not their "nature"; (2) their manifold functions in various contexts; and (3) the saliency of intertext and narrative voice to gauging their image. To elaborate briefly on the three points in sequence: Tolstaya's heroines and secondary female personae span the gamut as regards intelligence, morality, age, beauty, capacity for feeling, professional training, and so forth, but other, dominant aspects of Tolstaya's prose that instantly capture our interest serve to camouflage or subsume diversity, and so deflect us from it. For example, although a character like the eponymous Sonia externally bears all the earmarks of the stereotypically ridiculed, domestic spinster, her function in the narrative (which pits spiritual qualities against crass materialism) necessitates recognizable (i.e., conventional), demeaning physical particulars to contrast more forcefully with her admirable inner qualities. Those readers who by focusing on Sonia's bizarre physical appearance fail to notice her heroic dimension—as the sole repository of "soul" in the story—ally themselves with the shortsighted pragmatists whom the text implicitly discredits.

Feminine beauty, its desirability, and its relationship to women's social and psychological makeup—all issues that continue to vex feminists—receive varied treatment by Tolstaya, depending on both the given story and a woman's function within it. To cite a revealing case, of the two equally beautiful sisters in " 'On the Golden Porch,' " Veronika is portrayed in mythic, larger-than-life terms as an engulfing, oppressive force, while Margarita, depicted in less detail and grandeur, personifies diametrically opposing tendencies. In other words, here, as elsewhere, Tolstaya in her representation of female personae makes no consistent a priori assumptions, as misogynists typically do, about the connection between the visible and invisible, exterior and interior, or looks and character.

The densely intertextual nature of Tolstaya's prose, with its virtual elimination of a stable, central narrative voice, should discourage readers from a facile equation of ideas or attitudes articulated directly in her stories with authorial discourse and viewpoint. By and large, Tolstaya favors a complexly mediated presentation of character, whereby images of individuals emerge from conflicting statements and judgments by others within the narrative whose emphatically subjective discourse creates and evaluates a contingent reality. Tolstaya's liberal use of quasi-direct discourse (*erlebte Rede/style indirect libre/kosvenno priamaia rech'*), her double or multiple voicing, and her extensive deployment of irony all problematize the task of pinpointing an anchoring perspective and of gauging its reliability. Several of Tolstaya's stories, in fact, evidence her penchant for refracting likable or vivid characters through the subjective viewpoint of a negative counterpart, whereby the recording consciousness details traits that s/he interprets negatively, while on the basis of that information, with the aid of other incompletely suppressed perspectives, we arrive at a counter-reading ("Fire and Dust," "Heavenly Flame," "Sweet Dreams, Son").

If Tolstaya's sophisticated handling of narrative and voice complicate the process of unpacking her prose, unraveling her intertexts offers an equally daunting prospect. Without becoming embroiled in partisan polemics around Harold Bloom's and Roland Barthes's contrary theories of intertextuality (which, I believe, can find accommodation through synthesis instead of the exclusivity each embraces), one cannot sidestep the crucial role of intertextuality in Tolstaya's fiction. Because her prose is so richly steeped in parody, evocations of or variations on voices and tropes from Russian (and, less frequently, West European) fiction, poetry, songs, and folklore, reading stories like "Okkervil River" and "Loves Me—Loves Me Not," for instance, resembles the act of summoning up one's relationship to the full span of Russian culture and assimilating it into one's understanding of the Tolstayan text. Without a recall of Pushkin, Gogol, Lermontov, Russian romances, the Symbolists (vulgarized), Goethe, and entire literary and cultural traditions that one semi-recognizes without quite achieving exact identification, the two stories remain enigmatic, their accessibility and resonance circumscribed. Thus any reader combing Tolstaya's fiction for evidence of misogyny or feminism without possessing the cultural background requisite for grasping the context in which her characters and incidents are embedded dooms herself to misapprehension. The fourth chapter of my study illuminates this feature of Tolstaya's prose by focusing in detail on her intertexts and their function in the stories "Okkervil River" and "The Circle."

Although Tolstaya's extensive reliance on intertexts allies her with postmodernism, she ultimately emerges as a writer of traditional neohumanist values with a modernist technique. Her profoundly ironic distance from her own materials, her antipathy to closure, and her penchant for decentering and multivocalism never join forces in a comprehensive skepticism. Just as her parody of decadent verse (e.g., in "Loves Me—Loves Me Not"), her satirical treatment of kitsch, of unbridled flights of romantic fantasies, and of naive yearnings for culture never fully discredit these phenomena—indeed, one senses Tolstaya's own attraction to them—so her arsenal of mediating strategies never disguises her attachment (however ambivalent on occasion) to principles recognizable as definitive of Western humanism. Within Russian literature her links are above all with Gogol, Bely, Olesha, Bulgakov, and Nabokov, all impassioned proponents of the power and significance of art. And if her satirical framing of decadent and Symbolist aesthetics, urban love songs (*romansy*), and cultural clichés distances her from these phenomena, their repeated inscription in her texts renders them inseparable from her ambivalent perception of Russian culture, and particularly of its more radical manifestations of idealism and philistinism.

Tolstaya's style, not unlike Gogol's, has elicited delight and distress, primarily by its extravagant metaphors, quicksilver oscillation between the lyrical and affecting on the one hand and the grotesque or absurdly comic on the other,[2] rapid and seemingly unmotivated shifts in mood or tone, in tandem with myriad other unexpected leaps of a temporal, spatial, or discursive nature. Tolstaya juxtaposes and amalgamates ostentatiously incompatible elements while simultaneously exercising rigorous precision largely in the interests of a maximal condensation that places extraordinary demands on her readers, while vouchsafing them generous rewards. One of those rewards is the sheer pleasure of Tolstaya's richly hued humor, which spans the spectrum from robust, rollicking hilarity to sardonic debunking and gentle irony. And that humor not only unleashes energy, but beguiles and cajoles the reader into participation, even when it bursts forth in the midst of melancholy, profoundly meditative moments, or elevated lyricism, as it frequently does.

My study does not offer a unified reading of Tolstaya's entire oeuvre. In fact, it assiduously avoids a neatly packaged, smooth interpretation, in the conviction that Tolstaya's fiction enables her to follow through to its fictional conclusions the adoption of various perspectives on phenomena ranging from imagination, memory, time, art, and spirituality to consumerism, selfishness, egotism, vanity, and the like. Instead, the first seven chapters of my study isolate pairs or trios of narratives that I link thematically or structurally, so as to examine them from an angle pertinent to contemporary literary and theoretical debates.

Accordingly, Chapter 1 examines Tolstaya's interpolation of the Edenic myth as algorithm for her idyllic representations of childhood in " 'On the Golden Porch' " and "Rendezvous with a Bird." A contrasting view of childhood as a dark labyrinth defined by the limits or incommensurability of linguistic conventions is investigated in Chapter 2 on the basis of "Loves Me—Loves Me Not" and "Night." Tolstaya's reliance on traditional associations as she pits spirit against matter and the complexities she brings to that polarized antinomy form the core of Chapter 3, which treats "Sonia," "The Moon Came Out," and "Peters." Chapter 4 deals with the crucial role of intertexts in "Okkervil River" and "The Circle," while Chapter 5 argues that three of Tolstaya's stories lend themselves quite readily to a feminist reading insofar as they dismantle gender stereotypes: "Hunting the Wooly Mammoth," "The Poet and the Muse," and "Fire and Dust." Chapter 6 traces the ambivalence of Tolstaya's attitude toward art as a transcendent category, rife with pitfalls for the "uninitiated," as articulated in "Fakir" and "Okkervil River." Whereas Tolstaya's notion of literarization as violaton of literal truth appears in a predominantly alluring light in these two stories, Chapter 7 argues that "Heavenly Flame" and "Sweet Dreams, Son" highlight the destructive potential of narrativity. Chapter 8 takes a thorough look at the centrality of time in Tolstaya's fiction and its operation and significance, above all vis-à-vis the generic conventions of autobiography, while Chapter 9 discusses her exploitation of tropes, particularly metonymy and metaphor. The Postscript spotlights the commonality between Tolstaya's fiction and her journalism.

My invocations of theorists and critics as heterogeneous as Bakhtin, Barthes, Benjamin, Brooks, Culler, de Man, Genette, Jakobson, Ricoeur, and White signal neither appeals to purported authority nor displays of pseudo-erudition. Rather, they are part of my prevailing design and goal— to illustrate how part of Tolstaya's seductive appeal lies in the relevance to contemporary criticism of the issues that her texts implicitly or overtly engage and to which they give rise. Obviously, all my choices and groupings are provisional and could easily have assumed another form. For instance, I could have included "Okkervil River" among the texts subjected to a feminist reading. Similarly, most of Tolstaya's stories could be approached as narratives of love or dramatized struggles between matter and soul.

Finally, this study entirely omits several Tolstayan texts from consideration: "A Clean Sheet," "Serafim," "Limpopo," and "Plot." Limitations of space partly explain that neglect, but so does a dearth of rich response on my part. Quite simply, having little to say about them, I have opted for silence. I remain equally silent regarding Tolstaya's biography, not only because the facts of her "nonfictional" life have been reviewed too frequently to warrant further repetition, but also because my mode of reading Tolstaya's fiction contradicts that unmediated continuity so often posited between the empirical experiences of the author and her texts. Clashes, discrepancies, and discontinuities intrigue me far more, as the title of my study intimates.

In that regard I disagree strongly with Caryl Emerson—as thoughtful and intelligent a reader of manuscripts as one could hope for, and one whose critical suggestions in an in-house reading I took to heart, but ultimately did not transfer wholesale to the page. Protracted soul-searching and brainstorming convinced me that Caryl and I enjoy different Tolstayas. Hers, as Caryl herself phrases it, writes "integrated, lyrical, delicately etched, whimsical" prose. My TNT, by contrast, explodes conventions and traditions even as she acknowledges their potent appeal; she punctuates lyricism with a healthy gust of laughter or by wickedly sticking out her tongue; as a writer, she is flamboyant, irreverent, and intoxicating.[3] That is precisely why I have been imbibing her prose since the first draft that was "Peters." One woman's integration, then, is another woman's dynamite, and I thank Caryl all the more warmly for her intellectual largesse in the face of such differences, as well as for those incisive observations that *did* prompt me to expand, modify, or refine my thinking.

My most intense gratitude, however, is reserved for someone else with whom I have frequently disagreed about several of the narratives in question: Tolstaya herself. I thank her not only for the first thunderbolt contact with her prose but also for an entire decade of unparalleled "pleasure of the text." Given her dismissal of "women's fiction" as a category, it is gratifyingly ironic that her writing, above all else, played a key role in my decision, a dozen years ago, to concentrate my research on contemporary Russian women's culture. Although my study occasionally cites correspondence and conversations with Tolstaya, I wish to emphasize that my readings of her texts more often than not run counter to her self-commentaries and self-perceptions—a fact that has also occasioned brazen pleasures of complex sorts.

I am grateful to those loved ones who over the years read, listened to, argued with, and helped me to clarify and refine my thoughts on Tolstaya's fiction: Bożenka, Volodia Padunov, Uliana Gabara, Sophia Wiśniewska, and Kostia Kustanovich. During the 1980s, Brittain Smith in his "European" phase proved a wonderful reader. My affectionate appreciation goes to those thoughtful and talented graduate students at the University of Pittsburgh who have shared, if at a sensibly lower temperature, my tireless passion for Tolstaya's prose. To the many institutions that invited me to present talks on various aspects of Tolstaya's writing, and to the National Humanities Center at Research Triangle Park, where I wrote parts of this study and benefited from Alexander Zholkovsky's linguistic skills and critical resistance, as well as from Jane Tompkins's flare of passion for Tolstaya's creative gifts, I likewise render thanks.

* * *

Throughout, I rely on available translations, but amend them or provide my own when the given translation is inaccurate (as happens in Antonina Bouis's renditions) or does not convey an aspect of the original salient to my point. The Russian version usually follows the translation, but in those sections of the last chapter that analyze the instrumentation of Tolstaya's prose, I cite only the original, since even as skilled a translator as Jamey Gambrell cannot capture the rhythm and sound effects of Tolstaya's Russian. Whenever context does not eliminate all ambiguity as to whether a reference is to the original or the translation, the page number is preceded by E (English) or R (Russian) (e.g., E203). Citations from "Sleepwalker in a Fog," "The Moon Came Out," "Night," "Heavenly Flame," "Most Beloved," and "The Poet and the Muse" rely on Gambrell's versions (*Sleepwalker in a Fog*), with minor modifications; for the remaining stories I have used Bouis's translations (*On the Golden Porch*), but with significant changes.

In transliterating Russian I follow the Library of Congress system, but within the text proper omit all diacritics. The sole exception concerns names that have acquired a conventional spelling in the West, notably Tatyana Tolstaya, who appears as such within the chapters, but in Library of Congress transliteration (Tat'iana Tolstaia) within Russian sources cited in the scholarly apparatus.

Earlier versions of Chapters 1, 3, 5, 6, and 8 appeared, respectively, in the following publications: *Indiana Slavic Studies* 5 (1990): 97–114; *Slavic and East European Journal* 34, 1 (1990): 40–52; *Sexuality and the Body in Russian Culture*, ed. Jane Costlow, Stephanie Sandler, and Judith Vowles (Stanford: Stanford University Press, 1993): 204–220 (published with the permission of the publishers; original version © 1993 by the Board of Trustees of the Leland Stanford Junior University); *World Literature Today* 67, 1 (Winter 1993): 80–90; and *New Directions in Soviet Literature*, ed. S. Graham (London/New York: Macmillan, 1992): 36–62. I thank the publishers who hold copyright to the original incarnations of the pertinent chapters for granting permission to reprint.

✧ 1 ✧

Paradise, Purgatory, and Post-Mortems:
The Lapsarian Myth as
Universal Rite of Passage

Tatyana Tolstaya made her literary debut in 1983 on the pages of *Avrora* with the story, dedicated to her sister Shura (Aleksandra), that subsequently lent its title to her collection: " 'On the Golden Porch' " (" 'Na zolotom kryl'tse sideli . . .' ").[1] Since this miniature masterpiece of six pages and its companion piece, "Rendezvous with a Bird" ("Svidanie s ptitsei"),[2] her second publication, condense practically all the hallmarks of her writing, they afford a convenient introduction to Tolstaya's artistic world—a world structured by the regnant triad of cognition, time, and memory.

As elsewhere in Tolstaya's work, plot in " 'On the Golden Porch' " performs a minimal function. The story summarizes selectively a woman's reminiscences of several externally insignificant incidents from her childhood in the countryside, most of which involve a neighboring bookkeeper called Uncle Pasha. Such a deceptively mundane and highly compressed recapitulation, however, cannot even hint at the dazzling richness of the story, which, like a voluminous body packed into an undersized corset, strains at the contours of the confining form, its abundance threatening to burst the seams. The thematic wealth, the resonances, and the gourmandizing style (which elicited the uneasy opprobrium of critics accustomed to a diet of attenuated texts)[3] must have overwhelmed readers weaned on the blandness of Soviet prose.

Tolstaya casts the nets of her creativity wide and high. At the heart of the story reside no less than the eternal questions of life's meaning and the elusive multifariousness of the individual life, which the narrator as a young girl reformulates more concretely and reductively as the enigma of personality. Hence the children's counting rhyme that serves as the story's epigraph:

> On the golden porch sat:
> Tsar, tsarevich, king, prince,
> Cobbler, tailor.
> Who are you?
> Tell me fast, don't hold us up. (41)

> Na zolotom kryl'tse sideli:
> Tsar', tsarevich, korol', korolevich,
> Sapozhnik, portnoi,
> Kto ty takoi?
> Govori poskorei, ne zaderzhivai dobrykh liudei. (40)

The unusual genre of the epigraph, together with the plot surface of the text proper, prompted an interviewer to read the story naively as a commentary on the evanescence of childhood, in response to which Tolstaya asserted:

> The story . . . is about the attempt to grasp life. What is life? Who exactly is the neighbor Uncle Pasha: a tsar, tsarevich, cobbler, tailor? He's the first, the second, and the third. He's a henpecked husband, and a happy lover, and an impotent [helpless] old man. And we see him with the enraptured eyes of a child one moment, and the sober gaze of an adult the next, and each time he's different. And there's no answer to the children's counting rhyme: who are you?

> Rasskaz . . . o popytke postich' zhizn'. Zhizn'—chto eto takoe? Sosed diadia Pasha—kto on takoi: tsar', tsarevich, sapozhnik, portnoi? I to, i drugoe, i tret'e. On—i zabityi muzh, i schastlivyi liubovnik, i bessil'nyi starik. I my vidim ego to voskhishchennymi detskimi glazami, to trezvym vzgliadom vzroslogo, i kazhdyi raz on raznyi. I net otveta na detskuiu schitalochku: kto ty takoi?[4]

To have a children's chantlike ditty point to the ontological dimension of her narrative is characteristic of Tolstaya's subversive penchant for yoking that which convention deems incompatible. It evinces her attraction to grotesque, oxymoronic matings of all types, whether they be confined to a single narrative sphere (such as character, style, tone, or language) or simultaneously cut across two or more categories and strata.[5]

For the actual exploration of the mystery of life in " 'On the Golden Porch,' " however, Tolstaya draws prodigiously on two familiar domains rich in ontological tradition and imagery that also inform her second published narrative: the Edenic myth and folklore. The matrix metaphor that presides over " 'On the Golden Porch' "[6] unambiguously identifies childhood with the natural, uncorrupted world of prelapsarian innocence/ignorance. Tolstaya establishes the equation in the story's introductory sentences, which have an evocatively Biblical ring:

> In the beginning was the garden. Childhood was a garden. Without end or limit, without borders and fences, in noises and rustling, golden in the sun, pale green in the shade, a thousand layers thick. (41)

> V nachale byl sad. Detstvo bylo sadom. Bez kontsa i kraia, bez grani i zaborov, v shume i sheleste, zolotoi na solntse, svetlo-zelenyi v teni, tysiacheiarusnyi. (40)

Innumerable autobiographies conceive of childhood as a paradise destined to be lost, yet partly retained or recuperated as a source of inspiration for the remainder of one's life. For Kathleen Raine, the author of a fine-tuned re-creation of early years entitled *Farewell Happy Fields* (1973), the significance of childhood lies less in its personal experience than in its shared cultural inheritance as "[p]art of the Fable we know; Paradise and the Fall. And as surely as we each enact the Fall, so have we memories of Paradise. My own have been a refuge, a source of wisdom and poetry, inexhaustible to this day."[7] As Richard Coe justly observes, "Few childhoods, even among the most sordid and the most degrading, are entirely without *some* experience of paradise" (67). In the majority of cases, that paradise assumes the form of a verdant refuge awaiting exploration.

Tolstaya's lush garden of timeless eternity (Mircea Eliade's *illud tempus*) and sun-washed splendor lacks enclosure. It thus enables the protagonist and her companion to bite the metaphorical fruit through a voluntary traversal of symbolically saturated time and space so as to acquire firsthand knowledge of the body:

> They say that early in the morning they saw a *completely* naked man at the lake. Honest. Don't tell Mother. Do you know who it was? . . .—It can't be.—Honest, it was. He thought he was alone. But we were in the bushes.—What did you see?—Everything. (41)

> Govoriat, rano utrom na ozere videli *sovershenno* gologo cheloveka. Chestnoe slovo. Ne govori mame. Znaesh', kto eto byl? . . .—Ne mozhet byt'.—Tochno, ia tebe govoriu. On dumal, chto nikogo net. A my sideli v kustakh.—A chto vy videli?—Vse. (40)

This first, as yet unassimilated, loss of innocence conduces to others, arranged in an incremental sequence that Tolstaya orchestrates so as to emphasize the link between knowledge and retributive mortality prescribed by the lapsarian myth. Accordingly, the naked body of a man at the lake becomes the live equivalent of the anatomical illustration in the girl's biology textbook, which Tolstaya describes in terms of skin removed from red meat ("Sodrav po etomu sluchaiu kozhu, naglovatyi, miasnoi i krasnyi" [40]). From this textbook image, which attempts to actualize theoretical knowledge, Tolstaya rapidly modulates to the red meat fed a neighbor's cat ("Takim zhe krasnym miasom starukha Anna Il'inichna kormit tigrovuiu koshku Memeku" [40]), then culminates the image in the cat's decimation of sparrows ("V dushnykh zarosliakh krasnoi persidskoi sireni koshka portit vorob'ev. Odnogo takogo vorob'ia my nashli. Kto-to *sodral* [had torn off] skal'p s ego igrushechnoi golovki" [emphasis added (41)]). This chain of suffering flesh, pain, and death, which posits a continuity between the human and the animal spheres, initiates the child-protagonist into the world of mortality with all its attendant complexities. These are skillfully condensed by Tolstaya in the figure of Uncle Pasha, his women, and his dwelling, as emblems of elemental mystery, mutability, and death.

Tellingly, to reach Uncle Pasha's house, which is singled out contrastively from the rented dachas as "sobstvennyi dom," one has to descend "vniz-vniz-vniz" (down-down-down). As in Zamiatin's *We* (My),[8] the downward movement extends the story's cluster of Fall imagery, abetted by the description of Veronika Vikent'evna, who rules the house as "tsaritsa," "huge white beauty" ("belaia, ogromnaia krasavitsa"), and "luxurious, golden, *applelike* beauty" ("pyshnaia, zolotaia, *iablochnaia* krasota" [emphasis added]). With her crimson hands bathed in the blood of the berries she weighs ("the beautiful merchant's wife's fingers in berry blood" [43]/ "pal'tsy prekrasnoi kupchikhi v iagodnoi krovi" [41]) and the calf she slaughters in a barn, Veronika effects the narrator's horrified realization that death is life's deferred corollary and ineluctable end, an epiphany from which the girl instinctively recoils, but which she can only postpone: "Argh! Let's get out of here, run, it's horrible—an icy horror—shed, damp, death" (43) ("Proch' otsiuda, begom, koshmar, uzhas—kholodnyi smrad— sarai, syrost', smert' " [42]). The alliterative sibilants, of course, onomatopoetically conjure up the hiss of the Edenic snake, thus strengthening the matrix metaphor through auditory means.

Tolstaya amplifies Veronika's mythic proportions, transmitted initially through imagery of sovereignty, life, and death, by mythic and folkloric associations: the Cerberus-like yellow guard dog she acquires; the magical egg[9] she sells conditionally to the protagonist's mother, according to the formula of fairy-tale contracts; the enormous bed on glass legs that she shares with Uncle Pasha; and her nocturnal insomnia-inspired appearances in the garden, where her hearing takes on supernatural acuity and her posture with a pitchfork evokes not only implicit demonic associations but also an explicit comparison with Neptune. That comparison reinforces the lines from Pushkin's folkloric "Tale of the Fisherman and the Fish" ("Skazka o rybake i rybke"), of which Tolstaya interpolates four lines to analogize Veronika with the poor fisherman's domineering, greedy wife, who aspires to rule the sea:

They pour foreign wines for her,
She eats iced gingerbread,
Terrifying guards surround her,
Axes over their shoulders . . . (43)

Nalivaiut ei zamorskie vina,
Zaedaet ona prianikom pechatnym
Vokrug ee stoit groznaia strazha,
Na plechakh toporiki derzhat . . . (42)

Since Veronika-tsaritsa is both "merchant" ("kupchikha") and "the greedi-est woman in the world" ("samaia zhadnaia zhenshchina na svete"), within her character zone, to borrow Bakhtinian terminology, the idyllic gold of sunshine (emanating from the sun, traditionally cognate with a higher Unity, Oneness, the divine eye)[10] metamorphoses into the crasser gold of material wealth.

At this conjunction of mythic and folkloric planes, Veronika constitutes the first mysterious, ominous symbol of death (both spiritual and physical), and hers is the first literal (wholly unexplained) human death in the story. True to the polarized doublings of folklore formula, Veronika is the dark sister (the "Black Swan"), subsequently replaced by her physically identical but spiritually obverse younger sister Margarita (the "White Swan"). Asso-ciated antithetically with light (by virtue of its golden center, the daisy [*margaritka*] evokes the image of the sun), laughter, and youth, Margarita becomes Uncle Pasha's next love and liberates him from the imprisonment of Veronika's sterile materialistic influence: he places Cerberus in a trunk with mothballs, hospitably opens his house to children, takes in lodgers, and rediscovers the romance of youth as he casts a spell over his visitors by his rendition of Beethoven's "Moonlight" Sonata. In a quintessentially Tolstayan reversal, Uncle Pasha becomes the sleeping prince awakened on his glass-legged bed by Margarita's kiss.

The same forces that signal Uncle Pasha's youthful rebirth (Margarita, the magically released dog, spatial openness) accompany his death by freez-ing many years later. In a passage that fuses striking paronomasia with poignant overtones of Bulgakov's *Master and Margarita*, Tolstaya writes: "Uncle Pasha froze to death on the porch. . . . White snow daisies grew between his stiff fingers. The yellow dog gently closed his eyes and left through the snowflakes up the starry ladder to the black heights, carrying away the trembling living flame" (50) ("Diadia Pasha zamerz na kryl'tse. . . . Belye moroznye *margaritki* [emphasis added] vyrosli mezhdu ego oderevenevshikh pal'tsev. Zheltyi pes tikho prikryl emu glaza i ushel skvoz' snezhnuiu krupu po zvezdnoi lestnitse v chernuiu vys', unosia s soboi drozhashchii zhivoi ogonechek" [48]).[11] Uncle Pasha's death is pre-figured in his collection of clocks, stored in the wondrous room overflow-ing with mementos of the past, alongside the immemorial omens auguring all humankind's ultimate fate: the clock housing the two figures of "the Lady and the Chevalier, masters of Time" (49) ("Dama i Kavaler, khozia-eva Vremeni" [101]). Just as their chimes announce the departure of the narrator during a visit, so they toll Uncle Pasha's departure from life.[12]

The multiple deaths in " 'On the Golden Porch' "—of Veronika, Uncle Pasha, birds, and animals whose bodies/meat provide food for other spe-cies—instantiate the axiom that no one escapes mutability and the inexor-able flow of time that rules the universe. We all die our biological deaths and turn to dust; and in keeping with the magical transformations that reticulate throughout the story, Tolstaya literalizes the metaphor by having Uncle Pasha, narratively speaking, disintegrate into dust virtually over-night.[13] Yet, Tolstaya contends, people become immortalized in two ways. The first is through their participation in the universal process of life, hence the ostensibly cryptic paradox articulated early in the narrative: "Life is eternal. Only birds die" (42) ("Zhizn' vechna. Umiraiut tol'ko ptitsy" [41]). Hence also the magical dog (in the logic-defying spirit of fairy tales, he lives several decades) who carries away with him the quivering, vital flame of life ("drozhashchii zhivoi ogonechek").[14] Since he transports it "po zvezdnoi lestnitse v chernuiu vys'," presumably its destination is the heights beyond the Milky Way to which, maintains the poem conjured by Uncle Pasha's inspired performance of the "Moonlight" Sonata, the united bodies of lovers ascend:

> O Milky Way, light brother
> Of Canaan's milky rivers,
> Should we swim through the starry fall
> To the fogs, where entwined
> The bodies of lovers fly? (48)
>
> O Mlechnyi put', presvetlyi brat
> Molochnykh rechek Khanaana,
> Uplyt' li nam skvoz' zvevdopad
> K tumannostiam, kuda sliiano
> Tela vozliublennykh letiat! (46)

This extract from David Samoilov's remarkably free translation of Guil-laume Apollinaire's "La Chanson du mal-aimé" (included in his 1913 col-lection *Alcoöls*) reads as follows in the original five free-flowing, continuous lines:

Voie lactée o soeur lumineuse
Des blancs ruisseaux de Chanaan
Et des corps blancs des amoureuses
Nageurs morts suivrons-nous d'ahan
Ton cours vers d'autres nebuleuses.[15]

The apposite quotation focuses on death; on the transcendent ("voie lactée") and the earthly ("des blancs ruisseaux de Chanaan"), as embodied in Tolstaya's two contrasted sisters ("o soeur lumineuse"); and on the power of love, likewise central to Tolstaya's story. Moreover, the lengthy poem from which the passage is extracted provides additional resonance for Tolstaya's text, insofar as Apollinaire compares the love of the lyrical "I" to the phoenix that is reborn after death, stresses the fidelity and the capacity of Ulysses' dog to remember his beloved master, and insists on the primacy of memory for human experience.

The last has special pertinence for Tolstaya, for the second means whereby people attain immortality is through their resurrection in the memory of those who remain. That idea (expounded in Pasternak's *Doctor Zhivago*)[16] finds metonymical incarnation here in the old photograph of a family bearing the inscription: "Don't forget us. 1908" (46) ("Na dolguiu, dolguiu pamiat'. 1908 god" [98]), which the girl-narrator finds under the sideboard. Since elsewhere in the narrative we learn that the egg incident transpired in the summer of 1950, the photograph antedates the story's events by more than forty years. Presumably the family immortalized by a camera lives on in someone's memory, just as Uncle Pasha leads a vital existence in the recollections of the narrator, in a suggestive parallelism that momentarily conflates the mimetic mode with the diegetic. The protagonist-narrator's retrospective portrait re-creates Uncle Pasha's life, shaping it, and in the process offering complex insights into the nature of time, memory, and perspective.[17]

Time operates in contradictory and fascinating ways in Tolstaya's universe. In the Edenic state of childhood, time, appropriately, stands still; or rather, its felt significance derives exclusively from direct experience (Henri Bergson's *durée réelle*).[18] It may be contracted and expanded subjectively, independently of scientific time measured in standard units according to mathematical principles. Such temporal relativity empowers the child-narrator of " 'On the Golden Porch' " to say "When we move up (in a hundred years) to the eighth grade" (42) ("Kogda [cherez sto let] my pereidem v vos'moi klass" [40]) and to marvel at Uncle Pasha's clocks as enthralling objects intrinsically no different from the other bric-à-brac in his storage room. With adulthood, however, time becomes a conventionally quantifiable commodity, directly linked with aging and death, of which it is a relentless reminder. That is why, when after a protracted absence the grown-up narrator visits Uncle Pasha, out of her profoundly time-bound consciousness she privately registers: "I'm getting old!" ("Kakaia zhe ia staraia!"), and Prufrock-like doles out her hours, saying: "You want to show me your treasures? Well, all right, I have five minutes for you" (49) ("Ty khochesh' pokazat' mne svoi sokrovishcha? Nu tak i byt', u menia est' eshche piat' minut" [47]). Only now does she perceive the clock's Lady and Chevalier as "masters of Time," reacting automatically to their chimes with the words "Sorry, Uncle Pasha. Time for me to go" (50) ("Prosti, diadia Pasha. Mne pora" [48]). Through the bifocal point of view built into retrospective narration, Tolstaya stresses time's incalculable effect on one's perceptions, among them, one's perception of time itself.

According to Tolstaya, then, humankind passes from the cognitive paradise of childhood, through the purgatory of adulthood, to the post-mortem of one's posthumous revival, effectuated by others' reminiscences. For Tolstaya, it is usually the backward glance that enables a full, meaningful assessment of one's own experience and others' place within it. Memory makes possible an intimate if only partial and subjective repossession that leads to understanding, for, just as an object loses clarity when it is brought too close to the viewer, so, paradoxically, one attains a profound knowledge of one's experiences only after they are over.[19] The story's narrator, therefore, senses that time works fundamental changes but cannot appreciate and structure their significance until long after the fact, when she has gained the perspective of distance. She notes: "Life changed the slides ever faster in the magic lantern" (48) ("Zhizn' vse toroplivee meniala stekla v volshebnom fonare" [47]). This magic lantern of perception, which recalls Pushkin's "magicheskii kristall" and Marcel's bedside lamp in the Combray section of Marcel Proust's *A la Recherche du temps perdu*,[20] implicitly posits imagination as the colorful consort of cognition and constitutes the lenses through which she looks out onto the world: "And, looking back once, with unbelieving fingers we felt the smoked glass behind which our garden waved a hankie before going down for the last time. But we didn't feel the loss yet" (49) ("I, oglianuvshis' odnazhdy, nedoumevaiushchimi pal'tsami my oshchupali dymchatoe steklo, za kotorym, prezhde chem uiti na dno, v poslednii raz makhnul platkom nash sad. No my eshche ne osoznali utraty" [47]). With the recognition of loss, the effort of recuperation through memory begins, as hindsight yields new and fluid perspectives.

Perspective in general, like the patterns in a kaleidoscope, shifts continuously in Tolstaya's world, for myriad phenomena (of which time is only the most obvious and influential) impinge upon it nonstop. Life by definition is process, entailing ceaseless change that makes a static, unalterable perspective impossible, or at least incommensurate with the flux of life. Epistemological indeterminacy along the horizontal axis (temporality) as well as the vertical (spatiality) is thus a fundamental law of existence. Tolstaya conveys the potential for endless successive and synchronous perspectives on a given phenomenon by orchestrating several synchronic points of view that ostensibly are mutually exclusive. Thus Uncle Pasha appears as a "small, meek, henpecked" "old man" (43) ("malen'kii, robkii, zatiukannyi" "starik" [42]), a fifty-year-old bookkeeper whose little feet get crushed by Veronika's heavy white body, but also as "Tsar Solomon" (45), "Caliph for an hour, enchanted prince, starry youth" (48) ("Khalif na chas, zakoldovannyi prints, zvezdnyi iunosha" [46]). Inorganic matter likewise metamorphoses according to changing subjectivities. Thus Uncle Pasha's storeroom at first shimmers like Aladdin's fabulous cave, brought to vibrant life by a resplendent catalogue of sensual images:

O Uncle Pasha . . . ! You hold the Horn of Plenty in your mighty arms. A caravan of camels passed with spectral tread through your house and dropped its Baghdad wares in the summer twilight. A waterfall of velvet, ostrich feathers of lace, a shower of porcelain, golden columns of frames, precious tables on bent legs, locked glass cases of mounds where fragile yellow glasses are entwined with black grapes, where Negroes in golden skirts hide in the deep darkness, where something transparent, silvery bent. (47)

O diadia Pasha . . . Rog izobiliia derzhish' ty v moguchikh rukakh! Karavan verbliudov prizrachnymi shagami proshestvoval cherez tvoi dom i rasterial v letnikh sumerkakh svoiu bagdadskuiu poklazhu! Vodopad barkhata, strausovye per'ia kruzhev, liven' farfora, zolotye stolby ram, dragotsennye stoliki na gnutykh nozhkakh, zapertye stekliannye kolonny gorok, gde nezhnye zheltye bokaly obvil chernyi vinograd, gde mertsaiut neprogliadnoi t'moi negry v zolotykh iubkakh, gde izognulos' chto-to prozrachnoe, serebrianoe. (45)

Yet the same room glimpsed from a later perspective yields a diametrically contrasting picture—of a graveyard piled with worn, vulgar, lifeless objects:

All this secondhand rubbish, these chipped painted night tables, crude oilcloth paintings, odd-legged flowerpot stands, worn plush velvet, darned tulle, clumsy fakes from the market, cheap beads? (49)

Vsia eta vetosh' i rukhliad', obsharpannye krashennye komodiki, topornye kleenchatye kartinki, kolchenogie zhardin'erki, vytertyi pliush, shtopanyi tiul', rynochnye koriavye podelki, deshevye stekliashki? (47–48)

By emphasizing the interpretive nature of cognition and especially its vulnerability to mutation through time, Tolstaya implies that the post-mortems we conduct entail not a systematic, objective dissection and evaluation, but a thoroughly subjective act of creation, an artful reconstruction of subjectively assimilated material. The transforming powers of memory and desire guide these re-creations, and their vividness and sharpness of outline, paradoxically, increase with the passage of time. Apropos of this contradiction, Tolstaya has commented:

> What interests me is that a person whom nobody needs while he's alive becomes more and more necessary after death, and his memory grows like a shadow at sunset.

> Menia interesuet . . . to, chto chelovek nikomu ne nuzhnyi pri zhizni, posle svoei smerti stanovitsia vse nuzhnei i nuzhnei, i pamiat' o nem rastet, kak ten' na zakate.[21]

The perspectivism of which subjective recollection is a major facet has its stylistic parallel on the narrative level, as the story's conclusion attests. Immediately after Lenskii's death by duel in Chapter VI of *Eugene Onegin*, Pushkin muses on the hypothetical future fates that might have awaited the poet.[22] Tolstaya transfers that series of alternatives onto a stylistic plane, offering in quick succession three distinct epitaphs suffused with genre tonalities and philosophical implications.[23] The first—a lyrical, visually poeticized image of death—asserts transcendence through the immortality of the soul or spirit (in the passage with the miraculous dog cited above). By contrast, the second stresses in ludicrously mundane terms the material basis of life, the finality and degradation of death, and the casual indifference of those who survive us:

> The new owner—Margarita's elderly daughter—poured Uncle Pasha's ashes into a metal can and set it on a shelf in the empty chicken house; it was too much trouble to bury him. (50)

> Novaia khoziaika—pozhilaia Margaritina doch'—ssypala prakh diadi Pashi v zhestianuiu banku i postavila na polku v pustom kuriatnike—khoronit' bylo khlopotno. (48)

The third perspective, which provides the story's closure, restores grandeur to death by universalizing it through an existential trope, the mythic power of which derives from centuries of elaboration:

And the golden Lady of Time [who, as Time's Mistress, functions as a direct antipode to Margarita's daughter—H.G.], *having emptied the cup of life*, will strike it against the table, sounding Uncle Pasha's last midnight. [emphasis added]

I zolotaia Dama Vremeni, *vypiv do dna kubok zhizni*, prostuchit po stolu dlia diadi Pashi posledniuiu polnoch'. (48)

The triplex treatment has a curiously ambiguous effect. On the one hand it underscores the finality of death and in that sense provides closure. The lexicon ("*posledniuiu* polnoch'") closes the circle opened at the story's beginning ("*v nachale* byl sad"). Yet the sheer repetition in various keys implies the potential for other, still different, stylistic formulations, thereby destabilizing the reader's sense of a final, uncontested resolution. Coupled with the motif of transcendence through love, death blurs into something indefinite and susceptible to narratability.

Although Tolstaya excludes the element of memory from her second published story, "Rendezvous with a Bird" ("Svidanie s ptitsei"), she structures it around a parallel Edenic/folkloric paradigm for roughly the same purposes. The profoundly mythicized world of "Rendezvous" similarly dramatizes the child protagonist Petia's transition to adulthood through his access to knowledge of mortality and the flesh. The story rests on multiple layers of myth located at different planes of significance that intersect at the pivotal moment of revelation. The governing paradigm here, as in " 'On the Golden Porch,' " is the inexhaustible myth of the Fall. Until his lapse into awareness, Petia enjoys a blameless state of ignorance as he plays with his younger brother in the garden, daydreams over his food, and construes the world around him through the formulae of story-book legends. That untroubled perspective on phenomena is shattered definitively by two crucial interrelated discoveries that Tolstaya presents as obverse sides of the same coin. Awakened by a chilling prophetic dream, Petia trespasses upon two shocking sights that catalyze his cognitive transformation: his grandfather's corpse lying in bed (mortality as universal divine punishment) and the bodies of Uncle Boria and Tamila, likewise in bed, patently in a position of sexual intimacy ("knowing" through "knowing" in both Biblical senses). In symbolically eloquent reaction, Uncle Boria, like Adam before him, covers his and Tamila's nakedness,[24] while Petia flees, "he threw himself down under the wet *tree* oozing rain" (130; emphasis added) ("brosilsia pod mokroe, sochashcheesia dozhdem *derevo*" [123]), and immediately afterward surveys the world around him through irrevocably altered eyes: "The dead lake, the dead forest: birds had fallen from the trees and lay feet up; the dead empty world was filled with gray, thick, oozing depression. Everything was a lie. . . . No one could escape his fate. It's all true, child. That's how it is" (130) ("Mertvoe ozero, mertvyi les; ptitsy svalilis' s derev'ev i lezhat kverkhu lapami; mertvyi pustoi mir propitan seroi, glukhoi, sochashcheisia toskoi. Vse—lozh'. . . . Nikto ne uberegsia ot sud'by. Vse— pravda, mal'chik. Vse tak i est' " [123–24]). The Petia who returns home at story's end has been painfully educated out of blithe, carefree ignorance forever.

As in her first story, Tolstaya again contrasts pre- and postlapsarian states, through a juxtaposition of Petia with his younger brother Lenechka. To underscore the disparity in their spiritual and cognitive evolution, Tolstaya uses identical imagery to convey both Lenechka's retention of paradisiacal unawareness and resultant autonomy ("he was still little and his *soul* was *sealed* like a chicken *egg*: everything just rolled off" [127]/"on eshche malen'kii, i *dusha* u nego *zapechatana*, kak kurinoe *iaitso*: vse s nee skatyvaetsia" [120], emphases added) and Petia's forcible jolt out of time-lessness into the realm of mutability: "his *soul* was boiled like *egg white* hanging in clumps on the *trees* rushing towards him" (130) ("*dusha* svarilas', kak *iaichnyi belok*, kloch'iami povisala na nesushchikhsia navstrechu *derev'iakh* [123], emphases added).[25] The image of the soul as egg originates in Alkonost's "magic egg," the descriptive details of which (rosy glass with gold tones) evoke the transparency and riches traditionally linked with a symbolism of transcendence, as amply illustrated in both folklore and the Bible.[26] Within the framework of this code, transgression makes the transparent glass of purity and primal vision opaque, just as Petia's desolate soul loses its egg-transparency once he attains knowledge.

As in her first story, Tolstaya interpolates a series of subordinate but salient features from folklore into the overarching schema of the Edenic myth. Here too they crystallize around the female figure who first acquaints the child protagonist with mortality: Petia's exotic neighbor Tamila. Tamila's image straddles the two myths that regulate the story's clusters of conceptual metaphors, for although her persona defines itself in folklore *topoi*, she fulfills a pivotal function in the dynamics of the Edenic myth. Tamila elaborates a comprehensive mythology to elucidate both the universal human condition and her own mythic origins. She patterns her autobiography on the conventional fairy-tale plot of a young maid (innocence) dwelling on a mountain (associated with the sacred, the spiritual, ascension) who is carried off by a dragon (symbol of "things animal," "the primordial enemy," identified with the snake).[27]

From the outset Tamila's symbolic significance finds expression in the magical trappings and objects constellated around her: the sundial, with its earlier function of tabulating time; the dragon's insignia on her black robe;

her rings, with their ominous snake and toad (her talisman!);[28] her smoke, and the mysterious "panacea" she drinks; the mystic numbers three and seven;[29] and the glass egg ("rozovoe volshebnoe") shot through with golden sparks. Tamila initiates Petia not only into these emblematic phenomena, which represent a fallen world, but also into the evil and suffering, doubts, and enmity that derive from the Fall. In her cosmic scheme, the trinity that oversees human life consists of three of the four mystical "birds of paradise":[30] (1) Finist, the "bright falcon" of fairy tales,[31] who, Tamila relates, used to visit her until they quarreled (115). That detail presages ominous developments, for it signals that the phoenix-like rebirth through love evoked by the legendary bird will remain outside the story's events, as indeed it does.[32] (2) Sirin, the sweet-voiced death-bearer, with whom Petia and his grandfather have the metaphorical rendezvous that supplies the story's title. And (3) Alkonost, whose magic egg brings its possessor eternal misery:

> And there's another bird, Alkonost. It gets up in the morning at dawn, all rosy and transparent, it sparkles and glimmers. [. . .] It lays one egg, very rare. Do you know why people pick lilies? They're looking for the egg. Whoever finds it will feel a sense of longing his whole life. But they still look for it, still want it. (122)

> A to est' eshche ptitsa Alkonost. Ta utrom vstaet, na zare, vsia rozovaia, prozrachnaia, svetitsia, s iskorkami. [. . .] Neset odno iaitso, ochen' redkoe. Ty znaesh', zachem liudi lilii rvut? Oni iaitso ishchut. Kto naidet, na vsiu zhizn' zatoskuet. A vse ravno ishchut, vse ravno khochetsia. (116)

In accepting the egg, then, Petia tacitly acquiesces to embark on a journey toward spiritual and cognitive revelation. His first contact with Tamila marks a watershed in his interior odyssey. Tolstaya notes: "He used [. . .] to think that miracles happened only on distant islands [. . .] . But the world, it turned out, was wholly imbued with mystery, sadness, and magic, rustling in the branches, swaying in the dark waters" (123) (On ran'she [. . .] dumal, chto chudesa—na dalekikh ostrovakh [. . .] . A mir, okazyvaetsia, ves' propitan tainstvennym, grustnym, volshebnym, shumiashchim v vetviakh, kolebliushchimsia v temnoi vode" [117]). The successive phases of Petia's gravitation toward knowledge develop consonantly with the story's modal paradigm, with the next, as yet unrecognized stage, replicating the dynamics of " 'On the Golden Porch' ": Petia chances upon the dead bird, which prefigures the imminent fate of his grandfather: "He carefully rode around a dead crow—a wheel had run over the bird, its eye was covered with a white film, the black collapsed wings covered with *ashes*, and the beak frozen in a bitter avian smile" (127) ("Ostorozhno ob''ekhal dokhluiu voronu—kto-to razdavil ptitsu kolesom, glaz zakryl beloi plenkoi, chernye svaliavshiesia kryl'ia pokryty *peplom*, kliuv zastyl v gorestnoi ptich'ei ulybke" [120, emphasis added]). This accidental encounter adumbrates both Petia and his grandfather's rendezvous with the bird (Alkonost *and* Sirin) to which the story's title alerts us. Petia's personal discovery of death (his grandfather's) and of flesh-knowledge (through Tamila and Uncle Boria) clarifies the significance of the objects that earlier perplexingly linked his grandfather with Tamila: her black cushions and his oxygen bags, described as "black oxygen cushions" ("chernye kislorodnye podushki" [118]). The moment of epiphany offers a similarly belated realization that the smoke which throughout the story seems to connect Tamila and Uncle Boria only superficially and by misleading contrast (Petia discriminates between them qualitatively) in fact provides clues to both the physical nature of their connection and their symbolic ties with the dragon.[33]

What at first may appear as operatic decoration or fictive play calculated to entertain a child proves to carry prophetic weight on a symbolic plane when validated by later events: possession of Alkonost's egg does lead to Petia's experience of gnawing misery, his induction into the adult world of strife; Tamila's snake does witness Petia's access to knowledge, a rite of passage enabled by its owner; the removal of her toad-ring does have negative consequences for both Tamila and Petia, exposing her in her demythicized aspect as an earthly creature of "forbidden" appetite, and plunging Petia into the pain-ridden sphere of adulthood. And in Tolstaya's universe, adulthood is synonymous with adulteration.

The folkloric mythology in which Tamila's image and created world are steeped, then, differs decisively from the third realm of myth in the story, which Tolstaya handles in a more localized and less freighted way, to shape Petia's flights of imagination and to bolster in a minor key the exfoliation of the matrix metaphors. The legends of Atlantis and the Flying Dutchman, which recur as conflated leitmotifs in Petia's daydreams, do not form the mythic backbone without which the narrative would collapse. In that sense they play an ancillary and much simpler role than that of the lapsarian and folklore myths (joined, in any case, by their shared preoccupation with paradise, soul, and im/mortality).[34] Yet they do have a symbolic relevance to the story's dominant concerns. The lost continent of Atlantis may be read, after all, as a proleptic or prophetic vision of unrecoverable innocence, particularly since the metaphor is spawned within Petia's consciousness. His fanciful thoughts as he contemplates the breakfast cereal placed before him expand into an epic metaphor communicated via quasi-direct discourse: "a melting island of butter floated in the sticky

Sargasso Sea. Go under, buttery Atlantis. No one will be saved [presaging the story's concluding insight that no one *can* be saved—H.G.]. White palaces with emerald scaly roofs" (117) ("taiushchii ostrov masla plavaet v lipkom Sargassovom more. Ukhodi pod vodu, maslianaia Atlantida. Nikto ne spasetsia. Belye dvortsy s izumrudnymi cheshuichatymi kryshami" [122]). The passage is spun out for over a dozen lines before closing with a reference to the divinity with which Alkonost later will resonate ("looks *longingly* to the east") ("s *toskoi* smotrit na vostok" [emphasis added]).

In like manner, the Flying Dutchman represents a variant on humankind's eternal search for the beatific peace of paradise lost. It is hardly fortuitous, then, that "the Flying Dutchman" is what Petia mentally christens the boat on which he fantasizes sailing with Tamila to seek out the lost continent: "Then they would board 'The Flying Dutchman,' the dragon flag on the mast, Tamila in her black robe on the deck, sunshine and salt spray, and they would set sail in search of Atlantis, lost in the green, shimmering briny deep of Atlantis" (122–23) ("A potom oni siadut na Letuchii Gollandets, flag s drakonom—na verkhushke machty, Tamila v chernom khalate na palube,—solntse, bryzgi v litso,—poedut na poiski propavshei, soskol'znuvshei v zelenye zybkie okeanskie tolshchi Atlantidy" [116]). Although these auxiliary myths may be expendable, they enrich the narrative and fortify elements of the primary myths that impart meaning and structure to the narrative's events.

With her third story, "Sonia," Tolstaya abandoned a full-scale deployment of myth as algorithm. Although later works, such as "Seraph" ("Serafim"), contain mythic elements, their concentration is diluted and their function restricted. As a result, the stories' texture loses some of the extraordinary density that distinguishes Tolstaya's first two publications. In other respects, however, the two narratives that marked Tolstaya's literary debut provide an accurate index of her prose in general. They evidence her metaphysical bent, her interest in "eternal questions" and, perhaps as a consequence, the absence in her fiction of that direct engagement with the burning issues of the day that characterizes so much of glasnost literature.[35] This does not mean that Tolstaya excludes the *realia* of Soviet life. On the contrary, most of her stories contain vivid details about Soviet housing, stores, food, long lines, black-market or unofficial dealings, the service sector of Soviet society, its system of perquisites and useful connections (*blat*), contemporary sexual mores, and so forth, but she treats these synecdochically and relegates them to what Henry James aptly called a "habitable background."

Tolstaya's first two publications also are typical of her oeuvre in their textual complexity and the cultural challenge they offer, for a solid knowledge not only of Russian but also of European and classical literature, as well as folklore, is a prerequisite for understanding her prose even on the most elementary level. Although Tolstaya's values are traditional insofar as they overlap with humanistic principles, evidence her ecumenical faith, and thus position her within a continuum in Russian culture, her style, paradoxically, belongs to postmodernism, which for Fredric Jameson, among others, involves "a radical break, both with a dominant culture and an aesthetic."[36] Soviet readers more readily embraced the Platonic model of the writer as "seer" than as Aristotelian "maker" (*homo faber*).[37] And Tolstaya's irony, macabre humor, decentered narrator, time derangement, rhetorical devices, and so forth, struck many of them as irreverent, puzzling, overly self-conscious, and "aristocratic"—a reaction doubtless encouraged by both her familial antecedents and the ingrained habits of a reading public more accustomed to deciphering political codes smuggled into texts than coping with sophisticated narrative play and wide-ranging intertexts.

According to Tolstaya, what stimulated her first literary efforts in the early 1980s was the dreary lexical poverty of Soviet prose. Appalled at the ever-narrowing range of vocabulary that nervelessly repeated itself from one author to the next, Tolstaya wished to revive the tradition that last flourished in the Soviet Union during the 1920s: that of individual style based on juxtaposition of, and shifts among, various linguistic levels. As she puts it:

> The academician Lev Shcherba identified four linguistic layers: the elevated, the neutral, the familiar, and the vulgar. The existence of these layers is obvious. What's more important, essentially, isn't the process or the object a given word denotes, but our relationship to that word. What matters is the emotional aura surrounding the word. Literature, unlike technical, informal texts, works not with actual objects, but with their emotional coloration and with the contrasts produced by the "clashes" in these colorations. Even within the parameters of a small vocabulary, if we start combining words from different layers, then we'll get a stylistic oxymoron. That produces a specific emotional effect. You have something vivid that stirs your emotions. Good writers work on specific shifts from one layer to another, on the combination of various layers. They use these leaps and shifts all the time. A writer's individual style above all manifests itself in such choices—they're a measure of his taste, sense of balance and harmony or intentional disharmony.[38]

Tolstaya's own calibration of stylistic levels bypasses a half-century of homogenizing Soviet authorial practices, forging links with the 1920s, specifically Iurii Olesha, Ivan Bunin, and Mikhail Bulgakov; it has much in common with the verbal play of Nikolai Gogol, Andrei Bely, and Vladimir Nabokov. Doubtless that accounts in part for the controversy her prose elicited in the Soviet press. In a country where writers, paid by the page, pragmatically opted for length at the expense of depth, Tolstaya consistently strived for maximal condensation.

Whereas I. Grekova and Andrei Voznesensky hailed Tolstaya as an exceptionally gifted newcomer to Russian fiction,[39] others faulted her for being cold and unfeeling and for succumbing to stylistic excesses, particularly to immoderate reliance on metaphor.[40] What doubtless disconcerted many readers while fascinating others is not only the startling surface discrepancy between Tolstaya's themes and choice of characters, on the one hand, and her style, on the other, but also the unexpected tonal leaps she mentions in her interview that evoke a clash of emotional responses (à la Gogol's "Overcoat" ["Shinel' "] and Bulgakov's *Master and Margarita*). Tolstaya explores her favorite themes of life's meaning, time's passage, imagination, memory, isolation, materialism, and misanthropy through the specific fates of characters whom many readers find absurdly pathetic or aggressively bizarre. Moreover, she presents them ambiguously. Externally, these seemingly less than average beings—often children, old women, and hapless men—lead a solitary, eventless existence, misunderstood by and and alienated from those around them (e.g., Marivanna, Zhenechka, Shura, Uncle Pasha, Peters). Yet the rapid shifts in Tolstaya's style—which veers between ridicule and pathos, naturalism and lyricism—preclude a single, stable perception of their character zone. Moreover, even as Tolstaya writes marginalized lives of emotional deprivation, her style provides an energetic denial of the melancholy in life, for its lush, pulsating colors suggest the amplitude of human and especially artistic potential. Although " 'On the Golden Porch' " and "Rendezvous with a Bird" indisputably differ from her subsequent fiction on account of their wholesale absorption of myth, they are nonetheless stylistically representative inasmuch as they brim with flamboyantly original metaphor, Homeric catalogues, exuberant humor, fantasy, poetic cadences, rhythmic syntax—the full panoply of available rhetorical devices.[41]

This verbal feast is served up by a narrative that begs for Bakhtinian analysis, for it consists of multiple voices not easily distinguishable from each other or identifiable as to provenance. Nor are they set off by conventional typographical markers.[42] It is above all the fragmented, multivocal narration that slides in quicksilver fashion from one mood or viewpoint to another, and yet another, scattering sighs, apostrophes, and exclamations as it stretches out into paragraphs, that invites comparison with Gogol, Bely, and Nabokov. The echoes from Pushkin, Lermontov, Tiutchev, Fet, Blok,

Olesha, Bulgakov, fairy tales, songs, and romances intercalated in her prose further amplify the choral effect that stamps her texts with her unique signature the way a watermark individualizes paper. The extravagant density of this verbal texture, its capacity for creation, ultimately assert the robust forces of life and suggest that what some critics have mistaken for aloofness inscribes Tolstaya's impassioned faith in language and the imagination. To foreground language itself as the hero of her texts, Tolstaya effaces her presence as author identifiable with a narrative voice by systematically multiplying voices whose origins remain open to conjecture. If in her interviews and journalism Tolstaya's "I" finds direct and forceful expression, it undergoes endless mediation in her fiction. The chief mediating devices in her first two stories are myth, intertext, and quasi-direct discourse (here anchored predominantly in a child's perspective).[43] Although the proportions among these elements vary from story to story, they nonetheless serve as Tolstaya's basic means of authorial self-exclusion in later works.

✧ 2 ✧

Language and the Soul's Dark Night in Childhood

As almost all commentators on Tolstaya's stories dealing with child-hood have remarked, her child's world constitutes a realm of wondrous enchantment, an Aladdin's cave of "perfect moments" accessed through a radiant imagination undimmed by logic, convention, or taboos. Maturation, with its attendant growth of (self-)consciousness, therefore, tends to be synonymous with an overwhelming sense of loss, with an attenuation of inventive powers at an ever-increasing remove from the immediacy of experience. Not all of Tolstaya's visions of childhood, however, are sunwashed Arcadias. Both "Loves Me—Loves Me Not" ("Liubish'—ne liubish' ") and "Night" ("Noch' "), in fact, expose its underbelly.[1]

Set, not accidently, in an urban environment that contrasts pointedly with the pastoral rhythms of " 'On the Golden Porch' " and "Rendezvous with a Bird,"[2] these two evocations of childhood foreground its fears, bewilderment, and desolation in an alien universe imperfectly governed by adults. The animism that elsewhere in Tolstaya's work transmutes early experiences into a series of indelible adventures conjures up dark, minatory forces in "Loves Me—Loves Me Not" and "Night"; the atmosphere recalls the dysphoric trials of a Hans Christian Andersen fairy tale, where horrors outweigh delights. Both texts juxtapose the microcosm of a mute animal haven to the macrocosm of a terrifying, menaced vulnerability.[3] And in both stories the child's point of view shapes the presentation of events, via first-person narrative in "Loves Me—Loves Me Not" and via Tolstaya's favorite narrative mode of quasi-direct discourse in "Night."

By borrowing her title of "Loves Me—Loves Me Not" from the formula ritually recited as one strips the petals from a flower to determine whether one's affection is reciprocated, Tolstaya from the outset pinpoints the universal thirst for love as a focal concern in the story. Indeed, the *siuzhet* traces the cumulative effects of lovelessness and mutual incomprehension between the five-year-old girl narrator and her governess Mar′ia Ivanovna

(Marivanna). These culminate at story's end in the latter's tearful departure from the household that hired her services. Rude, disobedient, and contrary, the little girl contemptuously ridicules Marivanna ("old, fat, silly," "silly old twit"), extending her hatred even to the woman's possessions as totems of a negative presence:[4] her hat with a veil, her hole-ridden gloves, and the cookies she feeds pigeons in the city park. Marivanna, in her turn, seems utterly oblivious to and disinterested in the needs of a five-year-old. Their activities "together," consisting principally of Marivanna's ecstatic reminiscences about her former life with "Uncle Georges" or declamations to the stupefied child of Georges's "decadent" lyrics, serve only to separate them. The two antagonists inhabit different tenses: Whereas the narrator/protagonist is attuned, childlike, to the present and the future, all of Marivanna's points of reference exist in the past, originating with the dead Uncle Georges. Their failed, adversarial relationship appears all the bleaker because Tolstaya flanks it by two contrastively successful ones: Marivanna's with Katia (the paragon of a former charge who loves her as her "dearest nanny"); and the little girl's with her beloved old Nanny Grusha.

The story's iterative references to love and its irrational nature amplify the theme: Pushkin, the narrator observes, "*loved* her [Nanny] very much too, and wrote about her and called her 'my ancient dove' " (4) ("ee [nianiu Grushu] tozhe ochen' *liubil* i pisal pro nee: 'Golubka driakhlaia moia' " [3]);[5] Marivanna recalls of Uncle Georges, "He *loved* me madly, madly" (5) ("On bezymno, bezymno menia *liubil*" [4]); of the lampshade purchased with her father at the flea market, the little girl anticipates, "we'll come to *love* it" (9) ("my ego *poliubim*" [8]);[6] witnessing the tearful, happy reunion between Marivanna and Katia, she protests, "Hey, girl, what's the matter with you? Rub your eyes! It's Marivanna [. . .] stupid, old, fat, silly" (12) (Ei, devochka, chto ty? Protri glaza! Eto zhe Mar'ivanna! [. . .] glupaia, staraia, tolstaia, nelepaia!" (11), which elicits a riposte from an unidentified source, "But does *love* know that?" ("No razve *liubov'* ob etom znaet?"),[7] followed by the protagonist's soundless wail: "I'm much better than that girl. But Marivanna doesn't *love* me like that. The world's unfair" (12) ("Ia gorazdo luchshe etoi devochki! A menia-to Mar'ivanna tak ne *liubit*. Mir nespravedliv" [11, emphases added]). In sum, the legitimate complaints of both Marivanna and the narrator (the former, of recalcitrance, spite, and poor manners; the latter, of neglect, tediousness, and stupidity) are rationalizations for what ultimately affronts them most: feeling unloved and slighted by the other.

Their inability to communicate with each other is conveyed through their contrasting discourses. With a child's inherent inclination to concreteness, the little girl takes literally Marivanna's metaphorical, periphrastic euphemisms (e.g., of Uncle Georges, "he was run over by the wheel of fortune. Because he was in debt and crossed the street improperly" [4]/"ego pereekhalo kolesom fortuny! Potomy chto on zaputalsia v dolgakh i nepravil′no perekhodil ulitsu!" [3]), and in her fits of negation she invents the kind of neologisms that Kornei Chukovskii showcased in *From Two to Five* (*Ot dvukh do piati*): for example, "No hello," "No revoir" ("Ne zdras′te," "Ne revuar!").[8] Her anomalous discourse provides, in linguistic terms, an index of her child's perspective, of the impermissible that is permissible in a child before s/he enters the discursive community of adults.[9] At the opposite end of the spectrum, Marivanna speaks in lofty tones, rhapsodizes over mysticism, the sublime, refinement, her own past and preferences, and, more importantly, regales the girl with readings from Georges's poetry. That poetry, in which Tolstaya hilariously parodies decadent *topoi*, dwells above all on death.

Given its orientation, Uncle Georges's poetry of seething passions, twisted violence, cryptic juxtapositions, and overbold imagery could hardly be less suitable for an impressionable child. Samples of his verses include a reworking of Goethe's "Erlkönig" as a dialogue of six stanzas between a petrified child and a nanny, who replaces the father in Goethe's original ballad:[10]

> "Nanny, who screamed so loud outside,
> Flashing past the window,
> Creaking the porch door,
> Sighing under the bed?"
>   [. . .]
> "Sleep, child, don't worry,
> The door is strong, the fence is high,
> The thief won't escape the block,
> The axe will thud in the night."
>
> "Nanny, who's breathing down my back,
> Who's invisible and climbing
> Ever closer up my
> Crumpled bed sheet?"
>
> "Oh, child, don't frown,
> Wipe your eyes and don't cry.
> The ropes are pulling tight,
> The executioner knows his job. "(6)
>
> "Niania, kto tak gromko vskriknul,
> Za okoshkom promel′knyl,
> Na krylechke dver′iu skripnul,
> Pod krovatkoiu vzdokhnul?"
>   [. . .]

"Spi, ditia, ne vedai strakha,
Dver' krepka, vysok zabor,
Ne minuet vora plakha,
Prozvenit v nochi topor."

"Niania, kto mne v spinu dyshit,
Kto, nevidimyi, ko mne
Podbiraetsia vse vyshe
Po izmiatoi prostyne?"

"O ditia, chto khmurish' brovki,
Vytri glazki i ne plach'.
Krepko stianuty verevki,
Znaet remeslo palach." (5)

As the little girl wryly observes, "after hearing a poem like that, who'd be brave enough to lower her feet from the bed, to use the potty, say?" (5) ("kto posle takikh stikhov naidet v sebe sily spustit' nogi s krovati, chtoby, skazhem, sest' na gorshok!" [5]). Marivanna's recital of a lubricious pseudo-Modernist poem by Uncle Georges ("Not white tulips/In bridal lace" [14]/ "Ne belye tiul'pany/V venchal'nykh kruzhevakh") provokes a similar reproof from Nanny Grusha: "What horrors/passions at bedtime for the child" (15) ("Strasti kakie rebenku na noch' " [14]). And the lyric by Uncle Georges that precedes Marivanna's final leave-taking once again yokes amorous escapade with death: "Princess Rose grew weary of life/And ended it at sunset" (16) ("Printsessa-roza zhit' ustala/I na zakate opochila" [14]).

The versifying gambler–lover–poetaster, in fact, embodies death throughout the story: we first learn of him as someone who, after being "run over by the wheel of fortune," "hanged himself because he had a bad bladder" (4); Marivanna lives in her communal apartment with her "hanged uncle" (7); in that apartment, he "runs his hands over the glass, peering out" (13); and in order to read the last-quoted poem, "the pale uncle comes out dressed in black" (15). Thus by foisting recollections of Georges and his poems onto her refractory charge, Marivanna force-feeds a relentless diet of scenarios about death to someone who by definition finds mortality conceptually inaccessible.[11] Psychologists, critics, and writers concur that an authentic apprehension of death necessitates a rite of passage from childhood to adolescence and, in some cases, adulthood.[12] Death does not customarily figure among the myriad phenomena that can inspire terror in children because in those rare cases when they acknowledge it as a reality they disavow its applicability to themselves.[13]

Marivanna's solipsistic obsession with Uncle Georges and his scribblings not only alienates her from her charge but makes her cruelly insensitive to a child's irrational fears, which stem partly from an imagination unballasted by the kind of reasoning that evolves only with adulthood. Imagination here, unlike in Tolstaya's "Edenic stories," is double-edged, and the emphasis in this instance falls on its darker side. Throughout, the little girl is shown as the victim of primal terrors generated by animistic beliefs.[14] Accordingly, she unhesitatingly credits a lampshade with quasi-human emotions and the dead with the standard attributes of the living ("Marivanna goes back to her place, a communal apartment, where, besides her, also live Iraida Anatolievna [. . .] and the hanged uncle" [7]/"Mar'ivanna ukhodit nochevat' k sebe, v kommunal'nuiu kvartiru, gde, krome nee, zhivut eshche: Iraida Anatol'evna [. . .] i povesivshiisia diadia" [6]). During the darkness of night the child hides under the bedclothes from all the evil spirits who threaten her safety. By assigning them proper names (Zmei [Snake], Sukhoi [the Dry One], Indrik and Khizdrik, Glaza [Eyes]) and particularizing their appearance and behavior more precisely than those of any human in the story, Tolstaya indicates the degree to which a child perceives these nocturnal phantoms as a palpable reality:

> Everyone knows that under the bed, closer to the wall, is the Snake: in laceup shoes, cap, gloves, motorcycle goggles, with a hook in his hand. The Snake isn't there during the day, but by night he coagulates from twilight stuff and waits very quietly: who'll dare lower a leg? And out comes the hook! He's unlikely to eat you, but he'll drag you in and shove you under the plinth, and you'll fall endlessly, under the floor, between the dusty partitions. Other species of noctural creatures guard the room: the fragile and translucent *Dry One*, weak but terrible, who stands all night in the closet. [. . .] Behind the peeling wallpaper are *Indrik* and *Khizdrik*; one is greenish, the other gray, and they both run fast and have many feet. [. . .] but the most horrible is the nameless one who is always behind me, almost touching my hair (*Uncle knows!*). (7, emphases added)

> Pod krovat'iu, blizhe k stene—vsem izvestno—lezhit Zmei: v shnurovannykh botinkakh, kepke, perchatkakh, mototsiklennykh ochkakh, a v ruke—kriuk. Dnem Zmeia net, a k nochi on sgushchaetsia iz sumerechnogo veshchestva i tikho-tikho zhdet: kto posmeet svestit' nogu? I srazu—khvat' kriukom! Vriad li s"est, no zatashchit i propikhnet pod plintus, i beskonechno budet padenie vniz, pod pol, mezhdu pyl'nykh pereborok. Komnatu storozhat i drugie porody vechernikh sushchestv: lomkii i poluprozrachnyi *Sukhoi*, slabyi, no strashnyi, stoit vsiu noch' naprolet v stennom shkafu. [. . .] Za otstavshimi oboiami —*Indrik* i *Khizdrik*—odin zelenovatyi, drugoi seryi, oba bystro begaiushchie, mnogonogie. [. . .] no samyi-to strashnyi—tot bezymennyi, chto vsegda za spinoi, pochti kasaetsia volos (*diadia svidetel'*!). (6)

Tolstaya presents the five-year-old's nocturnal apprehensions, here exacerbated by the Gothic coloration of Uncle Georges's pastiche ("Having frightened me with her uncle's poems, Marivanna leaves" [7]/"Napugav diadinymi stikhami, Mar'ivanna ukhodit" [6]), as a dread of violence from malevolent forces ("they don't attack from the front"/"speredi ne napadaiut").

This image of the child as a passive, helpless victim under assault recurs in a related network of visual and auditory metaphors during her sickness, which translate her fever into a buzzing honeycomb, a squadron of airplanes, and a persistent drum roll that surrounds her threateningly from all sides ("banging on red drums," "my heart can't take any more, it'll burst" [7]). That defenselessness surfaces again when, wounded by Marivanna's undisguised preference for Katia, the little girl laments: "The world's unfair. The world's upside down. I don't understand anything! I want to go home!" (12) ("Mir nespravedliv. Mir ustroen navyvorot! Ia nichego ne ponimaiu! Ia khochu domoi!" [11]). And it climaxes, significantly, in the pivotal scene where she and Marivanna find themselves alone in the twilight city streets. In the thickening shadows (associated with Uncle Georges), the child's anguish at her solitude, helplessness, and sense of abandonment attains existential proportions:

> An hour of depression for adults, of depression and fear for children. I'm all alone in the world, Mama has lost me, we're going to get lost any second now. [. . .] Hurry, hurry home! To Nanny! O Nanny Grusha! Darling! [. . .] I'll huddle against your dark skirts, and your warm old hands will warm my frozen, lost, bewildered *heart*. [. . .] Lord, the world is *so frightening and hostile*, the *poor, homeless, inexperienced soul huddling* in the square in the night wind. *Who was so cruel, who filled me with love and hate*, fear and depression, pity and shame, but *didn't give me words: stole speech*, sealed my mouth, put on iron padlocks, and threw away the keys? (13, emphases added)

> Chas toski dlia vzroslykh, toski i strakha dlia detei. Ia odna na vsem svete, menia poteriala mama, seichas, seichas my zabliudimsiaaaaaaa! [. . .] Skorei, skorei domoi! K nianechke! O nianechka Grusha! Dorogaia! [. . .] Ia prizhmus' k temnomu podolu, i pust' tvoi teplye staren'kie ruki otogreiut moe zamerzshee, zabludivsheesia, zaputavsheesia *serdtse*! [. . .] Gospodi, *kak strashen i vrazhdeben mir*, kak *szhalas'* posredi ploshchadi na nochnom vetru *bespriiutnaia, neumelaia dusha*! *Kto zhe byl tak zhestok, chto vlozhil v menia liubov' i nenavist'*, strakh i tosku, zhalost' i styd—*a slov ne dal: ukral rech'*, zapechatal rot, nalozhil zheleznye zasovy, vybrosil kliuch! (12)

While the interior monologue begins within the little girl's discursive mode, its modulation to a jeremiad unmistakably leads the reader out of it.

Gerard Genette's concept of focalization, which distinguishes between who sees and who speaks within a narrative, helps to clarify Tolstaya's major infraction here of the mode that otherwise dominates throughout. "Who sees," or, more accurately, feels the emotions of panic, forlornness, and impotent resentment articulated in this passage is indisputably the little girl. Yet the discursive markers (abstract generalization, conceptual metaphor) clearly disqualify her as the one "who speaks."[15] Like the earlier intrusive generalization, "But does love really know that?" (12) ("No razve liubov' ob etom znaet?" [11]), the final paragraph, with its echoes from Pushkin's poem "Futile gift, chance gift" ("Dar naprasnyi, dar sluchainyi" [1828]),[16] assumes a stance and tone incompatible with a five-year-old's mental processes and above all her verbal formulations. Although it would be absurd to claim that the rest of the text approximates bona fide children's speech, Tolstaya nonetheless manages to maintain that illusion within a basically adult narration through systematically interspersing direct utterances by the protagonist ("Eat your own crummy cream of wheat!" [11]/"Esh'te sami vashu poganuiu kashu!" [10]), tracing certain patterns of thought and behavior (willful misconduct calculated to irritate adults that nonetheless captures their attention), and registering specific actions ("I stick out my tongue at her" [5]/"Ia pokazyvaiu ei iazyk" [5]) that are all generally recognizable as childlike. Having sustained the fiction of a child's reporting viewpoint for such an extended stretch, why does Tolstaya conspicuously shift narrative gears here? Exactly at the moment when the little girl's anguish sets the stage for a profound self-revelation, Tolstaya, like the Unknown ("Kto") implicitly reproached in the monologue, withdraws the power of narrative voice from her. Such a silencing gesture is rendered all the more ironic by the gist of the passage, which laments the incommensurateness of language's expressive capabilities with the child's inner realm of passions and sensations. If, as Bakhtin postulates, language is constitutively intersubjective, then the social category of children has been excluded from the dialogized heteroglossic interplay that enables the utterances capable of directly articulating a subjectivity.[17] In seeming to be motivated by that lack, Tolstaya's strategy—the abrupt displacement of narrative voice—underscores the absence of such a language. Paradoxically, the shift also distances the child from the reader by transforming her into an object of compassion where formerly she had been a compass, a refractory but communicative guide of that reader's responses.

So acute is the child's desperation that it continues to color all her perceptions even after her reinstatement in the cozy refuge of home. Under its lingering impact, she reinterprets even familiar surroundings in the subjective terms of her own tragic desolation ("Go away, all of you, leave me alone, you don't understand anything!" [15]/"Uidite vse, ostav'te menia, vy nichego ne ponimaete!" [14]): projecting her panic onto the illustrations at the bottom of her bowl, she identifies with the children about to be seized by the geese and swans, defenseless because the depicted girl's hands have faded, making it impossible for her to protect herself or her little brother (E14). As in the earlier flea-market episode, these impressions blur into temperature-induced hallucinations as the tearful protagonist succumbs to feverish sleep.

Although the little girl aspires to a discourse of subjectivity, ultimately the language that she best understands and that the story implicitly privileges is not verbal. Rather, it is the mute communication of physical gesture—body language prompted by animal instinct, exemplified in her relationship with Nanny Grusha. Frozen in terror at the prospect of being stranded forever in the dark night of Marivanna's company, the little girl yearns for Nanny Grusha's protective, wordless comfort:

> Nanny will unwind my scarf, [. . .] and take me into the *cavelike warmth of the nursery*, where [. . .] my bitter childish tears will drip into the light blue plate [. . .] . And, seeing that, *Nanny will also cry*, and sit close, *and hug me*, and won't ask, but *will understand with her heart, the way an animal understands an animal, an old person a child, and a wordless creature its fellow.* (13, emphases added)

> Nianechka razmotaet moi sharf, [. . .] uvedet v *peshchernoe teplo detskoi*, gde [. . .] zakapaiut gor'kie detskie slezy v golobuiu tarelku [. . .] . I, vidia eto, *nianechka zaplachet i sama*, i podsiadet, i *obnimet*, i ne sprosit, i *poimet serdtsem, kak ponimaet zver'—zveria, starik—ditia, besslovesnaia tvar'—svoego sobrata.* (12)[18]

Marivanna's interactions with the little girl are exclusively verbal, consisting of interrogatives, sigh-punctuated reminiscences, and verse recitals that relegate the child to spectatorship of *her* world, with its pretensions and complaints. Nanny Grusha, who instinctively understands the child and does not instrumentalize her to satisfy her own needs, operates chiefly on the physical plane of nurture to make the child emotionally secure. In the context of the story, then, Nanny's ignorance of French has a broader significance, for language as a formal set of rules—as the medium of the macrocosm with its universal prescriptions, theories, and abstractions—is not her forte; her mode of communication is bodily, tactile—that of the domestic microcosm, a domain in which individualized, immediate experience plays a more prominent part.[19]

"Loves Me—Loves Me Not," then, examines the possibilities and limits of language in human intercourse largely through a child's relationship to the adult world around her. Language in its richest sense here coincides with the Bakhtinian notion of utterance as an evolving means of addressed self-expression whereby communication with others is enabled by context and others' responsive understanding, their active receptivity to dialogue. Thus Marivanna remains alien ("*chuzhaia*") to the child, as does her discourse, invariably reported on the narrative level in quotation marks or distanced through double voicing to signal her irreconcilable Otherness.[20] Neither adversary permits the other's voice to enter her discourse as anything but a foreign element unsupported by a tacit gesture of openness. The little girl's despair at her inability to articulate her psychological state measures not so much her verbal circumscription as her companion's resistance to dialogue with her, which the child intuitively grasps. In Bakhtinian terms, Marivanna fails to acknowledge the human other in the child, while demanding precisely that acknowledgement for herself. That is partly why her closest ties are to the dead Georges and the "dead" activity of repetitious recitation.

Aleksei Petrovich, the retarded adult, hence "child," in "Night," shares the five-year-old's animistic perception of the world, her dread of its incalculable hazards, and her reliance on a protective figure for a sense of security. He, too, submits to existential terror in the dark outdoors, then finds the verbal expression adequate to the insight vouchsafed by that alienation.

To cast Aleksei's cognitive and mental faculties in a childlike mode, Tolstaya draws once again on folklore. Accordingly, from the outset she has him conceive of night as a mythic/psychological principle of nonlife boasting its own underworld kingdom of dragons, dwarfs, and mushrooms: "the gates of the nighttime realm have slammed shut; dragons, mushrooms, and frightening dwarfs have plunged below the earth once again, life triumphs" (67) ("zakhlopnulis' vorota nochnogo tsarstva; drakony, griby i strashnye karliki snova provalilis' pod zemliu, zhizn' torzhestvuet" [95]).[21] In the same vein, he mythicizes the lascivious neighbor into a mermaid, endowed with the paradigmatic traits of ambiguous, seductive allure, slipperiness, and skill at entrapment. People, objects, and various other phenomena appear not as individual instances of categories but as entire categories or essences: Man, Woman, Leg, Smell, Rules.[22] Moreover, Aleksei's reactions to objects and people resemble children's insofar as he apprehends them undifferentiatedly. As Coe has astutely remarked, frequently "the supreme ecstasies of childhood arise out of contact with the inanimate" (113). What arouses Aleksei's most intense pleasure and agony are the little cardboard pillboxes he glues together to earn money. His love for them leads him to violate Maternal Law (the only authority he knows) by surreptitiously concealing two samples under his pillow and to fly into a murderous rage at the realization that consumers discard them: "Mamochka runs over, calms him down, leads the enraged Aleksei Petrovich off, takes away the knife, tears the hammer from his convulsed fingers" (71) ("Mamochka bezhit, uspokaivaet, uvodit raz′′iarennogo Alekseia Petrovicha, otbiraet nozh, vyryvaet molotok iz ego sudorozhno skriuchennykh pal′tsev" [96]). These devices collectively convey Aleksei's estrangement from the "norms" of the adult world, from the macrocosm of his society.

Contrasted to this infinitude of uncertainties and perils, communicated in such subjective spatial metaphors as the open sea, dark labyrinths, and a forest of fallen trees, is the relatively safe microcosm of Aleksei's immediate universe supervised by his mother. His sole link with the world outside their communal apartment, she is simultaneously his bulwark against its intimidating unknowns, as Tolstaya emphasizes by couching her maternal persona in an imagery of shelter and steerage: medieval castle, ship's captain, guiding star, protective bird's wing, and, implicitly, nurturing animal ("Mamochka leads Aleksei Petrovich by the reins into a warm den, into a soft nest, under a white wing" [76]/"Mamochka vedet pod uzdtsy Alekseia Petrovicha v tepluiu *noru*, v miagkoe gnezdo, pod beloe krylo" [98]). For Aleksei, this eighty-year-old tower of comforting flesh is the intrepid explorer who has mastered a domain beyond his comprehension, the omniscient sage who legislates his mode of existence both indoors and out: "Mamochka knows best. I'm going to listen to Mamochka. Only she knows the safe paths through the thickets of the world" (72) ("Mamochka luchshe znaet. Budu slushat′ Mamochku. Tol′ko ona znaet vernuiu tropku cherez debri mira" [97]).

Aleksei's sense of self-definition, of what he can claim as his territory within the world, is expressed according to the classic formula of pre-socialized children: the smaller and more womblike, the safer and better:[23]

> Aleksei Petrovich has his own world—in his head, the real one. Everything's allowed there. But this one, outside, is bad, wrong. And it's very hard to remember what's good and what's bad. They've learned, they have good memories. But for him it's hard to live by someone else's Rules. (70)

> U Alekseia Petrovicha svoi mir—v golove, nastoiashchii. Tam vse mozhno. A etot, snaruzhi,—durnoi, nepravil′nyi. I ochen′ trudno zapomnit′, chto khorosho, a chto plokho. Vyuchili, u nikh pamiat′ khoroshaia. A emu trudno zhit′ po chuzhim Pravilam. (96)

If in the spatial scheme of ever-expanding circles of existence the widest sphere offers the greatest exposure to danger, while the familiar, if imperfectly mastered, middle terrain of enclosed space at least guarantees the asylum of maternal safekeeping, then the smallest—the invisible arena of Aleksei's inner life—is the site of his most intense and complete experiences. There he transcends "someone else's Rules," specifically by surmounting spatial restrictions along the vertical plane—again, in folkloric terms. Fairy tales, rhymes, and such children's texts as *Alice in Wonderland* and *Through the Looking Glass* contain numerous examples of miraculous expansion and shrinkage.[24] These transformations merely exteriorize the child's psychological sense of power and control over her/his environment, on the one hand, or helplessness in the face of complex and intractable surroundings, on the other. When Aleksei teeters on the psychologically rich border between sleep and wakefulness, these options merge in a physical sensation that synchronizes two polarized movements, movements that logically would seem to be mutually exclusive:

> The sky is all sprinkled with stars [. . .] : little shining beads [. . .] . When Aleksei Petrovich lies in bed and wants to fall asleep, his legs start growing on their own, down, down [evoking, but now in positive terms, his hysterical panic in elevators, where "they're pulling, pulling on (his) legs, dragging them down" (71)—H.G.], and his head grows up, up, to the black dome, up, and sways like the top of a tree in a storm, while *the stars scrape his skull like sand*. And the second Aleksei Petrovich, inside, keeps shrinking and shrinking, compressing, he disappears into a poppy seed, into a sharp needle tip, into a microbe, *into nothingness, and if he's not stopped, he'll vanish there completely*. But the external, *giant Aleksei Petrovich* sways like a pine log mast, grows, scratches his bald spot against the night dome, doesn't allow the *little one* to disappear into a dot. And these two Aleksei Petroviches are one and the same. (73–74, emphases added)

> Nebo vse zasypalo *zvezdami* [. . .] : *malen'kie* siiaiushchie biserniki [. . .] . Kogda Aleksei Petrovich lezhit v posteli i khochet zasnut', nogi u nego sami nachinaiut rasti vniz, vniz, a golova—vverkh, vverkh, do chernogo kupola, vse vverkh, i raskachivaetsia, kak verkhushka dereva v grozu, a *zvezdy peskom skrebutsia o ego cherep*. A vtoroi Aleksei Petrovich, vnutri, vse s''ezhivaetsia, s''ezhivaetsia, szhimaetsia, propadaet v makovoe zernyshko, v ostryi konchik igolki, v mikrobchika, *v nichto, i esli ego ne ostanovit', on sovsem tuda uidet*. No vneshnii, *gigantskii Aleksei Petrovich* korabel'noi sosnoi raskachivaetsia, rastet, chirkaet lysinoi po nochnomu kupolu, ne puskaet *malen'kogo* uiti v tochku. I eti dva Alekseia Petrovicha—odno i to zhe. (98)

The *fabula* of "Night" translates these diametrical oppositions—of involuntary diminishment to the point of self-elimination versus empowerment through limitless extension—into two pivotal episodes explicitly connected with the section cited above: Aleksei's encounters in the dark after his solitary flight into the street; and his attempt to become "a Pushkin." These disparate, ostensibly antithetical routes converge in the story's conclusion, and it is worth examining Tolstaya's strategy for leading up to that convergence.

The first episode recounts how Aleksei snatches money from a table to buy the ice cream that his mother earlier denies him on account of his sore throat. Once outside, he surrenders to a growing terror on several counts: his guilt about his theft, coupled with his animistic reading of the world, conjures up a classic children's fantasy of wolves waiting to pounce on him ("In the entryways wolves stand in black columns: they're waiting" [75]/"V podvorotniakh chernymi sherengami stoiat volki: zhdut" [98]);[25] his typically bizarre behavior (his fly is unzipped, he walks backward,[26] and he peers at women's legs) earns him several blows from the women's male escorts; and, finally, disoriented, bleeding, and panic-stricken, he cannot find his way in the dark ("Mamochka, Mamochka, where are you? Mamochka, the road is black, the voices are silent, the paths lead into a deep swamp! Mamochka, your child is crying, dying, your one and only, beloved, long-awaited, long-suffered!" [75]/"Mamochka, Mamochka, gde ty? Mamochka, cheren put', molchat golosa, v glukhoe boloto vedut tropinki! Mamochka, plachet, umiraet tvoe ditia, edinstvennoe, nenagliadnoe, dolgozhdannoe, vystradannoe!" [98]). In one of her startling rhetorical shifts, Tolstaya metonymically resurrects the above-quoted passage as she brackets the moment in a cosmic perspective with an empathetic apostrophe of, narratively speaking, problematic origins:

> Aleksei Petrovich leans against a drainpipe, spits something black, whines. *Little one, so little,* alone, you got lost on the street, *you came into this world by mistake. Get out of here, it's not for you*! Aleksei Petrovich cries with a loud howl, lifting his disfigured face to the stars. (75, emphases added)

> Aleksei Petrovich privalilsia k vodostochnoi trube, pliuet chernym, skulit. *Malen'kii, malen'kii,* odinokii, zabludilsia na ulitse, *po oshibke prishel ty v etot mir! Ukhodi otsiuda, on ne dlia tebia!* Gromkim laem plachet Aleksei Petrovich, podniav k zvezdam izurodovannoe litso. (98)

The apostrophe links this passage specifically with the earlier description of Aleksei's sensation of shrinking so radically as wholly to disappear, while the diegetical frame echoes elements from the antithetical sensation of expanding upward into the star-filled sky. In both sections a key element is the night, which not only adverts to the story's title but also provides its closure. Characteristic of Tolstaya's authorial practises is her method of inscribing night as an undulating motif in the story so that it steadily acquires incremental associations. By story's end the word "night" is so freighted with conceptual accretions that it can legitimately pass for the poem that Aleksei believes he has composed in merely iterating the word ten times.

At the story's opening, night is metaphorically conceived as an underworld kingdom of nonlife that surfaces when it grows dark; its "guests" stage a performance aided by transparent, ambiguous props ("prizrachnyi, dvusmyslennyi rekvizit" [95]). Night is next evoked obliquely through the stars scattered across the sky (R97) that introduce Aleksei's mystic experience of dwindling and enlarging (R97). Reprising the earlier stage metaphor, the next mention of night projects it as the backdrop (replete with such "ambiguous props" as wolves, atomized body parts, and the sounds of fire engines) for Aleksei's traumatic solitary confrontation with the outside world, which leaves him devastated and prompts the apostrophe that stresses his smallness. Thus night carries associations of death, illusion, contradiction, fragmentation, and solitariness; it connotes uncontrollable, powerful forces that inflict pain and terror, crushing Alexsei and reducing him to a miscroscopic point; hence "Mamochka, plachet, umiraet tvoe ditia" (98). Paradoxically, Aleksei's illumination is an insight into darkness ("He knows everything, he has understood the world, understood the Rules. [. . .] Lightning *illuminates* Aleksei Petrovich's brain!" [76, emphasis added]/ "On vse znaet, on ponial mir, ponial Pravila. [. . .] Molniia *ozariaet* Alekseia Petrovicha!" [98–99]). The epiphany that the universe is a nocturnal desert, that we dwell in the human "heart of darkness," however, contains within it a redemptive element figurally represented by the stars that logically and narratively are inseparable from the metaphor of night. The stars, against which Aleksei's head brushes during his vision of expansion, to which he lifts his head as he summons his mother, and which metaphorically define his mother's role in his life ("putevodnaia zvezda"), respond to his supplication: his mother delivers him from the macrocosm of abstract, impersonal indifference to the microcosm of individual love and creaturely nurture ("Mamochka vedet pod uzdtsy Alekseia Petrovicha v tepluiu noru, v miagkoe gnezdo, pod beloe krylo" [98]).

Aleksei's impulse to articulate his epiphany in a poem intertwines this episode with the Pushkin motifs embedded in the narrative. Enlisted in his traditional tropological capacity as a metonomy for art and creative expression, Pushkin enters the text via the square named after him.[27] As Aleksei and his mother pass the architectural landmark of the Opekushin monument to the poet,[28] Pushkin's "example" inspires Aleksei to attain the status of

writer (" 'I'm going to be a writer too' " [73]/" 'Ia tozhe budu pisatelem' "
[97]). Further stimulus is provided by his mother's reading, during the
evenings, of Pushkin's "Winter Evening" ("Zimnii vecher"), the first stanza
of which Tolstaya quotes in full:[29]

> A storm with mist engulfs the skies,
> And whirls the drifting snow,
> First like a beast it howls and cries,
> Then like a child sobs soft and low. (73)

> Buria mgloiu nebo kroet,
> Vikhri snezhnye krutia;
> To, kak zver', ona zavoet,
> To zaplachet, kak ditia. (97)

Its pertinence to Aleksei's situation and to his final insight undoubtedly
motivates Tolstaya's choice of Pushkin lyric. At its biographical simplest,
the poem shows the poet indoors in the company of his old nurse, contemplating the stormy twilight outdoors. Specific analogies between Pushkin's
text and Tolstaya's literary treatment of Aleksei's plight, principally
through binary juxtapositions, abound.

Both works contrast the ominous atmosphere of a darkening, boundless
exterior to domesticated, enclosed space. Within the landscape of both, the
focus falls on the sky. Both present an older female figure as a potential
source of solace. And Pushkin's similes for the sounds of the storm are
reproduced in the two images of Aleksei that Tolstaya spotlights—sobbing
child and howling animal: "First like a beast it howls and cries,/Then like a
child sobs soft and low" ("To, kak zver', ona zavoet,/To zaplachet, kak
ditia") in Pushkin's poem; "Aleksei Petrovich cries with a loud howl,"
"your child is crying, dying" ("Gromkim laem plachet Aleksei Petrovich,"
"plachet, umiraet tvoe ditia") in Tolstaya's story. Accordingly, when his
mother reads "Winter Evening" aloud, Aleksei exhibits intense pleasure at
exactly that couplet and, moreover, imitates the storm's howl (97). Pushkin,
then, serves as Aleksei's model; just as Pushkin masters his experience
through the mediation of poetic composition, so Aleksei manages to find
the minimalist verbal form for distilling his revelatory ordeal of spiritual
terror and *Angst*, thereby gaining retrospective possession of it. With
Pushkin's aid, Aleksei Petrovich successfully completes the process of
comprehension, assimilation, and articulation that constitutes a child's rite
of passage en route to adulthood.

Although "Loves Me—Loves Me Not" and "Night" lack the ebullient
verbal playfulness of Lewis Carroll's Alice stories, in them, as in *Alice in
Wonderland*, "[t]he problem of personal identity is closely connected with

the idea of estrangement from language" (Flescher, 134). Both texts associate a child's existentialist terror not only with a crisis of self-expression but also with unbounded, alienating space. Both pit that anxiety-generating macrocosm against the asylum of a nurturing microcosm with a resident guardian. And both rely on folklore and poetry to convey a child's apperception of the world, its forces, and its means of communication.

Unlike the majority of Tolstaya's stories, "Night" strives for, and achieves, bona fide closure. In fact, it lends itself admirably to a tight, coherent reading of the type de Man calls totalizing, whereas "Loves Me—Loves Me Not," with which it otherwise has so much in common, ends on a future-oriented anticipatory note ("We've got the summer ahead"/("U nas vperedi leto") that intimates the start of another narrative and leaves the reader suspended. While an episode is over, the "complete story" has not been told. Such, at least, is the inference that "Loves Me—Loves Me Not" fosters, and perhaps the absence of a comparable intimated incompleteness in "Night," with its strong sense of finality, accounts for the claustrophobic gloom that shrouds the story.

✦ 3 ✦

Tolstayan Love as Surface Text

Warum bemachtigt sich des Kindesinns
So hohe Ahnung von den Lebendsingen,
Das dann die Dinge, wenn sie wirklich sind,
Nur schale Schauer des Erinnerns bringen?
Hugo von Hofmannsthal, *Der Tor und der Tod*

Whereas, according to the banal lyrics of a popular song, "love makes the world go round," in Tolstaya's fiction, love, or its facsimile, overturns the world, for it conduces above all to frustration, torment, and thought of suicide. Indeed, three of Tolstaya's Leningrad stories that purportedly concentrate on romantic love more accurately spotlight her protagonists' incapacity to realize love or to have it reciprocated.[1] Furthermore, in all three cases—"Sonia" (1984), "Peters" (1986), and "The Moon Came Out" ("Vyshel mesiats iz tumana") (1987)—their thwarted romantic aspirations seem to be an extension of the characters' more general inability to establish human intimacy within bounds that convention deems healthy.[2] Figures representing majority opinion or dominant values in the pertinent texts perceive all three characters as laughable failures, and, whatever Tolstaya's human compassion,[3] as author she depicts these apparent eccentrics and their amatory endeavors in terms that underscore the pitiful and grotesque—an unsettlingly ambiguous blend that for the Slavist involuntarily evokes Gogol's alienating portrayal of Akakii Akakievich in "The Overcoat" ("Shinel' ").[4]

Tolstaya casts the eponymous protagonist of "Sonia," her third published story, in a markedly carnivalized mold that on the surface at least divests her of recognizable normalcy and certainly of traditional heroinism. Likened to a horse, a witch, and a doll, Sonia in physical appearance presents a startling spectacle that invites and indeed provokes ridicule:

a head like a Przewalski's horse (Lev Adolfovich noted that), under her jaw the huge dangling bow of her blouse sticking out from the stiff lapels of her suit, and the sleeves were always too long. Sunken chest, legs so fat they looked as if they came from a different person's set, and clumsy, pigeon-toed feet. She wore her shoes down on one side. (147)

golova, kak u loshadi Przheval'skogo (podmetil Lev Adol'fovich), pod cheliust'iu ogromnyi visiachii bant bluzki torchit iz tverdykh stvorok kostiuma, i rukava vsegda slishkom dlinnye. Grud' vpalaia, nogi takie tolstye—budto ot drugogo chelovecheskogo komplekta, i kosolapye stupni. Obuv' nabok snashivala. (139)

The peculiarity of Sonia's exterior is matched by her unpredictable, tactless behavior and apparently limitless fatuity. Her ludicrous foibles, in fact, prime the reader to accept the extraordinary situation that Tolstaya orchestrates and culminates in a truly fantastic denouement: namely, as punishment for one of Sonia's idiotic indiscretions, her acquaintance Ada Adolfovna masquerades as Nikolai, a married father of three children who falls in love with Sonia at first glance and, overcome by passion, initiates a romantic correspondence with her. Completely duped by the scheme, Sonia not only maintains her impassioned side of the epistolary exchange, but when the grueling war years finally bring her face to face with the imaginary Nikolai, she fails to recognize him as Ada and dies happy in the conviction that she has saved her beloved's life.

While Tolstaya's surface text seems merely to deride a creature with a universal reputation as a gullible misfit,[5] upon closer examination the ostensibly unrelated details of Sonia's fragmented biography actually mesh into a concrete, aesthetically unified embodiment of a principle participating in a profound philosophical dialogue. Through Sonia's experiences Tolstaya's narrative offers a meditation on the clash between two distinct ontological categories: crude material reality that is amenable to empirical verification, on the one hand, and the infinitely more complex, intangible realm of spirit or essence that eludes all processes of final corroboration, on the other. The two poles of that irreconcilable opposition are incarnated respectively in Ada Adolfovna and Sonia, finding vivid expression in the tropes, images, and objects that Tolstaya clusters around each persona. The introductory paragraphs of the story establish the thematic core through the polarized juxtaposition of "incorporeal" ("bestelesnyi"), "soul" ("dusha"), "imperishable" ("netlennaia") and "deathless" ("bessmertnaia") with "crude, corporeal" ("grubymi, telesnymi"), climaxing in the telling simile "Chasing you is like catching *butterflies* with a *shovel*" (145, emphasis added) ("Goniat'sia za vami—vse ravno chto lovit' *babochek*, razmakhivaia *lopatoi*" [136]). *Ada Ad*olfovna's name, which evokes a double hell, and the comparisons of her to a snake ("po-zmeinomu elegantnaia," "etoi zmee Ade Adol'fovne," 139, 141), the stress on her physical traits (141) and on the glut of concrete possessions that surround her (136, 145), as well as the cruelty of her sadistic joke ("Lev called it 'a plan from Ades' " [149]/"Lev ego nazyval 'adskim planchikom' " [141])—all proclaim her symbolic function as a representative of lowly perishable matter, of phenomena. Sonia, by contrast, personifies the imperishable world of noumena, as her name (Sofia = divine wisdom)[6] indicates, and in that comprehensive symbolic framework the primacy of inner qualities renders her physical incongruities irrelevant.

From the very outset, in fact, Tolstaya disembodies Sonia, dissociating her from things physical, and infuses her image with details redolent of spirituality or interiority: "Only the name remains—Sonia" (143) ("Tol'ko imia ostalos'—Sonia" [136]), "*the crystal* of Sonia's stupidity" (146, emphasis added) ("*kristall* Soninoi gluposti" [138]), and "that sensitive instrument, Sonia's soul" (146) ("chutkii instrument Soninoi dushi" [138]). Sonia loves and protects children, nurtures adults through her superb meals (her culinary specialty, significantly, consists of animals' *innards* ["*trebukha*," 139]), works as a "curator" ("*khranitel '*") at a museum—the Russian term conjures up a guardian angel—and finds emotional sustenance in an emphatically Platonic love,[7] to which she voluntarily pledges and maintains eternal loyalty (143) and which enables her to intuit exactly when her beloved needs her ("a loving heart [. . .] feels such things" [152]/ "liubiashchee serdtse [. . .] chuvstvuet takie veshchi" [144]). After saving "him" at the probable price of her own life, she experiences only joy ("[she] blessed her lucky fate" [153]/"blagoslavila svoiu schastlivuiu sud'bu" [145]), and she leaves behind a legacy of love letters and other emblems of unwavering commitment described in a lexicon evoking transcendence ("the packet of Sonia's letters, an old package wrapped with twine, crackling with dried flowers [presumably the symbolic forget-me-nots sent by the imaginary Nikolai—H.G.], yellowed and translucent, like dragonfly wings" [153]/"pachku Soninykh pisem, vetkhii paketik, perekhvachennyi bechevkoi, potreskivaiushchii ot sukhikh tsvetov, zheltovatykh i prozrachnykh, kak strekozinye kryl'ia" [145]).

The polarization of the dichotomous spheres of human existence personified in Ada and Sonia communicates itself through two additional devices: directly, through Tolstaya's symmetrical contrast of their motives for penning the letters: "And so two women in two parts of Leningrad, one in hate, the other in love, wrote letters to each other about a person who had never existed" (151) ("I dve zhenshchiny na dvukh kontsakh Leningrada, odna so zloboi, drugaia s liubov'iu, strochili drug drugu pis'ma o tom, kogo nikogda ne sushchestvovalo" [144]); and obliquely, through the brooches both women wear. Ada's destructive proclivities have their analogy in the large cameo pinned at her throat, which depicts a battle scene: "on the cameo someone is killing somebody; shields, spears, the enemy gracefully fallen" (153) ("na kamee kto-to kogo-to ubivaet: shchity, kop'ia, vrag iziashchno upal" [145]; it bears remembering that elegant grace is one of Ada's explicitly named traits). In eloquent contrast, the "sole adornment" ("edinstvennoe ukrashenie") of the externally hideous but spiritually superior Sonia is an enamel brooch in the form of a white dove (pure soul),[8] which she encloses with the prophetic letter to Nikolai avowing her readiness to sacrifice her life for him (R143). In the prolonged struggle waged between coarse matter and elevated spirit, the latter ultimately proves victorious, as Tolstaya intimates in several ways. Curiously, Ada in time begins to resemble the "phantom" (*fantom*, 141) Nikolai ("She had even begun to turn a little into Nikolai" [E151]/"ona uzhe sama stala nemnogo Nikolaem" [144]), and the paralysis to the waist that she reserves for Nikolai's possible future condition (R142) eventually overtakes Ada herself (R145–46). Thus fantasy proves sufficiently potent to transfigure tangible reality. Moreover, when all is said and done, Sonia's love for the nonexistent Nikolai effects Ada's salvation and vouchsafes Sonia genuine happiness. Furthermore, Ada's reluctance to surrender the package of mysteriously preserved letters implies that Sonia's fate has made an indelible impact on her; as the narrator observes, "it's hard to read other people's souls: it's murky and not everyone knows how to do it" (152) ("chitat' v chuzhoi dushe trudno: temno i dano ne vsiakomu" [144]). These pointed details and Sonia's association with three winged creatures—butterfly,[9] dove, and dragonfly—that suggest spirituality and the power of sublimation, coupled with the closing sentence of the story, "After all, doves don't burn" (154) ("Ved' golubkov ogon' ne beret" [146]), restore Sonia to her rightful role as the triumphant, sublime (if externally ridiculous) agent of those spiritual values that reassert their mysterious power in a world of skeptical materialism and cynical indifference.

"Peters," which launched Tolstaya into the forefront of contemporary literature by winning her numerous admirers, offers a male variant of Sonia at a lower plateau of spiritual development, and with three modifications. Whereas Sonia is the object of the narrative, depicted wholly from the outside, in the later story Tolstaya presents events principally from Peters's viewpoint (via quasi-direct discourse or *erlebte Rede*);[10] although both narratives are retrospective, the backward movement in "Sonia" is comprehensive, entailing a multi-stage reconstruction of Sonia's life posthumously from memory second- or third-hand, whereas reminiscences in

"Peters" are confined to his childhood years, which the story's opening summarizes in broad, selective strokes; finally, Peters, his desperation notwithstanding, emerges as a grayer character, appreciably flatter and narrower in potential than Sonia, whose inner resources he lacks. Sonia's impregnable faith in, and self-sacrificing actualization of, an ultimate love independent of physical gratification lies beyond Peters's conceptual, imaginative, and behavioral capacities. Yet parallels between the two abound.

Like Sonia's, Peters's outward appearance arouses mirth, compassion, or contempt (stout and thick in the waist, he has a broad, womanish, pink belly, flat feet, and tiny eyes); to an incomparably greater degree than Sonia he suffers from loneliness and absence of human contact as well as romantic–sexual deprivation; others ridicule and take advantage of him; and his author portrays him in a manner sufficiently mixed to have elicited protests against her cruelty from a number of critics (e.g., Zolotonosov, 59). Just as in the earlier narrative, however, only the story's surface traces the protagonist's romance, that is, Peters's pursuit of love and his unavailing efforts to overcome estrangement. At a more profound level, Tolstaya orchestrates a battle between the primal powers of life/Eros and death/Thanatos fought in Peters's psyche.[11] In fact, Peters's struggle against, and submission to, the forces of oblivion structure the narrative from beginning to end, just as the contest between the phenomenal (Ada Adolfovna) and the noumenal (Sonia) shapes the internal dynamics of "Sonia."

The encapsulation of Peters's childhood establishes the terms of the conflict: Death manifests itself as stasis, sterile order and convention, the moribund past, self-negation, and imprisonment within restrictive space, with the room as a metaphor for the individual self. These are all associated with the story's presiding image of death—Peters's grandmother, who rears the boy as his substitute mother. Consequently, Peters's childhood unfolds among adults in cluttered rooms that function as tombs housing caveats and relics of the past:

> Peters walked in measured tread down the hallway, past old trunks, past old smells, into rooms where [. . .] green cheese slumbered under a green cover on the table and homemade cookies gave off an aroma of vanilla. While the hostess put out the small silver spoons, worn away on one side, Peters wandered around the room, examining the dolls on the chest, the portrait of the severe, offended old man with a mustache like a long spoke, and the vignettes on the wallpaper, or approached the window and looked through the thickets of aloe out into the sunny cold air where blue pigeons flew and rosy-cheeked children sledded down tracked hills. He wasn't allowed to go outside. (181)

Peters chinno shel po koridoru, mimo starykh sundukov, mimo starykh zapakhov, v komnaty, gde [. . .] na stole pod zelenym kolpakom spal zelenyi syr i vanil'iu veialo domashnee pechen'e. Poka khoziaika raskladyvala malen'kie, s''edennye s odnogo boku serebriannye lozhechki, Peters brodil po komnate, rassmatrival kukol na komode, portret strogogo, oskorblennogo starika s usami kak dlinnaia shpitsa, vin'etki na oboiakh ili podkhodil k oknu i gliadel skvoz' zarosli aloe tuda, na solnechnyi moroz, gde letali sizye golubi i s''ezzhali s nakatannykh gorok rumiannye deti. Guliat' ego ne puskali. (169)

His nickname Peters, with its evocation of an earlier culture, his confinement indoors (he will ever remain the outsider inside, gazing longingly out of the window onto life outdoors), his unchildlike tractability, quietness, and immobility ("His grandmother's female friends always liked him [. . .] a wonderful boy" [180]/"on vsegda nravilsia babushkinym podruzhkam [. . .] chudnyi byl mal'chik" [169]) all originate in his life-denying grandmother. The ancient game of Black Peter that she teaches Peters foreshadows the future consequences of such an unnatural childhood: whereas all the picture cards pair off, "Only the cat, Black Peter, had no pair, he was always alone" (182) ("Tol'ko kotu, Chernomu Peteru, ne dostavalos' pary, on vsegda byl odin" [170]), which indeed adumbrates Peters's later fate. As Peters subsequently recognizes, his grandmother robs him of his childhood ("Grandmother [. . .] ate up my childhood, my only childhood" [186]/ "babushka [. . .] s''ela moe detstvo, moe edinstvennoe detstvo" [174]), infantilizes and emasculates him, thereby trapping him in a psychological pattern of humiliating failure as man/lover.[12] She embodies the repressive civilization that Freud pits against our visceral impulse to attain satisfaction for the self.[13] Accordingly, her death signals the opportunity for Peters's resurrection, as is unambiguously registered by Tolstaya's single-line paragraph: "The day she was buried the ice broke on the Neva" (183) ("V den', kogda ee pokhoronili, po Neve proshel led" [171]).

As in folklore, Peters must pass through three such death-related experiences before he is finally reborn into life, hence his repetition of his formative relationship with his grandmother through his interaction with two surrogate death figures: Elizaveta Frantsevna and his nameless wife. Like his grandmother, Elizaveta Frantsevna gives him German lessons, seats him on an old sofa, feeds him, and plays the familiar, symbolic card game that leaves Peters with the lonely, unpaired tomcat. His dealings with her, as with his grandmother, end in pseudodeath ("The hell with life. To sleep, sleep, fall asleep and not wake up" [196]/"K chertu zhizn'. Spat', spat', zasnut' i ne prosypat'sia" [184]), immediately followed by a chance for rebirth ("Spring came" [196]). Ensnared in pattern, Peters once more neglects that chance by opting for living death through marriage to another variant of his grandmother: "he married a cold, hard woman with big feet, with a dull name" (197) ("zhenilsia na kholodnoi tverdoi zhenshchine s bol'shimi nogami, s glukhim imenem" [185]). Like his mistrustful grandmother, Peters's wife/death shadow fears and scorns humanity, "knowing that people are crooks, that you can't trust anyone; her basket smelled of stale bread" (197) ("znaia, chto liudi—moshenniki, chto verit' nikomu nel'zia; iz koshelki ee pakhlo cherstvym khlebom" [185]). Tolstaya makes the parallel implied by stale odor and human alienation explicit through the two women's identical physical habits ("She took Peters with her everywhere, grasping his hand firmly, as his grandmother had once done" [197]/ "Ona vsiudu vodila za soboi Petersa, krepko stisnuv ego ruku, kak nekogda babushka" [185]) and through the items associated with the woman ("the resonant, polite halls"/"gulkie, vezhlivye zaly"; "still, woolen mice"/"ostyvshikh sherstianykh myshei"; "dead yellow macaroni"/"mertvuiu zheltuiu vermishel'"; and "old people's brown soap"/"starcheskoe korichnevoe mylo" [185]). Their dreary shopping expeditions à deux conventionally pre cede a ritual of surrogate evisceration that all too painfully emblematizes Peters's self-destructive leanings and accentuates the homology of spouse and grandmother:

> And at home, under the watchful eye of the hard woman, Peters himself, with knife and ax, had to rip open the chest of the chilled creature and tear out the slippery purplish-brown heart, the red roses of the lungs, and the blue breathing stalk, so as to erase forever the memory of the one who was born and hoped, moved his young wings and dreamed of a green regal tail, of pearl grains, of the golden dawn spilling over the waking world. (197)

> I doma, pod vnimatel'nym vzgliadom tverdoi zhenshchiny, Peters dolzhen byl sam nozhom i toporom vsporot' grud' okhlazhdennogo i vyrvat' uskol'zaiushchee buroe serdtse, alye rozy legkikh i goluboi dykhatel'nyi stebel', chtoby sterlas' v vekakh pamiat' o tom, kto rodilsia i nadeialsia, shevelil molodymi kryl'iami i mechtal o zelenom korolevskom khvoste, o zhemchuzhnom zerne, o razlive zolotoi zari nad prosypaiushchimsia mirom. (186)

With his wife's departure and the onset of yet another spring, Peters awakens fully to life's potential, to "life—running past, indifferent, ungrateful, treacherous, mocking, meaningless, alien—marvelous, marvelous, marvelous" (198) ("zhizni—begushchei mimo, ravnodushnoi, neblagodarnoi, obmannoi, nasmeshlivoi, bessmyslennoi, chuzhoi—prekrasnoi, prekrasnoi, prekrasnoi" [186]).

Tolstaya interweaves Peters's programmed, neurotic attachment to the life-negating drives incarnated in the authority figure of his grandmother (Thanatos) with his persistent attempts to counter those inhibiting forces through a romantic pursuit of women (Eros). Significantly, his family background supplies the two alternate models of conduct vis-à-vis his grandmother: submission through death (Thanatos), as illustrated by his grandfather, or flight to Eros, as elected by Peters's parents, who abjure parental obligations to run off with their respective lovers.[14] Tolstaya, however, complicates the dynamics of both this classic formulation of antitheses, and her own narrative, through the deflection of Eros into Thanatos, that is, by revealing the interconnection as well as the conflict between the two. Earmarked for failure from his childhood, Peters inevitably yearns for women who remain inaccessible to him: the little girl with warts at his first party; his pretty coworker Faina; athletic Valia, trailing admirers in her wake; and the treacherous peri at the restaurant.[15] Their predictable rejection causes him to retreat to the melancholy safety of what he knows: his grandmother's cocoon of protective prohibition, of sexless, Oblomov-like hibernation that manifestly symbolizes death. Trained by her to find comfort in eating, Peters compulsively compensates for the frustration of one physical appetite (sex–romance) with the gratification of another, by mechanically ingesting food as solace. Whereas Peters's sexual–romantic forays take him out of doors into the windy streets and flower stalls (i.e., outside of himself), his failures drive him back to isolation indoors—into the self and, ultimately, into nonbeing (the room here, as in Franz Kafka's *Die Verwandlung* [1912], symbolically representing the innermost recesses of the self). So in "Peters," Eros works "in the service of the death instinct," to quote Herbert Marcuse, who understandably finds the ultimate relation between Eros and Thanatos as elaborated in Freud's *Beyond the Pleasure Principle* "obscure" (since the two originate in a common source) and adduces Otto Fenichel's argument that "if the 'regression-compulsion' in all organic life is striving for integral quiescence, [. . .] the death instinct is destructiveness not for its own sake, but for the relief of tension. The descent toward death [in that case] is an unconscious flight from pain and want."[16] Hence after the fiasco with Faina, Peters tries to commit suicide by putting his head in a gas oven (tellingly, an appliance used for the preparation of food), a solution refined in his subsequent death through identification when he moves into the chair in which his late grandfather used to rock. That identification with his oppressed grandfather becomes explicit after his third romantic debacle (failure to give Valentina his bouquet), which prompts the bitter, highly revelatory reflection that bares simultaneously the story's dialectical structuring principle and the illusory nature of the dialectic itself: "he should have married his own grandmother in due course and quietly rotted in the warm room to the ticking of the clock, eating sugar buns, his old stuffed rabbit placed in front of his plate for coziness and amusement" (191) ("nado bylo emu v svoe vremia zhenit′sia na sobstvennoi babushke i tikho tlet′ v teploi komnate pod tikan′e chasov, kusaia sakharnuiu bulochku i posadiv pered svoei tarelkoi—dlia uiuta i zabavy—starogo pliushevogo zaiku" [179]). In this conflation of Eros (*zhenit′sia*) and Thanatos (*tlet′*), the semantically freighted elements of mechanized time, food, and childhood toys cohere into a horrifying image of the regressive, externally reinforced infantilization that blighted Peters's childhood and adolescence.

With his third and definitive awakening, however, Peters breaks free from the fatal chain of action–reaction that has trammeled him from the outset. That liberation closes the story in a symbolic scene, wherein Tolstaya places her protagonist in his habitual childhood location—at the window, which he proceeds to open, finally permitting the current of life from the outside to invade his formerly shuttered sanctuary. This conclusion has provoked dissatisfaction in some quarters, especially among commentators who fault the last paragraph for its inconsistent, tacked-on quality.[17] Captious objections of that nature, however, simply betray their authors' incapacity to grasp that the marked shift in tone at story's end is not only justified but necessitated by Peters's enabling transition to a new phase of existence. Tolstaya unmistakably signals his soul's successful completion of its rite of passage through juxtaposing "the old Peters" with "the new children" (198/186) and through the symbolic imagery of thousands of birds taking flight (the aspiring spirit), the naked gold spring (innocent, rich promise), and the children, who intimate a resurrected Peters ("in the depths of his spiritual flesh something long forgotten, young and trusting, was stirring [. . .] and smiling" [198]/"v glubine dushevnoi miakoti uzhe ozhivalo [. . .] i ulybalos′ chto-to davno zabytoe, molodoe chto-to i doverchivoe" [186]). The story's ending celebrates the new Adam, the dawn of Peters's authentic life:

> *The old* Peters pushed the window frame—the blue glass rang, a thousand yellow birds flew up, and the *naked* golden *spring* gave a shout, laughing: catch me, catch me! *New children* played in the puddles with their little buckets. And, wanting nothing, regretting nothing, Peters smiled gratefully at life—running past, indifferent, ungrateful, treacherous, mocking, meaningless, alien—marvelous, marvelous, marvelous. (198, emphases added)

> *Staryi* Peters tolknul okonnuiu ramu—zazvenelo sinee steklo, vspykhnuli tysiachi zheltykh ptits, i *golaia* zolotaia *vesna* zakrichala, smeias′: do-

goniai, dogoniai! *Novye deti* s vederkami vozilis' v luzhakh. I nichego ne
zhelaia, ni o chem ne zhaleia, Peters blagodarno ulybnulsia zhizni. (186)[18]

An emergence from psychic darkness into light may be inferred also
from the title of Tolstaya's story "The Moon Came Out" ("Vyshel mesiats
iz tumana"), in which the Peters-like protagonist, Natasha, endures a similar
existence of unappeased longing.[19] As in the two works already discussed,
Tolstaya implants beneath the surface plot of a spinster's neglected solitude
a universal human drama—that of a psyche's inability to articulate and
fulfill its aspirations by translating them into action. Throughout the narrative, emotional expectations and spiritual potential find no outlet in physical
reality; this categorical gap between desire and actual experience discloses
the poles of the dialectic Tolstaya employs for the story's structure.

Whereas "Sonia" treats only several of its protagonist's adult years, and
"Peters" in a sense traces its hero's gradual (re)birth, "The Moon Came
Out" encompasses a broader temporal span, providing an unevenly paced
overview of Natasha's existence from childhood to middle age (fifty years).
The opening immediately establishes discrepancy as the key to Natasha's
life through the motif of unrealized expectations, of thwarted promise:

> The name [Natasha] promised large gray eyes, soft lips, a delicate silhouette,
> perky hair with highlights. But what came out was a fat, porous face, nose
> like an eggplant, a dejected chest, and short, bulging bicycle calves. (53)

> Imia obeshchalo bol'shie serye glaza, miagkie guby, nezhnyi siluet, veselye
> volosy s iskorkami. A vyshlo tolstoe, poristoe litso, nos baklazhanchikom,
> unylaia grud' i korotkie, krutye velosipednye ikry. (32)[20]

The unbridgeable chasm separating "promised" and "came out" widens as
the story progresses, for Natasha's life shrinks instead of developing with
each year, its movement charting a crablike crawl backward into the irre-
sponsibility of childhood (the regressive motion is emphasized by her surrogate parent, her grandmother). In contrast to Peters, who battles the
*de*formative claims of childhood and finally surmounts them, Natasha cannot or will not mature beyond the infantile stage of passive recipient and
sinks increasingly into quiescent inertness.

Patterned after a fairy tale, Natasha's early years are filled with dazzling
imaginings, dreams, and a sense of life's mysteries that she later recaptures
partially through dreams and recollections. The period of play in the countryside constitutes the peak of an existence that subsequently bears scant resemblance to life ("Long ago, in that now-disintegrated world, they played
the most delightful games [. . .]. Heavenly valleys, tall rose-colored grasses

swaying in the warm breeze [. . .]. And in the evenings, a never-extinguished sunset" [54]/"Togda, davno, v tom rassypavshemsia mire, na zelenykh luzhaikakh oni igrali v schastliveishie igry [. . .]. Raiskie doliny, kolyshu-shchie na teplom vetru rozovye travy [. . .], a vecherami—nikogda ne gasnushchii zakat" [32]). At this juncture Natasha has no foreboding of the cruelty of the universal human condition or of her lugubrious future, pro-phetically summed up in the children's counting rhyme from which the story borrows its title:

> The moon came out behind a cloud,
> He drew a knife and cried out loud:
> Now I'll stab you, now I'll hit,
> I don't care, 'cause you are IT! (54)

> Vyshel mesiats iz tumana,
> Vynul nozhik iz karmana:
> Budu rezat', budu bit',
> Vse ravno, tebe vodit'. (32)

The image of the moon ("horrid, yellow, horned" [54]/"strashnyi, zheltyi, rogatyi"[32]) reveals both the pain and suffering that attend life and the necessity of actively seeking, forging one's own unique destiny ("You are IT!"/"Vse ravno tebe vodit' ").[21] Only a bold response to the challenge of life, a refusal to accept passively its arbitrary laws, holds out the possibil-ity of freedom, as when one of the children daringly pronounces "Churiki!":

> Then for a second the horrific wheel of the world stopped running, stood rooted to the spot, the iron gates locked open, the fetters unfastened—and the little rebel himself froze in astonishment, brought up short inside the charmed, delicate rainbow bubble of sudden freedom. (54)

> Togda na mig zamiralo, ostanavlivalo svoi beg chudovishchnoe koleso mira, zastyvali, razdvinuvshis', zheleznye stvory, razmykalis' okovy—i malen'kii miatezhnik sam v izumlenii zastyval, obmiraia, v zakoldovan-nom, raduzhnom, khrupkom sharike svobody. (33)

Incapable of such bold rebellion, Natasha relinquishes active command of her own fate, subsisting on fantasies as she waits for life to dictate its terms. Her fancy, unlike Sonia's, remains sterile, for it never touches other lives, never influences the outer world of action, and hence substantiates the posited divi-sion between self and world that Sonia bridges and Peters learns to face. Perpetually arrested at a child's stage of development, Natasha never sloughs off palliative delusions about the protective shelter of adult ministrations. These seem to vindicate her torpid submissiveness and foster her apathy:

Grown-ups: large, warm pillars, reliable, eternal columns that held out glasses of milk and offered trays of latticed blueberry pie, that ran out with prickly wool sweaters in their outstretched hands and got down on their knees to fasten small dusty sandals. (55)

Vzroslye—bol'shie teplye stolby, nadezhnye, vechnye kolonny, protiagivaiushchie stakany moloka i pridvigaiushchie perecherknutye krestnakrest polotnishcha chernichnykh pirogov, vybegaiushchie s kusachimi sherstianymi koftami na vytianutykh rukakh i vstaiushchie na koleni, chtoby zastegnut' malen'kie pyl'nye sandalii. (33–34)

Once the magical colors of childhood fade,[22] Natasha cannot adjust to the loss of an emotionally protective environment and finds asylum in an unnatural stasis of withdrawal: "And Natasha lay for hours, covering herself with a blanket from head to toe so that neither humans nor the stars could discern her writhing soul or recognize the unmentionable" (56) ("I Natasha lezhala chasami, nakryvshis' s golovoi odeialom, chtoby ni liudi, ni zvezdy ne razgliadeli korchashchuiusia ee dushu, ne raspoznali to, o chem ne govoriat" [34]). Even when her one and only suitor, the energetic Konovalov ("his eyes bearing a questioning blue fire" [56]/"nesia v glazakh goluboi voprositel'nyi ogon'" [34), seeks some sign of affirmation from her, Natasha remains blankly unresponsive; as in "Peters," Tolstaya concretizes her disinclination to interact with the outside world in the image of an architectural/spatial structure, here specifically denoting a defensive confinement: "But Natasha battened down all the hatches, caulked all the cracks, and stood like a mute black tower, and Konovalov's blue flares fizzled out against her cold surface" (56) ("No Natasha zakhlopnula vse zaslonki, zamurovyvala vse lazeiki, stoiala glukhoi chernoi bashnei, i golubye vspyshki Konovalova gasli na ee kholodnoi poverkhnosti" [34]). With Konovalov's departure, Natasha slips even further into the forlorn solitude of dreams and recollections of a happier, externally fortified past, uncomplicated by existential demands. If, as Marcuse explicates Freud, the truth of memory "lies in the specific function of memory to preserve promises and potentialities which are betrayed and even outlawed by the mature, civilized individual, but which had been fulfilled in his dim past and which are never entirely forgotten" (Marcuse, 19), Natasha fails to derive benefit from memory's function by converting its contents into action. Her solution is to harbor wishes without agitating for their realization, in the inarticulate belief that *someone* will take care of her. Jung characterizes the phenomenon of such a faith in both cultures and individuals as the supervention of habit, degenerating into spiritual inertia that eventually leads to stagnation, and psychic regression to infantilism (*Symbols*, 232).

As a geography teacher Natasha similarly cannot articulate her imaginative flights ("No govorit' ob etom ona ne umela") and proves an ineffectual
pedagogue owing to her insularity as well as her irrational fears of ridicule
and exposure. Her very choice of profession is painfully ironic, in fact, for
as someone permanently locked in the spatial and temporal circle of both
her awkward, unattractive body and her earliest years, she could hardly
be less effective in guiding students through a discipline concerned, inter
alia, with vast expanses, remote places, and the traversal of both. Whereas
geography by definition demands movement, a readiness to branch out,
Natasha knows only inward retreat or stasis and continues to wait timidly
for experience, entertaining adventurous wishes without risking pursuit of
their fulfillment: "Time was passing, her heart beat, and no one arrived to
love Natasha" (59) ("Vremia shlo, serdtse bilos', i nikto ne prikhodil
liubit' Natashu" [34]).

Natasha's sole effort to translate her hopes into reality takes place, tellingly, in the unfamiliar setting of Moscow, constituting her only genuine
foray into geography—physical movement through space. That milestone
incident comes too late, for Petr Petrovich, like Peters's sexual targets,
proves an inappropriate object of her affections, being already married, a
father, and, moreover, totally oblivious to her sexual–romantic interest in
him. Their farewell at the railroad station marks Natasha's definitive, irreversible transition to sexless senescence: "And behind Natasha, holding her
firmly by the shoulder, stood old age, like a stern, patient doctor who has
prepared his usual instruments" (63) ("A za ee spinoi, krepko derzha
Natashu za plecho, strogim terpelivym vrachom stoiala starost', prigotoviv
svoi obychnye instrumenty" [35]).[23] The death of possibilities—the possibility of leading a full, active existence, of realizing her sexual–romantic
reveries—hovers persistently over Natasha's adulthood, as Tolstaya emphasizes through the images of death that she interweaves into Natasha's life:
Natasha's parents, the earth, her grandmother, and her neighbor Morshanskaia
all die; in proposing to her, the old widower Gagin asks Natasha to replace
his late wife; Natasha's dead parents communicate with her through her
dreams, which they persistently inhabit:

> you see yourself, squatting, with a yellow silk ribbon in your hair, and on
> the bench, ornamented by black beetles, *your dead parents are sitting
> and waiting.* [. . .] on the white ceiling the undeciphered abracadabra—the
> futile missive from *her dead father*—is melting. (58, emphases added)

> ty vidish' sebia-samoe, sidiashchuiu na kortochkakh, s zheltym
> shelkovym bantom v volosakh, i na skameike, uzorchatoi ot koroeda,

sidiat i *zhdut mertvye roditeli.* [. . .] taet na belom potolke neprochitannaia abrakadabra —tshchetnoe poslanie *mertvogo ottsa.* (34)

In the communal corridor of Natasha's apartment, "over the exit, rising like a plague *cemetery* up in arms, the black *skulls* of electric meters huddled together" (59) ("nad vykhodom, kak na potrevozhennom, vstavshem na dyby chumnom *kladbishche,* sbilis´ v kuchu chernye *cherepa* elektricheskikh schetchikov" [34]), and Natasha's points of reference become "Grandmother, asleep in Serafimovskii *Cemetery*" (63) ("Babushka, spiashchaia na Serafimovskom *kladbishche*" [35]) and "the *cemetery* where old lady Morshanskaia was buried [and] [w]here was also a Konovalov [. . .] and the little tombstone angel [. . .] urged silence" (64, emphases added) ("*kladbishche,* gde khoronili starukhu Morshanskuiu, [gde] tozhe lezhal odin Konovalov [. . .] i nagrobnyi angelok [. . .] prizyval k molchaniiu" [35]). That silence sums up Natasha's unarticulated inner world, which never engages with life's energetic forces, whereas Sonia's inner self emphatically does, in the process effecting lasting change while also bringing her untold joy. At story's end, Natasha, like Peters, approaches the window, but in marked contrast to him, makes no move to open it, resigned to her role of impotent child, of hapless observer: "Natasha would go up to the window and listen, and nothing, nothing could be heard but the din of passing life" (65) ("Natasha podkhodila k oknu i slushala, i nichego, nichego ne bylo slyshno, krome gula idushchei zhizni" [35]).

If read in the order of their publication, these three stories, which consistently juxtapose inner and outer spheres of being, reflect a steady progression toward a shadowed vision, a decreasing faith in the human powers of transcendence, accompanied by a gradual reduction in the arena of psychic endeavor. Whereas the energy emanating from Sonia's expansive spirit extends across a city, Peters's manages only to fill a room, and Natasha's never leaves the encasement of her body. Whereas Sonia saves another's life, Peters merely prepares to reclaim his own, while Natasha through passivity disavows hers. "Sonia" asserts the sovereignty of our psychic world, for Sonia's spiritual exaltation relegates visible experience, the world of matter, to the domain of insignificance. Such an assured ordering of categories cedes in "Peters" to an acknowledgement of the complex interplay between them, to an unresolved and painfully achieved confrontation with the manifestations of that symbiosis. In "The Moon Came Out" that confrontation never eventuates, for emotion and spirit remain immured in matter (here diminished to the contours of Natasha's physical body), unable to expand within, escape from, or transcend its limitations. The images of transcendence in "The Moon Came Out," principally in the form of a gaze or object directed heavenward,[24] comprise a plane that recedes beyond the events of the story, precisely as intimations of what is never attained. That province triumphs in "Sonia" and exists as potential in "Peters," but is absent in "The Moon Came Out." In all three works, it may be detected only by readers sensitized to the ontological quest that comprises the heartbeat of Tolstaya's fiction, located beneath the surface of her texts.[25]

✧ 4 ✧

The Eternal Feminine's *Liebestod*
Transposed to Baser Clef

Following, perhaps unconsciously, in Iurii Tynianov's footsteps,[1] Linda Hutcheon recently defined parody as "a form of imitation [. . .] characterized by ironic inversion, not always at the expense of the particular text," as "repetition with a critical distance, which marks difference rather than similarity." According to this formulation, parody entails "ironic transcontextualization," whereby a transfer to a new context produces dialogue or double coding. Any codified discourse, including, naturally, texts canonized within a cultural tradition, is susceptible to parody in this sense.[2] For instance, postmodern architects such as Robert Venturi and Charles Moore "have self-consciously restored the idea of architecture as a dialogue with the past," exploring forms that bespeak a preoccupation with historical memory and modes of communication (Hutcheon, "Modern Parody and Bakhtin," 93). In the sphere of literature, Iris Murdoch, Umberto Eco, Jorge Luis Borges, and Vladimir Nabokov have pursued a similarly code-reflexive track. Among Soviet writers of the 1980s, no one, with the possible exception of Andrei Bitov, produced fiction that had stronger stylistic affinities with this group than Tatyana Tolstaya.[3] To read Tolstaya's stories is to enter an echo chamber in which voices from various, primarily Russian, sources become destabilized, their original status undergoing modification through the interplay of perspectives and verbal variants that can, and frequently do, generate parodic distance. Sundry Soviet commentators mistook that ironic distance for aristocratic condescension, for coldness or cruelty on the author's part, and criticized Tolstaya accordingly.[4] An examination of Tolstaya's parodic skills exposes the myopia of her detractors. And, more importantly, it yields instructive insights into her authorial practices while concurrently suggesting a fruitful approach to her fiction in general.

"Okkervil River" ("Reka Okkervil'," 1985) and "The Circle" ("Krug," 1987), two of Tolstaya's most tightly constructed stories, not only offer excellent examples of parody according to my operating definition but also stand in dialogic relationship to each other. The narratives share a number of traits that invite comparative reading: male protagonists well past their youth convinced that their singular destinies will be realized through an ideal woman—à la Goethe's *das Ewig-Weibliche*; the theme of sublime romantic love; the pervasive image of circularity; the symbolic use of music; and elaborate, conscious intertextuality.[5] These features supply the common ground that also casts the disparities between the two texts into sharper relief.[6]

As usual with Tolstaya, plot in "Okkervil River" is so incidentless as to verge on the incidental.[7] Simeonov, a middle-aged translator of unnecessary texts, obsessively listens to old romances performed by Vera Vasilevna, a female singer from the distant past. These fan his fantasies about their extraordinary love, by comparison with which his real-life reluctant couplings with Tamara and other women seem utterly inconsequential. Learning that Vera Vasilevna is still alive, Simeonov visits her, expecting to encounter a fragile, abandoned representative of a bygone era. Instead, the chanteuse proves to be a robust vulgarian given over to appetite and surrounded by male cronies who tend to her comfort and in the process ensure their own. Disillusioned, Simeonov retreats to his apartment, where the velvety tones of Vera Vasilevna's recorded voice once again stimulate his adulation and rapturous flights of fancy.

The title "Okkervil River," which evokes the river north of Leningrad, points immediately to the primacy in the story of the literary myth of Petersburg. Simeonov resembles Akakii Akakievich of Gogol's "Overcoat" insofar as externally he, too, is a nondescript, middle-aged, isolated pen pusher cherishing a grotesque passion for an improbable love object under the chilly skies of the European capital. The story's more profound and illuminating debt, however, is to the masterpiece that single-handedly spawned the myth: Pushkin's *Bronze Horseman* (Mednyi vsadnik). In the figure of Simeonov, Tolstaya conflates Pushkin's Peter the Great and Evgenii; she implicitly analogizes the Neva with the Okkervil River; and she rewrites the tragedy of Parasha's death as simultaneously a comic resolution and a figment of the imagination. Indeed, the opening and closing sections framing the story achieve two aims vital to the work: (1) they pinpoint Tolstaya's concerns through reference to the signs of the Zodiac and simultaneously universalize them through use of the plural; and (2) they solidly establish the narrative's links with Pushkin's text. The story begins:

> When the sun moved into the sign of Scorpio, it grew incredibly windy, dark, and rainy. The wet, streaming city, its wind banging against the

glass outside the defenseless, uncurtained bachelor's window, [. . .] seemed to be Peter's evil plan, the revenge of the huge, bug-eyed, big-mouthed, and toothy carpenter tsar, [. . .] chasing and gaining on his weak and terrified subjects in their nightmares. The rivers, rushing out to the windblown and threatening sea, bucked and with hissing urgency opened the cast-iron hatches and quickly raised their watery backs in museum cellars, licking at the fragile collections that were crumbling into damp sand, at shamans' masks made of rooster feathers, at crooked foreign swords, at beaded robes, and at the sinewy feet of the angry museum staff brought from their beds in the middle of the night. On days like that, when the rain, darkness, and window-bending wind reflected the white solemn face of loneliness, Simeonov [. . .] would wipe dust with his sleeve from the table. (17–18)

Kogda znak zodiaka menialsia na Skorpiona, stanovilos' sovsem uzh vetreno, temno i dozhdlivo. Mokryi, struiashchiisia, b'iushchii vetrom v stekla gorod za bezzashchitnym, nezanaveshennym, kholostiatskim oknom, [. . .] kazalsia togda zlym petrovskim umyslom, mest'iu ogromnogo, pucheglazogo, s razinutoi past'iu, zubastogo tsaria-plotnika, vse dogoniaiushchego v nochnykh koshmarakh, [. . .] svoikh slabykh, perepugannykh poddanykh. Reki, dobezhav do vzdutogo, ustrashaiushchego moria, brosalis' vspiat', shipiashchim naporom otshchelkivali chugunnye liuki i bystro podnimali vodianye spiny v muzeinykh podvalakh, oblizyvaia khrupkie, razvalivaiushchiesia syrym peskom kollektsii, shamanskie maski iz petushinykh per'ev, krivye zamorskie mechi, shitye biserom khalaty, zhilistye nogi zlykh, razbuzhennykh sredi nochi sotrudnikov. V takie-to dni, kogda iz dozhdia, mraka, progibaiushchego stekla vetra vyrisovyvalsia belyi tvorozhistyi lik odinochestva, Simeonov [. . .] stiral rukavom pyl' so stola. (16)

Tolstaya reprises this picture of ominous turmoil in synoptic form at the story's end, when Vera Vasilevna's voice issuing from the gramophone figuratively soars above all earthly phenomena:

above everything beyond help, above the approaching sunset, above the gathering rain, above the wind, above the nameless rivers flowing backward, overflowing their banks, raging and flooding the city as only rivers can. (19)

nad vsem, chemu nel'zia pomoch', nad podstupaiushchim zakatom, nad sobiraiushchimsia dozhdem, nad vetrom, nad bezymennymi rekami, tekushchimi vspiat', vykhodiashchimi iz beregov, bushuiushchimi i zatopliaiushchimi gorod, kak umeiut delat' tol'ko reki. (28)

Peter the Great's momentous decision to reorient Russia's destiny by forcibly converting his abstract idea into the concrete grandeur of a "European" city; the city's propensity to flood; the solitary individual isolated in his modest domicile within the showcase of national splendor—Tolstaya appropriates all these elements from Pushkin but rings variations on them. Whereas Pushkin's *poema* juxtaposes, so as to contrast, the self-effacing clerk's humble dreams of domestic quietude with the tsar's grand, far-reaching vision of an imposing capital, Tolstaya conflates the two figures in her single hero. Just as contemplating the Neva inspires Peter's colossal dream of a dazzling European metropolis, so listening to Vera Vasilevna's ardent songs enables Simeonov to conjure up the magical world of the Okkervil River, where he and the songstress have their amatory encounters and his imagination performs the Petrine task of transformation:

> it was better *mentally* to plant long-haired willows on its banks, set up steep-roofed houses, release slow-moving residents, perhaps in *Dutch* hats [. . .], better to pave the Okkervil's embankment, fill the river with clean gray water, sketch in *bridges with towers and chains*, smooth out the *granite parapets* with a curved template. (21, emphases added)

> luchshe *myslenno* obsadit' ee berega dlinnovolosymi ivami, rasstavit' krugoverkhie domiki, pustit' netoroplivykh zhitelei, mozhet byt' v *gollandskikh* kolpakakh [. . .] luchshe zamostit' bruschatkoi okkervil'skie naberezhnye, reku napolnit' chistoi seroi vodoi, navesti *mosty s bashenkami i tsepiami*, vyrovniat' plavnym lekalom *granitnye parapety*. (20)

The un-Russian-sounding name of the remote Okkervil River (to which Tolstaya draws attention: "that distant, almost non-Leningrad river" [20]/ "etoi, pochti ne leningradskoi uzhe reki" [20]), Simeonov's imposition of his dream onto it ("No, no reason to be disillusioned by going to the Okkervil River, it was better mentally to plant long-haired willows on its banks" [21]/"Net, ne nado razocharovyvat'sia, ezdit' na rechku Okkervil', luchshe myslenno obsadit' ee berega dlinnovolosymi ivami" [20]), and Tolstaya's purposely ambiguous references to its turbulent waters emphasize its function as the new Neva and Simeonov's role as the Evgenized Peter.

Simeonov's Okkervil River originates in Vera Vasilevna's voice, in the sense that her singing prompts Simeonov to visualize *his* version of the river. That constructed body of water in turn becomes a subjective metaphor for her voice, the extraordinary force of which has the capacity to erect and destroy worlds, to sustain the creative imagination, and to inspire and promise eternal love. An ambivalent symbol that corresponds to the creative power of nature and of time, the river traditionally has signified fertility, on the one hand, and the irreversible passage of time, and consequently a sense of loss and oblivion, on the other.[8] That dualism reflects Vera Vasilevna's bifurcated function in the story as incorporeal voice and (very) corporeal woman, respectively. Hence the similes and metaphors likening her to such substantial phenomena as a naiad and a peri, while colorful descriptions of the water's movements—its protean, amorphous character—are confined to images for her voice. To underscore the potent nature of that voice, Tolstaya repeatedly associates it with the perfect circle of the records Simeonov plays ("an old and heavy disc, anthracite in color" [18]/"staryi, tiazhelyi, antratsitom otlivaiushchii krug" [138]; "but the free lone soul [. . .] is back in the dark magical circle filled with flames" [20]/"no vol'naia odinokaia dusha [. . .] uzhe tam, v temnom, ogniami napolnennom magicheskom krugu" [19]) and the apple-like roundness of its owner's high heels ("shoes with apple-round heels" [21]/"s kruglymi, kak iabloko, tufliami" [20]; "round heels clicking" [21]/"postukivaia kruglymi kablukami" [21]; "would walk away [. . .], swaying on her apple-round heels" [22]/"[ona] ukhodila [. . .], pokachivaias' na kruglykh, kak iabloko, kablukakh" [21]; "tripping [. . .] on her uncomfortable heels" [23]/"spotykaias' [. . .] na svoikh neudobnykh kablukakh" [22]; "the old-fashioned round heels fell in different directions" [28]/"pokatilis' v raznye storony kruglye starinnye kabluki" [27]).[9] The circular shape here evokes both the self-sufficient perfection of Simeonov's constructed paradise and its potential for eternal repetition. That potential inheres exclusively in the voice, which belongs to the Peter line of Tolstaya's story, for Simeonov's actual meeting with Vera Vasilevna makes him realize that the woman as projected and worshiped by him is dead (in keeping with the Evgenii side of the narrative): "Vera Vasilevna had died; she died long ago, killed, dismembered, and eaten by this old woman, the bones sucked clean" (28) ("Vera Vasil'evna umerla, davnym-davno umerla, ubita, raschlenena i s''edena etoi starukhoi, i kostochki uzhe obsosany" [27]). As in Pushkin's poema, then, the reification of Simeonov's/Peter's vision spells the death of Simeonov's/Evgenii's hopes.

Tolstaya adumbrates that death from the story's very first sentence, where she invokes Scorpio, the sign that carries associations with sexuality, and, more importantly, also corresponds to autumn—the period in the span of human life that lies under the threat of death (Cirlot, 268). Throughout the remainder of the narrative, death is signaled by the repeated symbol of chrysanthemums,[10] which not only accompany the "lovers' " first imagined meeting (E19, 20), but which Simeonov actually purchases for the singer when he finally sees her in person (E24). On two separate occasions Tolstaya emphasizes and makes explicit the symbolism of the flowers. The first explication, embedded in one of Simeonov's waking dreams, has a generalized lyrical character ("their white, dry, and bitter aroma is an autumnal one, a harbinger of fall, separation, oblivion" [20]/"ikh zapakh, belyi, sukhoi i gor'kii,—eto osennii zapakh, on uzhe zaranee predveshchaet osen', razluku, zabven'e" [19]), whereas the second harnesses the connotative properties to Simeonov's real-life dilemma during his nightmarish visit: "Vera Vasilevna had died [. . .] ; here are chrysanthemums for the grave, dry, sick, dead flowers, very appropriate, I've commemorated the dead, now I can get up and leave" (28) ("Vera Vasil'evna umerla [. . .] , vot khrizantemy na mogilu, sukhie, bol'nye, mertvye tsvety, ochen' k mestu, ia pochtil pamiat' pokoinoi, mozhno vstat' i uiti" [27]). The connection between death and white chrysanthemums is further strengthened and enriched through the motif of white bones that first anticipates ("Where are your white bones now?" [19]/"Gde teper' vashi belye kostochki?" [18]), and subsequently trails behind, the two illuminating references to chrysanthemums cited above: the flowers' "white scent" and the melancholy thoughts it engenders lead to Simeonov's rhetorical question "Whose soil chills your white bones?" (20) ("ch'ia zemlia studit vashi belye kosti?" [19]), while later during the encounter with Vera Vasilevna (who, indeed, is "white" [E25]), Simeonov mourns her metaphorical, irreversible dissolution. In a characteristic Tolstayan twist of irony, Simeonov confronts the mythic Vera Vasilevna's death on the real Vera Vasilevna's birthday.

Complicating the doubling of Simeonov's parodic identity as derived from Pushkin's *poema* are the Lermontovian quotations in Tolstaya's text, which belong to one of two categories: the romance recorded by Vera Vasilevna and the complexly recontextualized motifs from *Demon*. Both reinforce the thematics of the story and furnish ironic distance through double voicing.

Tolstaya cites only the first line of the romance based on Lermontov's poem, "No, it's not you I love so passionately" ("Net, ne tebia tak pylko ia liubliu") and treats it humorously, not only punctuating the words with exclamation marks to mimic the skipping action of the record, but also, through metonymy, transferring its movement to the singer: "Vera Vasilevna skipped, creaking and hissing, quickly spinning under the needle" (18) ("podskakivaia, potreskivaia i shipia, bystro vertelas' pod igloi Vera Vasil'evna" [16]).[11] Equating the two at this juncture is essential to Tolstaya's purpose of setting the stage for Simeonov's later disillusionment, through which the narrative ultimately posits the eternal nature of Vera's art and its power to generate imagined realities, while exposing the impermanence of tangible human form, doomed to mutability. Lermontov's three-stanza lyric of 1841, in fact, clarifies the nature of Simeonov's relationship to Vera Vasilevna, to her voice, and to himself. The entire lyric reads as follows:

No, it's not you I love so passionately,
The brilliance of your beauty is not for me,
In you I love past suffering
And my doomed youth.

At times when I look at you,
Gazing long into your eyes with my own,
I am involved in a secret conversation—
But it's not with you that my heart speaks!

I speak with someone dear from my youth,
In your features I seek other features,
In your lips, lips long mute,
In your eyes, the fire of now extinguished eyes.

Net, ne tebia tak pylko ia liubliu,
Ne dlia menia krasy tvoei blistan'e,
Liubliu v tebe ia proshloe stradanie
I molodost' pogibshuiu moiu.

Kogda, poroi, ia na tebia smotriu,
V tvoi glaza vnikaia dolgim vzorom,
Tainstvennym ia zaniat razgovorom,—
No ne s toboi ia serdtsem govoriu!

Ia govoriu s podrugoi iunykh let,
V tvoikh chertakh ishchu cherty drugie,
V ustakh tvoikh—usta davno nemye,
V glazakh—ogon' ugasnuvshikh ochei.[12]

The opening paragraph of the story corroborates the pertinence of the first stanza to Simeonov's real-life situation, for he experiences special pleasure in Vera Vasilevna's singing during bouts of acute loneliness on overcast days when he feels "particularly big-nosed and balding and feels his years around his face and his cheap socks far below, on the edge of existence" (18) ("osobenno nosatym, lyseiushchim, osobenno oshchushchaia svoi nestarye gody vokrug litsa i deshevye noski daleko vnizu, na granitse suchchestvovaniia" [16]). Vera Vasilevna provides the illusive self-definition he seeks, for the fantasies unleashed by her glorious voice transform Simeonov into an impassioned young lover.

The remaining two stanzas accurately prefigure his shocked reaction to Vera Vasilevna in the flesh. Her appearance and manner are so at odds with the poetic Vera constructed by his inflamed imagination ("you can't bring back anything now" [26]/"teper' nichego ne vernesh'" [26]) that to the alienated Simeonov, as to Lermontov's lyric "I," the two feminine presences become two distinct and irreconcilable entities. Whereas Lermontov's presumably autobiographical lyric juxtaposes two discrete women who played a romantic role in his life,[13] Tolstaya invokes the poem to dramatize the discrepancy between the posited artist in her ideal incarnation, on the one hand, and the actual woman, on the other. As the notorious example of Fet—a poet whose lyrics celebrated the wonders of nature even as he brutalized his serfs— illustrates, the expectation of continuity between an artist and his product is dictated by discursive modes alone; it is grounded in an assumptive unitary aesthetics that everyday reality seems to discredit. Fay Weldon neatly summarizes the distinction as one between "literary truth" and "home truth."[14]

Tolstaya similarly rearranges resonances from *Demon* (1829–41) in an ironic key. In Lermontov's unfinished *poema*, the skeptical spirit of negation undergoes a partial revival of faith and love when he glimpses the innocent Tamara. As he tempts her to succumb to him, his rhetoric conquers both the maiden's modesty and her guardian angel, upon whose departure the Demon literally kills Tamara with his kiss. In the ensuing verbal battle over Tamara's soul, a seraph vanquishes the Demon, depriving him of Tamara forever:

> And the vanquished Demon cursed
> His mad dreams,
> And once again, as earlier, was left,
> Haughty, alone in all the universe,
> Without hope and love!

> I proklial Demon pobezhdennyi
> Mechty bezumnye svoi,
> I vnov' ostalsia on, nadmennyi,
> Odin, kak prezhde, vo vselennoi
> Bez upovan'ia i liubvi! [II, 114]

From Lermontov's operatic extravaganza Tolstaya appropriates three elements: the Georgian princess Tamara; the titanic figure of the Demon; and the denouement, wherein his beloved's death casts the protagonist back into the unremitting despair of solitude. Reducing the cosmic dimensions of these materials, Tolstaya subjects them to ironic inversions. In diametric contrast to Lermontov's idealized exotic beauty (and to Simeonov's apotheosized Vera Vasilevna), Tolstaya's Tamara bears the mundane stamp of a domestic, motherly nurse attempting to hold onto Simeonov by catering to his creature comforts, "with washed laundry and fried potatoes and flowered curtains for the windows" (22) ("s postirushkami, zharennoi kartoshkoi, tsvetastymi zanavesochkami na okna" [21]). When Simeonov returns home crushed by the "loss" of Vera Vasilevna, he falls into faithful Tamara's cushioning embraces:[15] "Tamara—the darling!—was hanging around by Simeonov's door. She picked him up, carried him in, washed him, undressed him, and fed him a hot meal" (28) ("U dverei simeonovskoi kvartiry maialas' Tamara—rodnaia!—ona podkhvatila ego, vnesla, umyla, razdela i nakormila goriachim" [27]). Moreover, whereas Lermontov portrays the sublime Tamara as a symbol of paradise lost, of the original beatitude from which the Demon is eternally excluded and to which he aspires, Tolstaya's protagonist by and large evades Tamara's hapless overtures, for her smothering pursuit interferes with his full-time obsession with Vera Vasilevna.

Through the devices of multiplication and listing, Tolstaya reduces Tamara's significance in Simeonov's life to that of a minor object. Tamara is but one among several women whom Simeonov beds unenthusiastically on a semiregular basis, and Simeonov mentally includes her—in the generic plural, squeezed in between bird calls and cups—in the catalogue of items composing his banal everyday existence: "trolleys, books, processed cheeses, wet sidewalks, bird calls, *Tamaras*, cups, nameless women, passing years, all that is perishable in the world" (25, emphasis added) ("tramvai, knigi, plavlenye syrki, mokrye mostovye, ptich'i kriki, *Tamary*, chashki, bezymiannye zhenshchiny, ukhodiashchie goda, vsia brennost' mira" [23]). As part of the tangible but mutable and humdrum universe that surrounds Simeonov, Tamara belongs to a lower order of existence than the transcendent sphere magically opened up to Simeonov by Vera Vasilevna's divine voice, which, accordingly, consigns the phenomenal world to insignificance,

> rising from the depths, spreading its wings, soaring above the world, above the steamy body of little old Vera drinking tea from the saucer, above Simeonov bent in his lifelong obedience, above *warm, domestic Tamara*. (29, emphasis added)

> vosstaiushchii iz glubiny, raspravl iaiushchii kryl'ia, vzmyvaiushchii nad mirom, nad rasparennym telom Verunchika, p'iushchego chai s bliudechka, nad sognuvshimsia v svoem pozhiznennom poslushanii Simeonovym, *nad teploi, kukhonnoi Tamaroi*. (28)

In parallel fashion, Tolstaya demotes Lermontov's Demon to the secondary status of a supporting actor and also trivializes him by pluralization ("Simeonov listened to the arguing voices of two struggling demons" [23]/ "Simeonov slushal sporiashchie golosa dvukh borovshikhsia demonov" [23]) and by bringing the "demonic duo" down to earth both figuratively and literally. Whereas one of Tolstaya's demons retains his Lermontovian role of tempter, the other represents the appeal of common sense:

> one demanded he get the old woman out of his head, tightly lock the door, opening it occasionally for Tamara, and go on as before, loving moderately, longing moderately, in moments of solitude listening to the

pure sound of the silver horn singing over the unknown foggy river; the other demon—a mad youth with a mind dimmed by translating bad books—demanded that he walk, run, to find Vera Vasilevna. (23)

Odin nastaival vybrosit' starukhu iz golovy, zaperet' pokrepche dveri, izredka priotkryvaia ikh dlia Tamary, zhit', kak i ran'she zhil, v meru liubia, v meru tomias', vnimaia v minutu odinochestva chistomu zvuku serebrianoi truby, poiushchemu nad nevedomoi tumannoi rekoi, drugoi zhe demon —bezumnyi iunosha s pomrachennym ot perevoda durnykh knig soznaniem—treboval idti, bezhat', razyskat' Veru Vasil'evnu. (23)

Like Tamara's guardian angel, but in deliberately lowering terms that parody Lermontov's grandiloquent description of the parallel event, the demon of pragmatic literalism and reason, revolted at Simeonov's hyperbolic fantasies (" 'Go back,' his guardian demon sadly shook his head, 'Run for your life' " [25]/" 'Vernis',' pechal'no kachal golovoi demon-khranitel', 'begi, spasaisia,' " [24]; "What madness that time separated us. ['Ugh, *don't*,' grimaced his inner demon] [24]/"Kak bezymno proleglo mezhdu nami vremia! ['Fu, ne nado,' krivilsia vnutrennii demon]" [23]), abandons his charge when the latter surrenders to the lure of oppositional forces: "He rang. ('Fool,' said his inner demon, spat, and left Simeonov.)" (25) ("On pozvonil. ['Durak,' pliunul vnutrennii demon i ostavil Simeonova.]" [24]). In his cynical practicality, in fact, this demon bears more resemblance to the sardonic figure in Lermontov's unfinished self-parodying narrative poem *Fairy Tale for Children (Skazka dlia detei)* (1840), where Lermontov adopts an ironic stance toward the earlier maximalist effusions of his *Demon* ("Seething with the fire and strength of youth,/I formerly sang of a different demon"/"Kipia ognem i siloi iunykh let,/Ia prezhde pel pro demona inogo" [II, 74]).

In "Okkervil River," as in *Demon*, loss of the ideal beloved and all that she represents plunges the bereft lover into despair. For Lermontov's arch-Romantic protagonist, any possibility of future redemption and happiness vanishes together with Tamara, leaving him in dispossessed desolation once again. Potentially analogous consequences in "Okkervil River," by contrast, are robbed of tragedy: Simeonov finds temporary consolation in Tamara's waiting arms, then is visited by the mythic Vera Vasilevna in his dreams and the real Verunchik in his waking hours. At story's end Tolstaya leaves open the question of Simeonov's relations with both hypostases, giving the reader to understand, nonetheless, that some kind of reconciliation of the two may eventuate.

Such at least is the inference to be drawn when Tolstaya refers to Simeonov's "lifelong obedience" to "the bulky Verunchik" and asserts the supremacy of the singer's voice. A somewhat enigmatic passage earlier in the narrative, coupled with the singer's name, suggests that Simeonov's ideal Vera Vasilevna can be recaptured if his faith (*vera*) and imagination prove sufficiently resilient. During the grotesque birthday festivities supervised by Kissov/Potseluev (the traitor at a mock Last Supper), as Simeonov mentally reproaches the singer for having failed to save herself for him alone, Tolstaya writes: "She had betrayed him. Or had he betrayed Vera Vasilevna? It was too late to figure out now" (26) ("Ona prodala ego. Ili eto on prodal Veru Vasil'evnu. Teper' pozdno bylo razbirat'sia" [25]). Literally (if absurdly), Simeonov's betrayal consists of sexual infidelity with various women. On a more subtle level, however, he has betrayed the transcendent world of art—a world created by Vera Vasilevna with his active collaboration.

Until he succumbs to the temptation of a meeting with the corporeal Vera Vasilevna, Simeonov approximates an anchorite sequestered from the world ("O blessed solitude!" [19]/"O blazhennoe odinochestvo!" [19]) and consecrated to the worship of his immortal divinity, "the incorporeal Vera Vasilevna" (19), the Eternal Feminine with her intimations of unearthly joys.[16] Falling into the twin errors of materialism and vanity, Simeonov seeks tangible validation of his faith and instant recognition for his devoted service. Hence his betrayal of *vera* and Vera, who, as corporeal being, "had surrounded herself with *mortal, edible people*" (27, emphasis added) ("okruzhila sebia *smertnymi, s''edobnymi liud'mi*" [26]). The concluding image of Vera Vasilevna's disembodied tones rising above all earthly things, together with her resurrection in Simeonov's dream, however, implies that Simeonov's former state of ecstatic belief may yet be restored. Contemplation of the real Vera Vasilevna unavoidably evokes the imagined ideal, a process that, in a sense, illustrates how parody functions: an ironic inversion operating on the principle of similarity nevertheless spotlights difference; and its distance from the original embedded in it generates dialogue. For Simeonov that dialogue is conducted between the ideal Vera Vasilevna, a long-standing and familiar resident of his psychic realm conceived by him under the inspiration of her art, and the real Vera Vasilevna, who leaves a dirty ring around his bathtub and is a stranger seemingly unrelated to the exquisite voice and the sublime projection. Whether the two images of the women may be reconciled remains conjectural, but the story's concluding paragraph implies that Simeonov, now prepared to perceive as symbiotic what earlier seemed mutually exclusive, may integrate the ideal with the real.

The concept of the Eternal Feminine, the role of music, and circularity likewise inform Tolstaya's "Circle" ("Krug"), which may be read as a counterpart to "Okkervil River" or as its darker, more skeptical variant. In brief, "The Circle" recounts, largely in retrospect, Vasilii Mikhailovich's efforts to discover the secret of life's meaning and joy through a series of affairs with women. None of his amours, however, unlocks the mystery of existence. At story's end he dies unenlightened, vanquished, he believes, by the inescapable laws of determinism.

Not the story's title but the name of one of its personae indicates that the material parodied here by Tolstaya is the widely diffused myth of Tristan and Isolde, which Thomas Mann also ironized skillfully in his "Tristan."[17] Whether Tolstaya draws on the medieval poems of Beroul and Thomas (1160–70), on the somewhat later reworking by Gottfried von Strassburg that inspired Richard Wagner's renowned opera, on the prose compilation that served as a basis for the Russian *Tristan*, or on Wagner's libretto is difficult to determine and of minor significance.[18] What matters is less the discrepancies in detail and emphasis wrought by accretions and omissions in the sundry extant versions than the elements that constant repetition through the ages has codified into the myth's distinguishing traits. Those that pertain to Tolstaya's text belong to three categories: motifs, key plot incidents, and dominant concepts.

The cardinal motifs of the myth are undoubtedly the love potion drunk by the protagonists, the sea voyage, and (in Wagner's opera) the *Liebestod* that musically translates the work's regnant idea. Decisive moments in plot development include the lovers' first meeting, Isolde's betrayal of King Mark through her tryst(s)[19] with his nephew (the knight Tristan), the lovers' separation, and Tristan's expiration immediately after Isolde's return to him, followed by her own death. The tale of the two lovers, most commentators concur, demonstrates the fatality of passion, the sublimity of an overpowering, all-consuming love that cannot achieve full realization in this world; the noble pair find eternal union only in death, for, as Wagner declared, love in *Tristan and Isolde* is "desire without attainment; for each fruition sows the seeds of fresh desire, till in its final lassitude the breaking eye beholds a glimmer of the highest bliss; it is the bliss of quitting life, of being no more, of last redemption."[20] That the internal progression finally culminating in a renunciatory spiritualization of passion (an apotheosis that some critics have called a "greatly attenuated conception of oneness between man and woman")[21] in a sense contradicts Wagner's Act II, with its lush musical writhings of incremental sensuality, is a paradox that should not blind us to Wagner's intentions: to depict the loss of self through redemptive love.

Unlike several versions of the Tristan and Isolde myth, Tolstaya's text assigns central place to the male protagonist, Vasilii Mikhailovich. Like Tristan, he oscillates between the poles of yearning (*Sehnsucht*) and dying before finally succumbing to fate in the shape of death.[22] The story's opening and closing paragraphs universalize his destiny through generalized visual images imbued with cosmic symbolism. Just as Tristan's life consists of incessant peregrination over land and sea, so Vasilii Mikhailovich's temporal existence is captured in spatial terms. Both narratives mine the immemorial metaphor of life as a journey or voyage:

> The world is ended, the world is distorted, the world is closed, and it has closed around Vasilii Mikhailovich. At sixty a fur coat is heavy, stairs are steep, and your heart stays with you day and night. You've walked and walked, from hill to hill, past shimmering lakes, past radiant islands, *white birds overhead, speckled snakes underfoot,* and you've arrived here, and this is where you've ended up; it's gloomy and lonely here [. . .] . This is it, it's over. Here no grass grows. The soil has frozen, the road is narrow and stony, and ahead only one sign is lit up: exit. And Vasilii Mikhailovich isn't willing. (63–64, emphasis added)

> Mir konchen, mir iskrivlen, mir zamknut, i zamknut on na Vasilii Mikhailoviche. V shest'desiat-to let shuba tiazhela, stupeni kruty, a serdtse dnem i noch'iu s toboi. Shel sebe i shel, s gorki na gorku, mimo siiaiushchikh ozer, mimo svetlykh ostrovov, *nad golovoi—belye ptitsy, pod nogami—pestrye zmei,* i prishel vot siuda, a ochutilsia vot zdes'; sumrachno tut i glukho [. . .] . Vse eto, vse uzhe. Trava tut ne rastet. Zemlia pomerzla, doroga uzka i kamenista, a vperedi svetitsia tol'ko odna nadpis': vykhod. I Vasilii Mikhailovich byl ne soglasen. (61)

Although this introduction presents Vasilii Mikhailovich as Everyman, negotiating the carceral psychic space between the elevated and pure ("*white birds overhead*") on the one hand and the base and evil ("*speckled snakes underfoot*") on the other, the passage contains what at story's end one recognizes retrospectively as a clue to Vasilii Mikhailovich's individual situation: namely, the errant direction of his presumably chosen path, which bypasses everything associated with light on route to darkness: "you've walked [. . .] past shimmering lakes, past radiant islands." Light and darkness, of course, play a dominant role in Wagner's opera, which reverses standard associations: the lovers long for the darkness of night and ultimately of death, for only under its cloak can they attain their ecstatic union, since Night, in Wagner's mystic scheme of things, represents a transcendent state of being infinitely superior to the delusionary physical light of day.[23] Preserving the traditional link between day/light and life, and between night/darkness and death, Tolstaya constructs her modern Tristan as someone who lives neither in darkness nor in light but in the shadows of illusion, eschewing true illumination, yet fearing the darkness of oblivion. Her Vasilii Mikhailovich, in fact, is conceived as an anti-Tristan; not Tristan, merely *triste* (sad). Life for Tristan proves to be a tutelary experience whereby he learns to break free of the bankruptcy of earthly reality through the liberating option of death. For Vasilii Mikhailovich death merely means the final, intransigent gesture of predetermination, which he cannot convert into triumph for lack of spiritual resources. Tristan aspires to transcendence, Vasilii Mikhailovich to avoidance.

Although both Tristan and his Russian counterpart yearn to merge with a chosen woman, the terms of their desire are diametrically opposed. Tristan, the ideal knight dedicated to serving Mark and his country, to defending and protecting the weak, struggles to overcome his intense feelings for Isolde and thus remain faithful to his chivalric code. By contrast, all of the egotistical Vasilii Mikhailovich's transactions are launched and terminated out of rank self-interest. Isolde is Tristan's only, unique love—the incarnation of the Eternal Feminine that purportedly elevates man to spiritual self-perfection: for, according to Wagner, "it is woman, suffering and willing to sacrifice herself, who becomes at last the real, conscious redeemer: for what is love itself, but the 'eternal feminine' (das ewig Weibliche)."[24] Hence her betrayal of Mark, to whom she is promised as Queen, is glossed over in all versions of the myth, which, moreover, portray Mark as ultimately sympathetic to the noble pair. Vasilii Mikhailovich's creator, however, discredits the myth of the Eternal Feminine, equating Woman with thoughtless vanity, which requires that animals suffer and be slaughtered merely to provide cosmetics and fashionable clothing:

> Woman, woman, do you exist? . . . What are you? . . . High up a Siberian tree your hat blinks its eyes in fear; a cow gives birth in suffering so you can have boots; a lamb is sheared screaming so you can warm yourself with its fleece; a sperm whale is in its death throes; a crocodile weeps; a doomed leopard pants as it flees. (65)

> Zhenshchina, zhenshchina, est' li ty? . . . Chto ty takoe? . . . Vysoko na vershine na sibirskom derevne ispuganno blestit glazami tvoia shapka; korova v mukakh rozhaet ditia—tebe na sapogi; s krikom ogoliaetsia ovtsa, chtoby ty mogla sogret'sia ee volosami; v predsmertnoi toske b'etsia kashalot, rydaet krokodil, zadykhaetsia v bege obrechennyi leopard. (62)

Moreover, the early scenes of the story, which Tolstaya sets in the alienating environment of a beauty parlor, posit Woman as a dehumanized object that undergoes demeaning physical violations to be refashioned by despotic "producers of beauty":

> three women his own age squirmed in the hands of mighty blond *Furies*. Could he call *what* was multiplying in the mirrors "ladies"? With grow-

ing horror Vasilii Mikhailovich peered at *what* sat closest to him. A curly-haired siren planted her feet firmly, grabbed *it* by the head, and [. . .] *began choking her victim.* (64, emphases added)

tri ego rovesnitsy korchilis' v rukakh moguchikh belokurykh *furii*. Mozhno li nazvat' damami *to, chto* mnozhilos' v zerkalakh? S vozrastaiushchim uzhasom vzgliadyval Vasilii Mikhailovich v *to, chto* sidelo blizhe k nemu. Kudriavaia sirena, krepko upershis' nogami v pol, skhvatila *eto* za golovu i [. . .] *dushila svoiu zhertvu.* (61)

This site of hellish torments in pursuit of a frivolous cause extends the pattern of victimizer/sufferer (beautician → woman → animal) and demystifies Womanhood.

"The Circle" explodes not only the concept of the Eternal Feminine but also the hero's capacity to love at all: the most unknightly of creatures, Vasilii Mikhailovich marries out of lethargy, then proceeds to betray his wife with three women (Klara, Svetlana, and later Izolda),[25] with whom he embarks on affairs solely to circumvent what Fate has allotted him. According to him, Woman—the category, not an individual—will rescue him from boredom (hardly Wagnerian redemption) and, unveiling life's mystery, will wrest him from the common run of man ("[he] stared long and hard in the mirror at himself—the one and only" [66]/"[on] dolgo gliadel v zerkale na sebia—odnogo-edinstvennogo" [63]). The solipsistic egoist envisions women as "creatures" existing solely for his purposes:

> For sixty years he'd been waiting for them to come and call him and show him the mystery of mysteries, for red dawn to blaze over half the world, for a staircase of rays to rise from earth to heaven and archangels with trombones and saxophones or whatever they used to blare their unearthly voices to welcome the chosen one. (71)

> Shest'desiat let on zhdet, chto pridut, i prozovut, i otkroiut tainoe tainykh, chto polykhnet zarevo na polmira, vstanet lestnitsa iz luchei ot neba do zemli i arkhangely s trombami i saksofonami, ili chto tam u nikh polagaetsia, zavopiat nezemnymi golosami, privetstvuia izbrannika. (68–69)

If Tristan embraces the fate that transfigures him through cosmic fusion with his ideal Isolde, virtually all of Vasilii Mikhailovich's actions are a futile battle against the mortal destiny by which he feels entrapped ("Everything is predestined, and you can't swerve off the path—that's what tormented Vasilii Mikhailovich" [65]/"Vse predresheno, i v storonu ne svernut'—vot chto muchilo Vasiliia Mikhailovicha" [62]). A vigorous man of action who nevertheless surrenders joyfully to physical dissolution because it vouchsafes his purification, Tristan is innocent of manipulation, whereas the petty, timorous Vasilii Mikhailovich ludicrously tries to outwit fate by relying on his scant imaginative resources; hence the tedious liaisons that he initiates by calling women whose telephone numbers coincide with the seven digits imprinted on laundered sheets. When fate does send Izolda his way ("But the one who holds the skein of fate in his hands, who determines meetings [. . .] had already marked with a red X the intersections where he was to meet Izolda" [68]/"A tot, kto derzhit v rukakh svitok sud'by, kto predreshaet vstrechi [. . .] uzhe podmetil krestikom perekrestok, gde on dolzhen byl vstretit' Izol'du" [65]); "she would be the one to bring him out of the dark pencil case called the universe" [68]/"pust' ona i budet toi, kto vyvedet ego iz temnogo penala, imenuemogo mirozdaniem" [65]), Tolstaya's modern Tristan fails to appreciate his good fortune.

As in "Okkervil River," Tolstaya retains enough of the parodied text for the reader to appreciate her divergence from it. At his first, enchanted encounter with his "beloved," Vasilii Mikhailovich invites her for a drink, "and Izolda was like a wondrous silvery bird, which nature had created as one of a kind" (69) ("i Izol'da byla kak dikovinnaia serebrianaia ptitsa, izgotovlennaia prirodoi v edinstvennom ekzempliare" [66]). Like the overarching briar branches in the Tristan and Isolde myth that grow toward each other to form an inseparable bond between the graves of the dead couple,[26] Vasilii Mikhailovich's soul reaches out to Izolda through impassable space: "And Vasilii Mikhailovich, gasping in the dark, mentally sent his soul to Izolda, knowing that it would reach her *along the sparkling arc that connected them across the city*, invisible to the uninitiated" (69–70, emphasis added) ("I Vasilii Mikhailovich, zadykhaias' vo mrake, myslenno posylal Izol'de svoiu dushu, znal, chto ona doidet do nee *po sverkaiushchei duge, chto soediniaet ikh cherez gorod*, nevidimaia dlia neposviashchennykh" [67]). Following Tristan's Isolde, Vasilii Mikhailovich's commits herself to him unreservedly, asking for nothing except to remain at his side. And finally, like Tristan, Vasilii Mikhailovich glimpses his Izolda just before his death, having decided, "If I run into Izolda, I've come to the end of my road" (74) ("Esli vstrechu Izol'du, put' okonchen" [71]).

Throughout, however, Tolstaya debases these parallels and, moreover, transfers the lovers' relationship to a qualitatively different plane: (1) Whereas Tristan and Isolde are conjoined through eternal, unswerving love, Vasilii Mikhailovich breaks off his passing liaison with Izolda because she eventually bores him; and (2) the drink that Isolde proffers Tristan has considerable prominence both in the myth and in Tolstaya's text yet appears in different guises. Its status as a love philter in Wagner and earlier mythic variants becomes complicated in that its far-reaching consequences transform it into the death brew for which Tristan mistakes the liquid as he accepts the goblet. The potion, then, functions not as a material agency but as a symbol of predestination (Newman, 187), whereas in "The Circle" it appears in multiple alcoholic guises serving less grand purposes. It becomes the wine that, in a reversal of roles, Vasilii Mikhailovich offers Izolda when he catches sight of her at the market ("took Izolda by the arm and offered her some wine, and his words glistened with winy sparkle" [69]/ "vzial Izol'du za ruku i predlozhil vypit' vina, i vinnym bleskom sverknuli ego slova" [66]). Toward the story's end, which documents events transpiring two decades later, a boisterously drunk Izolda imbibes beer with fellow revelers at what is presumably the same market (i.e., the Tristan/Isolde circle of fate closes) and sings about her heart's joy before the police drag her away (E75). And when at that moment Vasilii Mikhailovich, who in his attempt to outguess fate had foretold that a meeting with Izolda would signal his end, finds his prediction fulfilled, Tolstaya presents his death through the resonant metaphor of drinking a cup of hemlock: "he gratefully accepted from gentle hands his well-earned cup of hemlock" (76) ("on s blagodarnost'iu prinial iz laskovykh ruk zasluzhennuiu chashku s tsikutoi" [73]). Thus, while retaining the associations with love and death that adhere to the myth's, and especially Wagner's, libation, Tolstaya transposes them to a baser, diminishing context.

Furthermore, "The Circle" problematizes the question of death through the figure of Izolda, whose character zone Tolstaya infuses with death throughout. Apart from the story's opening and conclusion, which are contemporary to the narrative, the bulk of the text consists of unobtrusively integrated blocks of flashback to twenty years earlier.[27] Immediately upon first mentioning Izolda within one such flashback that recounts the lovers' initial encounter, Tolstaya notes, "Now, of course, it was quite some time since she'd passed away" (68) ("Teper' ee, konechno, davno uzhe net" [65]). That shift to the present-day perspective, which constitutes Tolstaya's version of *Liebestod*, accompanies all subsequent references to landmarks in Izolda's relationship with Vasilii Mikhailovich. Just as in parody the materials comprising the parodic target must be posited for the sake of recognizability (Hutcheon, "Modern Parody and Bakhtin," 100) and consequently receive confirmation through (subsequently qualified) presence, so Izolda is kept textually alive, in a sense, through reiteration of her physical death. The death motif recurs when the narrative reports Izolda's last unambiguous contact with her lover: the poem she sends on his fortieth birthday, again followed by the comment "It was quite some time now that she'd passed away" (71) ("Teper'-to ee davno net" [68]). A third mention of the motif takes place after Vasilii Mikhailovich's bargain with fate: "But he was cheating: Izolda had passed away a long time ago" (74) ("No on khitril: Izol'dy davno uzhe ne bylo" [71]), and finally, at the very instant of Vasilii Mikhailovich's death: "But that couldn't be Izolda: she had passed away a long time ago" (75) ("Vprochem, eto ne mogla byt' Izol'da: ved' ee davno uzhe ne bylo" [72]). Ultimately it is impossible for the reader to ascertain beyond all doubt whether Izolda has actually died or not. Why Vasilii Mikhailovich presumes that she no longer exists is never clarified and, given his egocentrism, he might well equate her exit from his life with a departure from life in general. What is paramount here, however, is less Izolda's objective presence at this stage than the ironic dimension that results from the ambiguity (since neither alternative accommodates the couple's glorious expiration together, as in the myth). That ambiguity concerns the nature of predestination, around which Tolstaya builds her narrative.

One could justifiably claim that "The Circle" traces the path along which Tolstaya brings her protagonist around to death. Introduced as a sixty-year-old who cannot reconcile himself to extinction and at every turn fights to redesign the coordinates devised for him by fate, Vasilii Mikhailovich eventually accepts his cup of hemlock "gratefully" (76). Neither patient expectancy nor rebellion has averted the inevitable. Waiting for signs from above, such as the divine inspiration that illuminates artistic vision (Tolstaya invokes the "six-winged seraph" ["shestikrylyi serafim"] of Pushkin's poem "The Prophet" ["Prorok"]), and imposing significance on arbitrary phenomena through radical recontextualization, such as turning laundry marks into telephone numbers, have proved equally impotent:

> Vasilii Mikhailovich [. . .] realized that his attempt to escape the system of coordinates had failed. It wasn't a new, unheard-of route with breathtaking possibilities that opened before him, nor a secret path into the beyond, no; he had simply groped around in the dark and grabbed the usual wheel of fate, and if he went around it hand over hand, along the curve, he would eventually come around full circle, ending up with himself, from the other side. (67)

> Vasilii Mikhailovich [. . .] ponial, chto popytka vyrvat'sia iz sistemy koordinat ne udalas'. Ne novyi, nebyvalyi put' s sakhvatyvaiushchimi dukh vozmozhnostiami otkryvalsia emu, ne tainaia tropinka v zapredel'noe, net; on poprostu nasharil vpot'makh i ukhvatil obychnoe ocherednoe koleso sud'by i, perekhvatyvaia obod obeimi rukami, po duge,

po krugu dobralsia by v kontse kontsov do sebia samogo—s drugoi storony. (64)

The earth's sphere, the circle of fate, and the zero that constitute Vasilii Mikhailovich's inner world collectively stress the inescapability of repeated pattern, which characterizes the lot of humankind and imprisons the individual. True to the ironic paradox of the classic Oedipal paradigm, it is precisely by trying to elude his destiny that Vasilii Mikhailovich seems to actualize it, through a feeble endeavor to outmaneuver forces beyond his comprehension. He marshals his troops in the wrong battlefield, however: Tolstaya's imagery implies that Vasilii Mikhailovich has been given an extraordinary opportunity to transcend, if not avoid, mortality. That opportunity comes in the form of Izolda, who, like her mythic predecessor, is the hero's complementary other half and has the capacity to redeem him through love— but that potential goes unrecognized by her modern-day Tristan.

Although Tolstaya depicts Izolda as a rather pitiful, timid creature with frail blue arms[28] who roams the market stalls looking for left-over food, she endows her portrait with several details that nonetheless establish Izolda's identity as Vasilii Mikhailovich's "true love." Their two poems testify to their kinship: as a juxtaposition of the texts reveals, the poem he mentally transmits to her across the city has its direct counterpart in her farewell poem to him:

Night trains jangle in my throat,
It comes and grabs, and grows
   silent once more.
The crucified hangs above a deep
   hole
Where angels of death buzz like
   gnats:
"Give up! You're locked in a
   square,
We'll come, release you, and start
   over again."
O woman! Apple tree! Candle
   flame!
Break through, chase away,
   Protect, scream!
Hands tied, mouth contorted,
A black maiden sings in the
   dark. (70)
[HIS]

Here's a gift for you in parting:
Candle stub,
Shoe laces and plum pit.
Look closely and smile crookedly.
This was
Your love until it died:
Fire, and skipping, and sweet fruit
Above the abyss, and the brink of
   disaster. (71)

[HERS]

Nochnymi vagonami v gorle
  stuchit,
Nakatit—i khvatit—i vnov'
  zamolchit.
Raspiatyi, povis nad slepoiu dyroi,
Gde angely smerti zveniat
  moshkaroi:
"Sdavaisia! Ty zapert v kvadrate
  nochnom,
Nakatim—otpustim—i snova
  nachnem."
O zhenshchina! Iablonia! Plamia
  svechi!
Prorvis', progoni, ogradi, zakrichi!
I stisnuty ruki, i skriuchilo rot,
I chernaia deva iz mraka poet. (67)
[HIS]

Vot na proshchan'e dlia tebia
  podarok:
Svechi ogarok,
Shnurki ot tufelek i kostochka ot
  slivy.
Vgliadish'sia pristal'no i
  usmekhnesh'sia krivo:
Takoi byla
Tvoia liubov', poka ne umerla:
Ogon', i legkii beg, i sladkie plody
Nad propast'iu, na kraeshke bedy. (68)

[HERS]

The two lyrics clearly differ in tone and emphases: his pleads with her ("Woman") for salvation from his perceived role of trapped martyr suspended over the abyss of mortality; hers reproaches him for the transitoriness of his love. Yet common features link the poems: the catastrophic psychological setting ("nad slepoi dyroi," "Nad propast'iu"), the grimace ("skriuchilo rot," "usmekhnesh'sia krivo"), the notion of death as an ending ("angely smerti," "umerla"), and above all, the fruit and flame symbolizing love and the soul; the "iablonia" and "plamia dushi" of his poem dwindle to "kostochka ot slivy" and "svechi ogarok" in hers, signaling that hope for a new start, for spiritual rebirth through love, has deteriorated into disillusioned memories. Izolda's reworking of the imagery from Vasilii Mikhailovich's verses, which he communicates to her *telepathically*, suggests that an inner bond does indeed connect them. Moreover, the flame and the stub of the burned-out candle acquire importance in light of two passages: while Vasilii Mikhailovich pours out his heart to her in the expectation that she will reciprocate, Izolda seeks something independent of words: "she would be happy to sit forever at his side, burning like a wedding *candle, burning without extinguishing, with a steady quiet flame*" (70, emphasis added) ("vse by ei sidet' u ego izgolov'ia, vse by ei goret' venchal'noi *svechoi, goret' ne sgoraia, rovnym tikhim plamenem* [67]). The final self-portrait that Vasilii Mikhailovich momentarily glimpses before death is, tellingly, of someone crawling along a cold tunnel grimly extinguishing all the sparks along the way ("grimly smothering all the sparks that flashed on the way" [76]/ "ugriumo zataptyvaiushchego vse vspykhivaiushchie na puti iskry" [73])—

not the least of which is the "steady flame" of Izolda's love. That insight into his moribund life explains why the cup of hemlock he gratefully accepts is "well earned." While clinging to life, he has never fully lived it, just as he has never loved, while ostensibly craving and definitely receiving love. That is why, within the symbolic meaning of the story's title, when he completes the circle of his life, Vasilii Mikhailovich meets only himself (R72–73); all of his relationships have never taken him beyond the self. So although "The Circle" satirizes the notion of the Eternal Feminine in general, it implicitly seems to credit Izolda, at least, with the redemptive love that traditionally has been the sine qua non of that concept.

Woman as ideal and inspiration, then, finds qualified affirmation in both "Okkervil River" and "The Circle," even while undergoing parodic treatment. This doubling reflects what Hutcheon has called "the bi-directionality of the legitimacy of parody itself. The presupposition of both a law and its transgression bifurcates the impulse of parody: it can be normative and conservative, or it can be provocative and revolutionary" ("Modern Parody and Bakhtin," 101). In Tolstaya's two narratives, the provocation issues from an ironic uncrowning of hallowed myths through transcontextualizing debasement. Yet a normative tendency modifies this transgressive activity not only through the implicit recognition of a law that inheres in any parody, but through partial validation of elements from the specific myths being parodied. The two stories may be read as a dialogue between two voices at different stages on the path to skepticism. Whereas in "Okkervil River" Tolstaya achieves distance through a *synthesis* of available polarities (Pushkin's Peter the Great versus Evgenii)—a synthesis that can serve stylistically as a model for solving the work's key dilemma of reconciliation (between Vera Vasilevna as apotheosis and Vernuchuk as brute matter)— "The Circle" assumes a principally *antithetical* stance to its mythic sources, its very method thereby stressing the opposition, dissonance, and separateness that its inner movement highlights. In this dialogue between two voices represented by the two stories, the second voice is steeped much deeper in skepticism than the first and embraces a much darker vision. "Okkervil River" credits art with the capacity to extend one's imaginative compass and to offer restitution for, or tolerance of, an unpalatable reality. Life, as Hippocrates claimed, is short and art is long, but according to Tolstaya art can stretch life along the perpendicular, if not the horizontal, axis. "The Circle," by contrast, illustrates the barrenness of an existence closed upon itself, hence impervious to external stimuli and blind to their significance. If Vera Vasilevna's art endows Simeonov's life with moments of special radiance, he actively participates in that process of temporary transfiguration that ultimately may yield more lasting joys. Vasilii Mikhailovich, however, seeks revelation of a kingdom from which his psychic indigence inevitably excludes him, and which he cannot even recognize. Tolstaya's parodic transposition of tragic, cosmic, and arch-Romantic literary myths to a mundane register allows for an original, remarkably resonant treatment of eternal human dilemmas and for the partial incorporation into her texts of the works that have addressed these concerns for centuries. Her narratives thus illustrate one way in which story can subsume history.

✧ 5 ✧

Monsters Monomaniacal, Marital, and Medical: Tolstaya's Regenerative Use of Gender Stereotypes

In . . . the book of Egoism, it is written, Possession without obligation to the object possessed approaches felicity.

George Meredith, *The Egoist*

Amidst the welter of grotesque relationships proliferating in Tatyana Tolstaya's fiction,[1] romantic–sexual liaisons particularly stand out as oxymoronic misalliances cast in a Bakhtinian key.[2] More often than not, one or both partners involved seem highly implausible candidates for the type of coupling they contemplate, pursue, or enjoy, in large measure because social convention has accustomed us automatically to identify romantic scenarios with beauty, glamor, success, and the like. Tolstaya, however, intentionally swims against the current of custom, for the temperamental idiosyncrasies and outlandish physical appearance that as a rule discourage association with romance invariably characterize her lovelorn and love-seeking personae. Thus Peters, the pastry-gobbling "glandular washout," doggedly and futilely woos modish young sophisticates with mumbled reminiscences of his plush rabbit and vague references to German culture ("Peters"); the maladroit, equine-faced Sonia, with pigeon toes and a sunken chest, perishes in a bombardment while saving her beloved Nikolai, without noticing that in actuality he is a vengeful female acquaintance ("Sonia"); Simeonov scorns the (s)motheringly amorous overtures of Tamara in favor of obsessive fantasies about a singer from the distant past who, in person, proves to be a mountain of gluttonous flesh now preoccupied solely with physical gratification ("Okkervil River"); eighty-four-year-old Aleksandra Ernestovna, a thrice-widowed monument to time's passage, with drooping stockings and an improbable hat of floral overabundance, still dwells elegiacally on her ancient decision not to run off with her devoted admirer many decades ago ("Sweet Shura"), and so forth. In their fusion of extravagant Romance and risible pathos, these "odd couples" are polemical antipodes to Pyramus and Thisbe, Romeo and Juliet, Dante and Beatrice, Héloïse and Abelard, and other canonic exemplars of exalted love. To dismantle the immemorial constructs generated by, and generating, such cultural icons, Tolstaya capitalizes on readers' standard (and prejudiced) expectations, only to subvert them, democratizing Love and exposing its reliance on discursive modes, in the process achieving strong tonal and emotional effects.

That strategy of creative, irreverent sabotage likewise operates in a trio of narratives related to these works, though distinct from them, which dethrone specifically gender stereotypes through ironic double-voicing, literalization of metaphor, and parodic interpolation of myth: "Hunting the Wooly Mammoth" ("Okhota na mamonta") (1985), "The Poet and the Muse" ("Poet i Muza") (1986), and "Fire and Dust" ("Ogon' i pyl'") (1986).[3] The narrative impetus behind these stories derives from a reversal of stale formulae that have long regulated heterosexual relations: for example, a woman's "female essence" can be realized only in marriage; everyone "has a right to personal happiness" (i.e., marriage); marriage necessarily means domestication, the preservation of "the sanctity of Home and Family"; beauty and the projection of inaccessible "virtue" constitute a woman's passport to the haven of marital bliss, and so on. In addition to satirizing such notions, Tolstaya's trio explicitly discredits the prescribed gender identities buttressing these hollow but hallowed *idées reçues*, namely, womanhood as Muse, as inspiration for artistic (i.e., male) creativity; as sacred vessel, decorative dreamer, self-abnegating nurturer, and pedestaled helpmate. In all these cases the female protagonists engage in the reflexive sociocultural mimetism common to insecure individuals whose mental agoraphobia or reticent intelligence motivates their uncritical capitulation to their culture's dominant myths. These they internalize and disseminate in their turn, thereby upholding the constabulary of culture known as popular opinion or thought.

"Hunting the Wooly Mammoth" charts the narrow course of Zoia's relentless efforts to attain the universally sanctioned goal of "landing" a husband, optimally one with prestige ("Zoia didn't want to love withut guarantees" [57]/"liubit' bez garantii Zoia ne khotela" [56]). Within the presiding metaphor of the mammoth hunt, the hunter/hospital receptionist Zoia initially sets her impersonal sights on a surgeon but settles upon lesser game, the engineer Vladimir, as a compromise ("Zoia very much wanted to fall into a surgeon's bloody embrace. But an engineer was also fine" [53]/"Zoe ochen'-ochen' khotelos' past' v krovavye khirurgovy ob''iatiia. No inzhener—tozhe khorosho" [50]). Throughout, Zoia utterly dehuman-

izes Vladimir as an object defined exclusively in terms of her own teleology, and hence perceived as the adversarial prey earmarked for submission to her Purpose:[4]

> She [. . .] hated the two-bearded Vladimir, and wanted to marry him as
> soon as possible (55); Oh, how disgusting he was! Marry him, hurry up
> and marry him! (56); Zoia was hostilely silent [. . .] he, the viper, felt
> right at home (57); What a louse Vladimir was [. . .] Rules of the hunt do
> exist, after all (60); This man had never particularly appealed to her. No,
> let's be honest, he'd always repelled her. A small, powerful, heavy,
> quick, hairy, insensitive animal. (62)

> Ona [. . .] nenavidela dvukhborodogo Vladimira i khotela skoree uzhe
> vyiti za nego zamuzh (53); Okh, kakoi on byl protivnyi! Zamuzh, skoree
> za nego zamuzh! (54); Zoia vrazhdebno molchala [. . .] on, gad, prizhilsia
> (55); Podlets Vladimir [. . .] Est' zhe pravila okhoty (58); Nikogda etot
> chelovek ei osobenno ne nravilsia. Da net, chego uzh tam,—on ei vsegda
> byl otvratitelen. Malen'koe, moshchnoe, gruznoe, bystroe, volosatoe,
> beschuvstvennoe zhivotnoe. (60)

This reduction of the male to a purely referential function (which Tolstaya
intensifies by presenting him externally, through Zoia's eyes alone) exposes
the dehumanizing aspects of objectification by self-positing subjects. Vladimir becomes coopted and subsumed as alterity within an epistemologically
imperialistic system that denies him all autonomy. Paradoxically, that system originates in an internalized patriarchal structure that historically has
construed woman as Other. Zoia operates within that structure, her campaign unreflectingly presupposing both the validity of the timeworn clichés
within that binary paradigm and the efficacy of equally hackneyed patterns
of behavior sanctioned by it.

Zoia's solipsistic brutality communicates itself in the firmly grounded
animal imagery that helps build the narrative's connective tissue. From the
very outset, Tolstaya analogizes Zoia with a bee through the sound of her
name ("Zoia's a beautiful name, isn't it? Like bees buzzing by" [51]/
"Krasivoe imia—Zoia, pravda? Budto pchely prozhuzhzhali" [49]). A particularly apt, ambivalent association, given Zoia's delusive sweetness and
her capacity to sting, the image gains force through later repetition ("Zoia
buzzed like a bee" [56]/"Zoia zhuzhzhala pcheloi" [54]). By contrast, Vladimir is equated with the hapless mammoth portrayed in his artist friend's
symbolic painting, whose title the story appropriates:

> a wild craggy cliff, growths of cattails, and from the cattails emerges a
> wooly mammoth in slippers. Someone tiny is aiming at it with a bow and

arrow. On one side you can see the little cave: it has a light bulb hanging from a cord, a glowing TV screen, and a lighted gas burner. Even the frying pan is drawn in painstakingly, and there's a bouquet of cattails on the little table. (59)

dikaia skalistaia mestnost', khvoshchi, iz khvoshchei vykhodit mamont v tapochkakh. Kto-to malen'kii pritselilsia v nego iz luka. A sboku vidna peshcherka: tam elektricheskaia lampochka na shnurke, televizor svetitsia, gorit ogonek gazovoi plity. Dazhe skovorodka tshchatel'no narisovana, i na stolike—buket khvoshchei. (57)

The parallel requires little explication: just as in the larger scheme of things so-called civilization and its progress effected the mammoth's extinction, so the time-honored ritual of conjugal domestication renders the free-roaming male a doomed species: "Zoia set traps: she'd dig a pit, cover it with branches, and nudge him closer, closer toward it" (57) ("Zoia stavila zapadni: vyroet iamu, prikroet vetviami i podtalkivaet, podtalkivaet" [56]). Even the slippers in the painting have precise relevance for Vladimir's circumstances ("In the fall Zoia bought slippers for Vladimir" [56]/ "Osen'iu, Zoia kupila Vladimiru tapki" [54]).

Finally, the dove and pigeon simultaneously evoked by the term "golub' " become Zoia's radically subjective and specious correlative from the world of nature invoked to validate her recipe for happiness. The Russian language's failure to distinguish between the two (dove/pigeon) enables the image to connote spirituality and peace on the one hand and tamed subordination to human designs on the other. It also enables Tolstaya to spotlight the limitations of Zoia's earthbound pragmatism, for she can conceive of only the "lower" connotations:

A pigeon with a banded leg landed on the window and looked severely into Zoia's eyes. There, there you are! Even a pigeon, a lousy, dirty bird, gets banded. Scientists *in white coats*, with honest, educated faces, PhDs, pick him up, the little bird/dear, by the sides [. . .] , the pigeon with the fiery *wedding ring* rose from the darkness. (60–61, emphases added)

Na okno opustilsia golub' s okol'tsovannoi nogoi, strogo glianul v Zoiny glaza. Vot, vot—pozhaluista! Kakogo-to golubia—parshivuiu, sornuiu ptitsu—i togo kol'tsuiut. Uchenye *v belykh khalatakh*, s chestnymi, obrazovannymi litsami, kandidaty nauk, berut ego, golubchika, za boka [. . .] golub' s ognennym *obruchal'nym kol'tsom* vstaval iz mraka. (58)

Through the white coats, which recall Zoia's own garb in the hospital—a milieu that camouflages pain, dissolution, and death by a civilized veneer of sterility[5]—Tolstaya forges an eloquent parallel for Zoia's violent assault on

Vladimir's selfhood under the paradigmatic guise of dispensing and seeking "happiness with the man she loves." The story's conclusion, however, tears aside the veil of convention through the grisly metaphor of a prehistoric cave in which Zoia lassos her prey ("izverg," "zhivotnoe") and listens to it finally subside in defeat: "It puttered around for a while—whimpering, fussing—until it quieted down in the blissful empty silence of the great ice age" (62) ("Ono eshche vozilos′ kakoe-to vremia—skulilo, bespokoilos′, poka nakonets ne zatikhlo—blazhennoi, pustoi tishinoi velikogo oledeneniia" [60]).

Although in a characteristic original twist Tolstaya reverses the gender roles in the classic metaphor of love as hunt[6] and realizes the metaphor at several junctures, the effectiveness of these devices hinges on the reader's recognition of the image as a cultural stereotype. Moreover, that recognition empowers Tolstaya's concision and her audience's sensitivity to the double-voicedness of the narrative, which modulates constantly from Zoia's artless revelations of totalitarian impulses to the counter-voice of ironic distancing. Both voices, in their contrasting ways, and through the interplay between them, expose not only Zoia's undebilitated vulgarity but also her egotistic pragmatism—her determination to "land her victim" at all cost. She does so by following the steps of a time-tested strategy which presumes that a woman's beauty inherently entitles her simultaneously to the emblematic prerogatives of universal male adulation and a prestigious husband.

Zoia recruits her heaviest artillery from the arsenal of cultural history. It predictably consists of her looks and the simulation of elevated fragility and refinement. Narcissistically staging tableaux that give her center stage as the visual object of desire, she appeals to the male voyeurism that entails mediated possession without engagement. Thus during their first rendez-vous at a restaurant, she picks daintily at her dessert, "pretending that for some intellectual reason it wasn't very tasty" (52) ("delaia vid, chto ei po kakim-to intellektual′nym prichinam ne ochen′ vkusno" [49–50]). Later, she ostentatiously assumes a decorative pose of attitudinized contemplation, in a classic invitation to appropriation through the Male Gaze:[7]

> Zoia sat with a languorous air, a casual expression on her face, slightly mocking, somewhat dreamy—her face was supposed to reflect the fleeting nuances of her complex spiritual life—such as exquisite sadness or some refined reminiscence; she sat gazing into space, her elbows delicately resting on the table, her lower lip pouting, sending lovely smoke rings up to the painted vaulted ceiling. She was playing fairy. [. . .] Zoia was offended. Wasn't she a princess, albeit unrecognized? (53)

> Zoia sidela s tomnym vidom, sdelav nebrezhnoe litso, kak by slegka nasmeshlivoe, otchasti zadumchivoe—predpolagalos′, chto po litsu pro-

begaiut mimoletnye ottenki ee slozhnoi dushevnoi zhizni—vrode izyskannoi pechali ili kakogo-to utonchonnogo vospominaniia; sidela gliadia iakoby vdal', iziashchno postaviv lokti na stol i, ottopyriv nizhniuiu gubu, puskala k raspisnym svodam krasivye tabachnye kolechki. Shla igra v feiu. [. . .] Zoia obizhalas': razve ona ne byla printsessoi, khotia i neuznannoi? (50–52)

Tolstaya stresses Zoia's lack of subjective self, whereby she conceives of herself in purely visual, external terms, through the series of scenes projected by her imagination in which she cannot separate herself from the perspective of the objectifying male viewer: as the physically disheveled hence imperfect decoration merely accompanying Vladimir on an outing, hence not in her "true role" (R53) of heart-stopping beauty; as the "original" of the photograph of herself she slips into Vladimir's wallet (R54); as the pièce de résistance at an artistic gathering and the "subject" of a portrait that causes a sensation (R56–57); as the object of universal acclaim once the portrait becomes famous and she, as the "original," is sought after (R57); and, finally, as the incarnation of Unbounded Grief ("Bezgranichnaia Skorb' ") fit for depiction by a medieval artist (R59). Zoia's identity, then, seeks definition through material representation. Insofar as she walks through life with an invisible mental mirror in which she obsessively checks her reflection at every encounter with "a male subject,"[8] Zoia exemplifies what John Berger has defined as women's social presence:

> she comes to consider the *surveyor* and the *surveyed* within her as the two constituent yet always distinct elements of her identity as a woman.
> She has to survey everything she is and everything she does because how she appears to others, and ultimately how she appears to men, is of crucial importance for what is normally thought of as the success of her life. Her own sense of being in herself is supplanted by a sense of being appreciated as herself by another. (Berger, 46, emphasis in original)

Although Zoia gives every evidence of tactical indefatigability on the battlefield of sexual politics, she actually joins the fray out of profound existential insecurity. Her identity derives wholly from without, constituted by male attention as an acknowledgement of her desirability.[9] That contingent desirability comprises her essence. Without a yearning male gaze to verify her existence, Zoia becomes obliterated. Hence her loss of "self," both during the camping trip with Vladimir and his married coworkers ("All the engineers had their own women, no one *gazed* at Zoia with a special *look* or said 'Oh!' and she felt sexless, a camping buddy" [54–55, emphasis added]/"Vse inzhenery byli so svoimi zhenshchinami, nikto ne *gliadel* na Zoiu osobennym *vzgliadom*, ne govoril 'O!', i ona chuvstvovala sebia besplodnym briuchnym tovarishchem" [53]), and during their visit to Vladimir's painter friend:

> The host slid a radiant, as if unseeing *gaze* professionally over Zoia's surface. The *gaze* did not connect with Zoia's soul, as if she/it weren't even there. [. . .] they both [. . .] forgot about Zoia. [. . .] Zoia wasn't here or anywhere else, she simply didn't exist. (59, emphases added)

> Khoziain svetlym, kak by nevidiashchim *vzgliadom* professionala skol'zil po Zoinoi poverkhnosti. Zoinu dushu *vzgliad* ne zatseplial, budto ee vovse i ne bylo. [. . .] oba [. . .] o Zoe zabyli. [. . .] Zoi ne bylo ni zdes' i nigde, ee voobshche ne bylo. (57–58)

Zoia's colossal self-preoccupation articulates itself in her crass, appurtenance-based ideal of conjugal life, wherein during Vladimir's absence she relaxes picturesquely on the couch in an elegant robe (imported!), in front of a color TV ("let Vladimir buy her one"/"pust' Vladimir kupit"), by the rosy glow of a (Yugoslavian!) floor lamp, and sips a light beverage as she smokes something extraordinary ("let the patients' relatives give her some"/"pust' podariat rodstvenniki bol'nykh"), anticipating a flirtatious call from the "ideal" surgeon with whom she will engage in badinage (R53).[10] Satisfaction within marriage is thus equated with conspicuous consumption, the luxury items to be deposited on the altar of female beauty. Unable to envision any desires, any world, in fact, beyond her affirmation as an enshrined gift to mankind, Zoia ineluctably degrades herself and Vladimir into commodities for barter on the market of dehumanized pseudosexual relations that Marxist feminists identify with paradigmatic patriarchal institutions.[11] Hence the saliency of Susanne Kappeler's astute insight that "[t]he remorseless diffusion of gender stereotypes, of readymade and imperative life-styles, of regulated uniform 'relationships'—the ideological diffusion of 'mind images' of humans—through the remorseless diffusion of their material basis—consumer goods—renders human subjects increasingly marginal."[12] That Tolstaya conceives of Zoia's goal and modus operandi as a specific instance of a comprehensive cultural paradigm may be deduced from such comments as "But how to find out his intentions? Zoia didn't dare a direct question. *Many centuries of experience kept her from doing that.* One bad shot—and it was over, write it off" (57, emphasis added) ("Da kak uznat' ego namereniia? Na priamoi vopros Zoia vse-taki ne otvazhivalas'. *Mnogovekovyi opyt osteregal.* Odin neudachnyi vystrel—i vse, pishi propalo" [55]).

If "Hunting the Wooly Mammoth" spotlights the destructive consequences of manipulating life in accordance with internalized gender clichés,

"The Poet and the Muse" goes further by rendering those consequences literally fatal. Like the earlier story, "The Poet and the Muse" takes as its point of
departure two cultural bromides that the narrative proceeds to explode through
double-voicing, literalized metaphor, Homeric catalogues, and ironic citation of
biblical, folkloric, and mythic elements: (1) Woman as inspirational muse, and
(2) everyone's "right to personal happiness" ("pravo na lichnoe schast'e"
serves as a sardonic refrain).[13] The story's female protagonist, Nina, and its
plotline also echo "Hunting the Wooly Mammoth." As a doctor, Nina, like
Zoia, belongs to the medical profession; she likewise chooses the unsuspecting
victim of her implacable "love," launches a cold-blooded campaign to assume
ascendancy over all aspects of his life, and ultimately succeeds in destroying it
and eliminating him. Her presumption, which duplicates Zoia's, is that female
beauty per se merits the automatic conferral of happiness: "she'd earned the
right to happiness; she was fully entitled to a place in the line where it was
being handed out" (118) ("ona zasluzhila pravo na schast'e, ona imela vse
osnovaniia zaniat' ochered' tuda, gde ego vydaiut [113]); "justice demanded
that someone sing her praises" (119) ("bylo by prosto spravedlivo, chtoby
ee kto-nibud' vospel" [114]). Whereas Zoia is given to checking her own
image mentally, Nina observes herself quite literally in mirrors, to verify
her superiority over her female "friends" with the "standard-issue" hus-
bands for whom Nina harbors only contempt: "[she] would talk for a long
time, eyeing herself all the while in the dark glass of the kitchen door,
where her reflection was even more enigmatic, and more alluring in comparison with her friend's spreading silhouette" (119) ("[ona] dolgo govorila,
vse pogliadyvaia na sebia v temnoe steklo kukhonnoi dveri, gde ee
otrazhenie bylo eshche zagadochnee, eshche vyigryshnee i vygodno
otlichalos' ot rasplyvshegosia silueta priiatel'nitsy" [114]).

   With clinical precision, Nina diagnoses her own needs, the vapid terms
of which Tolstaya derides through (1) a listing device, which Gustave Flaubert used to comparable effect in *Madame Bovary*, and (2) a reaccented
application of motifs from the fairy tale "The Feather of Finist, the Bright
Falcon" ("Peryshko Finista iasna sokola"):

> she needed a wild, mad love, with sobs, bouquets, midnight phone vigils,
> nocturnal taxi chases, fateful obstacles, betrayals, and forgiveness. She
> needed a—you know—an animal passion, dark windy nights with
> streetlamps aglow, so that the *classical heroine's feat* would seem a mere
> trifle—wearing out seven pairs of iron boots, breaking seven iron staffs,
> devouring seven loaves of iron bread. (117, emphasis added)

> Nuzhno ei bezumnuiu, sumasshedshuiu liubov' s rydaniiami, buketami, s
> polunochnymi ozhidaniiami telefonnogo zvonka, s nochnymi pogoniami

na taksi, s rokovymi prepiatstviiami, izmenami i proshcheniiami, nuzhna takaia zverinaia, znaete li, strast'—chernaia vetrenaia noch' s ogniami, chtoby pustiakom pokazalsia *klassicheskii zhenskii podvig*—stoptat' sem' par zheleznykh sapog, izlomat' sem' zheleznykh posokhov, izgryzt' sem' zheleznykh khlebov. (113)[14]

This condensation of externals, of threadbare props and symbolic gestures divorced from essence, along with the verb "seem" (*pokazat'sia*), provides an eloquent measure of Nina's entrapment in appearance and form. That misguided attachment acquires an additional edge in the dismissive comparison with the "classical heroine's feat" from the fairy tale "The Feather of Finist, the Bright Falcon," in which the heroine undergoes genuinely harrowing ordeals to regain the "bright falcon" of a man she loves with wholehearted, unselfish devotion.[15] The jarring contrast between Nina and the beauteous maiden ("krasnaia devitsa") of the fairy tale reinforces the ironic tension that the narrative sustains throughout between the superstructure of overblown ideals and extravagant romantic display, on the one hand, and the base of savage repression activated by coarse, material self-interest, on the other.[16] The contradictory nature of this hybridization is captured brilliantly by Tolstaya's satirical encapsulation of Nina's first encounter with the poet Grisha:

> The near-corpse quickly abducted Nina's weary heart: the mournful shadows on his porcelain brow, the darkness around his sunken eyes, and the tender beard, wispy as a springtime forest—all this made for a magical scene. Invisible violins played a wedding waltz, and the trap sprang shut. Well, everyone knows how it usually happens. (120)

> Polutrup nemedlenno pokhitil Ninino zazhdavsheesia serdtse: skorbnye teni na ego farforovom chele, t'ma v zapavshikh glazitsakh, nezhnaia boroda, prozrachnaia, kak vesenii les, slozhilis' v volshebnuiu dekoratsiiu, nezrimye skripki igrali svadebnyi val'ts—lovushka zakhlopnulas'. Nu, vse znaiut, kak eto obychno byvaet. (114)

Without a thought for reciprocity (crucial to love, but irrelevant to summary annexation), Nina instantly determines to give Grisha her heart. As Tolstaya reinvigorates the exhausted metaphor through literalization ("Nina [. . .] took her heart from Grishunia's hands and nailed it to the bedstead" [121]/"Nina [. . .] vziala iz Grishuninykh ruk svoe serdtse i pribila ego gvozdiami k izgolov'iu posteli" [114]), she leaves pregnantly ambiguous at this stage the question of who better fits the role of savior, sufferer, and self-abnegator: "The thorny path lay ahead" (121) ("Ternistyi put' byl otkryt" [115]). That ambiguity feeds in part off Tolstaya's reversal of standard gender roles.

Feminist critics have exhaustively documented a particular strain in both literature and the visual arts obsessed with the moment when a male subject discovers (or perhaps uncovers) the female object of his libidinal drives as she is sleeping, or merely reclining, in a vulnerable pose particularly attractive to the voyeuristic/sadistic mentality. Works as dissimilar as Matthew Lewis's *The Monk* and the Gothic novel to which it is indebted, John Keats's voluptuous *Eve of St. Agnes*, and a host of fin-de-siècle paintings throughout Europe, not to mention countless examples of unabashed pornography, depict anticipated possession through the male viewer's omnipotent gaze directed at a prostrate woman—as a helplessly splayed object positioned for subjugation.[17] As the myth of Psyche and Cupid attests, the female variant of that scenario, in which the slumbering male body constitutes an object for female delectation, enacts less an assertion of sexual power than a craving for reassurance, an allaying of uncertainties.[18] Assigning Nina the active role and Grisha the passive function of reaction or resignation, Tolstaya embeds the male myth of possession within the larger narrative of romantic/marital entrapment. Like the heroes of the classic male formula, Nina unilaterally chooses Grisha on the basis of his looks (which stimulate conventional dreams fueled by bourgeois values) as the appropriate inhabitant of the doll's house in which she will psychologically incarcerate him. The unresisting Grisha, by contrast, seems indifferent to women's beauty (his affection for the talented but physically unprepossessing Lizaveta apparently surpasses his feelings for the beautiful Agniia); fulfills the standard feminine role of nurturer when Lizaveta falls sick (R116–17); weeps and gives freely of his emotions, which he readily expresses ("he gave himself out by the handful" [125]/"razbrasyval sebia prigorshniami" [116]); responds passively and emotionally to psychological imperialism ("only he was a frail thing: he cried a lot and didn't want to eat" [128]/"tol'ko vot slaben'kii on byl, mnogo plakal, i ne khotel kushat' " [118]); and succumbs to death for lack of toughness in withstanding the relentless attack on his selfhood. Like the fragile porcelain-browed (R117) virgin of fantasy abductions (Tolstaya briefly adverts to the experienced Nina's unsatisfying marriage and latest [?] affair but divulges nothing about possible sexual/romantic involvements in Grisha's past), the gentle, soft-hearted ("miagkii") Grisha struggles feebly, pines and whimpers, but ultimately resigns himself to the seemingly inevitable. Diminutives in the story ("blazhennen'ki," "slaben'kii," "rovnen'ko") are applied almost exclusively to him.

Saving Grisha's life in her capacity as doctor, Nina proceeds to devastate it as a woman, rearranging his entire existence, from the company he keeps to the poems he composes. Tolstaya uses military vocabulary to document

Nina's merciless campaign of terrorism, as she jealously edges his painter-friend Lizaveta out of his life ("*destroying* Lizaveta turned out to be as hard as *cutting* a tough apple worm *in half*. When they came to fine her for violating the residence permit in her passport, she was already holed up in a different place, and Nina *sent the troops* over there. [. . .] finally, Lizaveta evaporated to a mere shadow" [126, emphases added]/ "unichtozhit' Lizavetu bylo tak zhe trudno, kak *pererezat'* iablochnogo chervia-provolochnika. Kogda ee prishli shtrafovat' za narushenie pasportnogo rezhima, ona uzhe iutilas' v drugom meste, i *Nina poslala otriady* tuda. [. . .] nakonets Lizaveta soshla na net i stala ten'iu" [117]); dismisses all his friends from the apartment she now shares with Grisha ("Nina allowed Grishunia a final good-bye to his friends" [126]/"Nina razreshila Grishune v poslednii raz prostit'sia s druz'iami" [117]); oversees Grisha's poetry ("once a week she checked his desk and threw out the poems that were indecent for a married man to compose" [129]/"raz v nedeliu ona proveriala ego pis'mennyi stol i vybrasyvala te stikhi, kotorye zhenatomu cheloveku sochiniat' neprilichno" [118]); and insists that he create with remunerative publication in mind (" 'you should be thinking about a book. We live in the real world' " [128]/" 'ty dolzhen dumat' o sbornike, my zhivem v real'nom mire' " [118]). In effect, Nina becomes his censor, his warden ("Men are men; you have to keep an eye on them"),[19] and, finally, his executioner.[20] His eventual death as an indirect consequence of her repressive machinations is prefigured by her early dream of possessing him wholly as an object—a goal that Tolstaya captures in several revealing passages, as, for example:

> Oh, if only she could become the *fully empowered* mistress of the house once and for all, instead of just a casual, precarious girlfriend; if only she could put Grisha in a trunk, pack him in mothballs, cover him with a canvas cloth, bang the lid shut and sit on it, tugging at the locks to check: Are they secure? (124, emphasis added)

> O, esli by ona mogla stat' ne sluchainoi, zybkoi podrugoi, a *polnovlastnoi* khoziaikoi, polozhit' Grishuniu v sunduk, peresypat' naftalinom, ukryt' kholshchovoi triapochkoi, zakhlopnut' kryshku i usest'sia sverkhu, podergivaia zamki: prochny li? (116)[21]

Throughout, Tolstaya stresses the life-denying sterility of Nina's single-minded fixation on control, order, cleanliness, and domestic values: her apartment is "spotless" ("chisten'kaia"); the only facts we learn about her disappointing lover, the dermatologist Arkadii Borisovich (a profession inherently concerned with surface), is his fanatical preoccupation with sanitary conditions, which manifests itself in compulsive hand scrubbing (R113) and the use of face masks and rubber gloves to ward off infection—unsuccessfully! (R114); she mistrusts the "great unwashed" of bohemian life (R114); her "watchful gaze" ensures that guests wipe their feet carefully before entering the "crystal palace" of their apartment, maintained according to bourgeois ideals ("everything would be fine, warm, and clean, he'd be well fed" [127]/"vse budet khorosho, sytno, teplo i chisto" [117]). This strait-jacketed order is systematically placed in diametric opposition to the carefree vitality of the artistic circle that Grisha, Lizaveta, and Agniia typify—in Nina's hygienic eyes, a world of eccentrics, outcasts, mongrels, and vagrants ("all the holy fools, licensed and unlicensed, the geniuses and the outcasts"; "a carefree spirit, he was ready to embrace any street mongrel, shelter any *unsanitary* vagrant" [123, emphasis added]/"vse eti iurodivye, priznannye i nepriznannye, genii i otverzhennye"; "on, bespechnyi, gotovyi povisnut′ na shee u liuboi ulichnoi sobaki, prigret′ liubogo *antisanitarnogo* brodiagu" [116]). The two worlds collide at every turn. Whereas Lizaveta abandons herself unconstrainedly to an inspiration resembling frenzy as she daubs her "Talonist" canvases ("kogtizm"), Nina fastidiously protests, "Does she have to get so excited?" (124) ("A pochemu nel′zia spokoinee?" [116]). Whereas the beautiful actress-manquée Agniia admires Grisha's openhandedness and, like the rest of his crowd, deems him a genius, Nina shouts, "Did you understand me, sunshine? Don't dare write things like that!" (128) ("Ty menia ponial, solnyshko? Ne smei takoe sochiniat′!" [118]). Whereas Grisha prizes human contact to such a degree that in advance he sells his skeleton to the Academy of Sciences so that instead of lying alone in his grave "[he] would stand among lots of people [. . .] , and students—a fun crowd—would slap him on the shoulder, flick his forehead, and treat him to cigarettes" (130) ("[on] budet stoiat′ sredi liudei [. . .] i studenty—veselyi narod—budut khlopat′ ego po plechu, shchelkat′ po lbu, i ugoshchat′ papiroskoi" [119]), Nina despises his companions, whom she dehumanizes into categories of sanitation, as "unclean" ("nechist′"), "rubbish from a vacuum cleaner" ("musor iz pylesosa"). As the social anthropologist Mary Douglas argues in her classic study pointedly titled *Purity and Danger*, "Dirt is the by-product of a systemic ordering and classification of matter, insofar as ordering involves rejecting inappropriate elements. [. . .] our pollution behavior is the reaction which condemns any object or idea likely to confuse or contradict cherished classification. [. . .] our ideas of dirt also express symbolic systems."[22] Like the totalitarian state of E. Zamiatin's *We*, Nina militantly repudiates whatever threatens strict regimentation, predictability, and ready-made, invariable patterns. To borrow the nomenclature of Zamiatin's famous binary opposition, Nina advocates entropy and does everything in her power to crush energy.

Characteristically, Tolstaya literalizes the metaphor "they speak different languages" to drive home the couple's utter incompatibility: Nina interprets all of Grisha's metaphorical *cris de coeur* literally. When he couches his desperate sense of suffocation in the cosmic imagery of a garden gone to seed, razed forests, and a door frozen fast against which he pushes to the pounding of red heels resounding in the distance (R113), Nina's instant jealousy reveals the philistine literalist whose cognitive faculties are limited to matter: Whose red heels? Her nominal grief over Grisha's death, in fact, diminishes with her realization that his removal leaves more room in the apartment, room that another widow, for instance, happily converted into a showcase of bibelots, thereby profitably replacing one displayable object (a husband) with several.[23] Thus Tolstaya adumbrates the possible direction of Nina's future activity.

As she did in "Hunting the Wooly Mammoth," Tolstaya universalizes Nina's case through such remarks as "[she] was an ordinary woman [. . .] who had fought for her personal happiness, *as we were all taught to do*" (130, emphasis added) ("[ona]—obychnaia zhenshchina [. . .], borovshaiasia, *kak nas vsekh uchili*, za lichnoe schast'e" [119]). Or, when Nina decides to "have" Grisha, "the trap sprang shut. Well, *everyone knows* how it *usually happens*" (120, emphasis added) ("lovushka zakhlopnulas'. Nu, *vse znaiut*, kak eto *obychno* byvaet" [114]). Through such devices Tolstaya indicates that Grisha is a casualty of the annihilating force of gender stereotype pushed inflexibly to its logical limit. If Grisha ultimately succeeds in eluding Nina's complete possession, he does so at the cost of his life, because the stifling environment of Nina's sexual colonization leaves room only for posthumous autonomy. In Grisha, then, Tolstaya portrays a transgendered Clarissa, a victim of that aggressive desire that possesses its object through violation.

"Hunting the Wooly Mammoth" dramatizes a ghastly mismating predicated upon blind adherence to iron-clad convention. Tolstaya adds a new dimension in "The Poet and the Muse" by projecting a similar relationship against a background of bohemian camaraderie blithely indifferent to regulative blueprints of behavior. In "Fire and Dust" ("Ogon' i pyl' ") she posits that uninhibited, free way of life as a realizable alternative to yet another instance of doomed domesticity ruled by programmed thinking along institutionalized lines. The two antithetical models of existence find embodiment in Rimma and Svetlana. As their names intimate, Rimma (*Rim* = Rome) has been inculcated with the civic values that assign primacy to marriage, family, and stability. Armed with her identity as wife and mother, Rimma defers all other experience as she leisurely dreams of a materially comfortable future that entails accumulation but neglects experiential growth ("And meanwhile life wasn't completely real, it was a life of expectation" [102]/"A poka zhizn' shla ne sovsem nastoiashchaia, zhizn' v ozhidanii" [97]).

Conversely, her friend Svetlana (*Svet* = light/world) has a broader vision and ardently embraces whatever chance casts her way without sparing a thought for possible consequences. Since the narrative proceeds chiefly from Rimma's point of view,[24] the reader initially may align herself with Rimma's subjectivity, with her conformist values, and consequently may perceive the objectified Svetlana as a madwoman ("bezumnaia"), too indiscriminate with her sexual favors. Svetlana's indiscreet nickname of Pipka ("Little Cunt" or "Pussy"), her constant nakedness or near-nakedness ("poluodetaia" [98]),[25] her "black" mouth with its dreadful teeth,[26] and her association with fire—all signal her potent sexuality ("but a lot of men were attracted to her, and toward the end of a lively party they would often be one man short: amidst the noise, Pipka would have taken him off—always by taxi—to her place in Perlovka" [102]/"a ved' mnogim nravilas', i chasto k kontsu veselogo vechera odnogo iz muzhchin ne doschityvalis': Pipka pod shumok uvozila ego—vsegda na taksi—k sebe v Perlovku" [98]). Pipka's enigmatic origins and disappearances ("No one knew where Pipka would disappear to, just as no one knew where she'd come from—she just turned up, and that was that" [103]/"Neizvestno, kuda Pipka podevalas', kak neizvestno, otkuda ona voobshche vzialas'—voznikla, i vse tut" [98]), her bravura accounts of her fantastic adventures (" 'Just listen to her! A thousand and one nights!' " [104]/" 'Nu daet! Tysiacha i odna noch'!' " [99]),[27] her mysterious, evocatively named dwelling ("It was men like that whom Pipka usually took off to her semifantastic Perlovka, if it existed at all" [104]/"takogo obychno i uvozila Pipka v svoiu polufantasticheskuiu Perlovku, esli takovaia voobshche sushestvovala" [99]; "Then Petiulia disappeared too, and they assumed that Svetlana had taken him off to Perlovka. Anyone who ended up there would be gone for a long time and upon returning would take a while to get back to normal" 107]/"Potom propal i Petiulia, dogadyvalis', chto Svetlana uvezla ego v Perlovku. Vse, kto tuda popadal, ischezali nadolgo, i po vozvrashchenii byvali kakoe-to vremia ne v sebe" [102]), and the dramatic legends she trails behind her[28]—all ultimately coalesce into a beguiling image of life's infinitely rich possibilities, especially when one learns to subtract the distorting lens through which Rimma filters Svetlana's portrait. That plenitude Tolstaya evokes through the ancient imagery of sea and sirens, in which context Rimma remains a shorebound spectator (associated with inert objects and the dust of the story's title),[29] leading a life of perpetual postponement: "Life had passed by, and the voice of the future sang for others" (113) ("Zhizn' ushla, i golos budushchego poet dlia drugikh" [107]); "And the *siren* song deceptively whispering to the stupid swimmer sweet words of what would not be fell silent forever" (115, emphasis added) ("I penie *siren*, obmanno shepchushchikh glupomu plovtsu sladkie slova o nesbytochnom, umolklo navsegda" [108–9]).

Her antithesis Pipka, whose elements are, tellingly, fire and water, immerses herself in the boundless sea of human experience, leaping into the maelstrom without hesitation. Rimma's thoroughgoing conventionality and her smug condescension to Pipka ("Pipka's hardly a person, is she?"/"razve Pipka chelovek?" expands into a motif) erode as she gradually recognizes that her safe, orderly existence and philistine dreams have precluded her participation in such a life. Tellingly, in the midst of boisterous gatherings at her apartment, Rimma withdraws into fantasies about the future instead of joining in the immediacy of the present: "As usual, in the midst of the simple fare, the din of chatter, and the clink of forks, Rimma fell under a dreamy spell, seeing glorious visions" (104) ("Kak vsegda, na Rimmu posredi nezateilivogo zastol'ia, pod shum boltovni i zviakanie vilok, vdrug navalivalas' mechtatel'naia dremota, divnye snovideniia naiavu" [99]). For Rimma, in fact, life in its full sense never eventuates.

To contrast two alternate worldviews and modes of conduct, Tolstaya resorts to gendered models. Rimma's oppressively code-confirming beliefs find expression in quintessentially "feminine" dreams of domestic acquisition: Ashkenazii's room with fresh curtains, a renovated kitchen, a handsome husband with a PhD whose worth is gauged by the envy of her coworkers, clothes that will enhance her looks, and, for the children, activities rendered prestigious through their expensiveness, and so on. This upward mobility presupposes an essential stasis, with hearth and home as the reliable headquarters of an expanding empire sanctioned by timeworn social habits. Svetlana's way of life, by contrast, entails constant travels away from a *pied à terre* that seems more of a male harem than a domestic haven. Physical danger and vigorous sexual activity, the shedding of possessions (symbolized by her clothes), and receptivity to the unknown mark her multiple adventures in far-flung continents. Her periodic returns to Rimma's apartment, in fact, duplicate the structure of masculine movement in the majority of nineteenth-century Russian novels, where the arrival of the foot-loose male as the active principle triggers plot action.[30] As in "The Poet and the Muse," the conflicting poles of entropy and energy are translated into spatial categories: containment and interiors versus the illimitable vistas of the outside world.

Once more, then, Tolstaya mocks convention by discrediting the paradigm of stable home, marriage, motherhood, and domestic cares that most cultures have touted as women's definitive route to self-realization. As a tenable alternative Tolstaya postulates that which historically has been rejected on principle as entirely inappropriate or "unnatural" for a woman: an unattached life fired by sexuality, exposed to risk, and potentially spanning the gamut of human experience. Or, to recast the conflicting options in terms of literary genre, Tolstaya suggests that the tale of adventure, and not bourgeois drama, may offer a viable feminine narrative model. Such, at least, is the private epiphany at which Rimma arrives, spurred partly by Pipka's counterexample, which by story's end convinces Rimma that instead of seeking her own destiny she has marked time within the spurious safety of an untenable cliché.

Largely through Rimma's experience, "Fire and Dust" topples the aureoled Soviet image of Woman as tirelessly beaming Wife and Mother immovably rooted in the Bedrock of Family Happiness.[31] Implicit in the ironic undercutting of institutionalized roles here, as in the other two stories of the trio, is a plea for individualism, openness, and multiplicity that is stylistically abetted by a prose of dazzling luxuriance.[32] All three narratives, in fact, polemicize with gender assumptions through a partly stylistic assault on received wisdom regarding the disposition of sexes that is ostensibly based on intrinsic gender-marked traits. In dismantling the antediluvian mechanism of a gender assignment constructed by essentialization, Tolstaya extends her field of reference to encompass *all* forms of superimposition that constringe the life of the imagination and impede the discovery and expression of selfhood. Tolstaya's emphases, then, not only run counter to some of the regnant principles allying the majority of contemporary Russian women writers but flout fundamental tenets of conservative Soviet ideology.

To label Tolstaya a feminist or an activist seeking feminist redress is to misrepresent her dominant concerns, as several interviewers have discovered.[33] It would be just as inaccurate or irrational, however, to equate Tolstaya's fiction with her journalism or the opinions of her "interview persona." Any overlap that exists among those three categories cannot be absolute, and it is advisable to avoid what Mary Jacobus has called the "flight toward empiricism" that naively assumes "an unbroken continuity between 'life' and 'text.' "[34] In fact, some interviewers eager to trace consistency instead have encountered seeming contradiction. Throughout exchanges between Tolstaya and Western journalists and critics reticulate two leitmotifs pertinent to my reading of the three stories treated in this chapter: (1) Tolstaya's vehement assertion that she does not align herself with feminism, basically opposes it, equates it with the thwarted anger of overly militant, sexually confused women, and detects no evidence of it in the Soviet Union and post-Soviet Russia;[35] (2) the commentators' surprise or chagrin at what Westerners might well call conservative views on gender espoused by a writer with a deserved reputation for extreme liberalism or, perhaps, more accurately, subversive independence—an independence that Tolstaya, while in Russia, expressed forcibly and volubly, thereby incurring the disapproval of such ideologues as the misogynistic Vasilii Belov and the right-wing contingent of the Soviet Writers' Union.[36] To those readers who have never heard Tolstaya speak on women's issues, her apparently ultraconservative endorsement in *The New York Review of Books* of Francine du Plessix Gray's problematic volume *Walking the Tightrope* came as a shock.[37]

That scenario repeats itself, I believe, because of mutual incomprehension. Most Russians, even an educated, sophisticated Russian like Tolstaya, whose contacts with the West far exceeded those of the average Russian intellectual even when she resided in Moscow, have no inkling of what feminism in the West actually entails. After all, Western feminist publications, like most Western books and articles, rarely find their way into Russia. Consequently, Russians passing judgment on feminism are responding, for the most part, not to a highly diversified and substantial body of writings but to individual, random personalities, often encountered by chance and advocating a position so extreme or simplified as to create a false impression of the movement they purportedly typify. Instead of recognizing feminism as a complex social, political, and intellectual phenomenon driven by the characteristically Western principle of pluralism or multiplicity (a principle that flowered during the Renaissance, which bypassed Russia and thus is fundamentally alien to it), Russians reductively picture feminists as braless, mustached hags or harridans agitating for the wholesale metaphorical (if not literal) castration of men, whom they wish to crush or displace so as to relieve their own frustrations and indulge their lust for power, their lesbian inclinations, and so forth.[38]

A confessional–accusatory piece by Kay Ebeling presumptively called "The Failure of Feminism" published several years ago in *Newsweek* exemplifies the reductive mental processes at work in a writer whom Russians might misperceive as a disappointed former feminist. Instead, we have someone who thinks crudely and illogically, in addition to abrogating responsibility for her own actions:

> In 1973 I left what could have been a perfectly good marriage, taking with me a child in diapers, a 10-year-old Plymouth, and Volume 1, Number One of *Ms.* Magazine. I was convinced I could make it on my own. In the last 15 years my ex has married or lived with a succession of women.

> As he gets older, his women stay in their 20s. Meanwhile, I've stayed unattached. He drives a BMW. I ride buses.[39]

This remarkable stew of nonsequiturs and vulgarities[40] premised on unchallenged stereotypes of success would bewilder and appal any intelligent feminist. Feminism never exhorted women to leave "what could have been a perfectly good marriage." Instead of endorsing a rigid system of either/or's, it argued for examination and questioning, as opposed to unreflecting acceptance, of long-sanctioned formulas that stifled both sexes. It urged women to become full-fledged partners within marriage and to explore individual routes to self-fulfillment that did not *necessarily* entail marriage. *Ms.*, which played a key educational role in the early stages of feminism, was never intended as a Bible or a recipe for happiness, but as a source of information and a forum for debate. And, finally, nothing could be more alien to feminist thought than the crass notion that driving an expensive car and enjoying a succession of ever-younger lovers or wives measures success or fulfillment—or that riding buses and presumably not having a stable of lovers or a new husband denotes failure. A mainspring of the feminist movement, in fact, was a revulsion at precisely the kind of dehumanizing consumer mentality applied to both commodities and sexuality that Ebeling exhibits. Anyone who mistakes Ebeling for a disenchanted feminist of betrayed ideals instead of a faddist with a penchant for simplification and formulas will imbibe gross misconceptions about feminism. Unfortunately, those misconceptions are more accessible to a public whose numerous readership of *Newsweek* continues to multiply, while the audience for such feminist publications as *Signs*, *Difference*, and *Hypatia* is confined to the incomparably narrower, intellectually elitist sphere of academia.

The picture in the former Soviet Union is even bleaker. Disillusioned with the long-enforced ideology of Marxism-Leninism that has proved bankrupt, Russians simultaneously have lost faith in any comprehensive political program. Consequently, the likelihood of their grasping and allying themselves with the politics of feminism is extremely remote. Tolstaya, who readily admits to an "imperfect" knowledge of Western feminism,[41] categorically dissociates herself from it, yet frequently voices ideas and analyzes cultural phenomena in ways that converge with feminist interpretive strategies. For instance, the delay in Tolstaya's acceptance into the Writers' Union followed her spirited criticism of Belov's novel *Everything Lies Ahead* (Vse vperedi) for being "against the idea of women as human beings. He thinks all women are devils who should be destroyed because they seduce poor men."[42] "Looking upon a woman as an evil vessel," asserted Tolstaya, "betrays one's hypocrisy."[43] And at a conference in 1990 on contemporary Soviet–Russian literature, Tolstaya spoke about "Beauty and the Hooligan: Elements of Russian Subculture," arguing that male cultural icons such as Stenka Razin, Sergei Esenin, and Vladimir Vysotskii achieved their heroic status through ostentatious drinking and carousing, radical forms of violence against a female beauty, and the male bonding that resulted directly from those two forms of behavior.[44] A Westerner would probably characterize Tolstaya's words on both occasions as a classic feminist critique of repressive patriarchal practices. Yet after the conference Tolstaya unequivocally resisted the suggestion that in pinpointing an archetypal misogynistic ritual she had (perhaps unknowingly, and certainly unintentionally) given a feminist analysis of the problem.[45] The stumbling block, then, is not feminist theory or praxis but the label "feminist" per se, discredited, as David Ransel has noted, by developments in earlier phases of Soviet history.[46]

At its best, feminism strives to reexamine and dismantle authoritarian social institutions and facile assumptions that produce gender clichés. Tolstaya, with her fine-tuned sensitivity to the use, misuse, and abuse of discourse, writes a prose that pays homage to the formidable powers of language while ironizing the anesthetizing effects on the human psyche of catchwords, slogans, and other forms of ready-made discourse that symptomatize lack of individual awareness and responsibility. Among those texts in which her horror of cliché as philosophical and psychological imprisonment finds some form of articulation, the three discussed above lend themselves admirably to a feminist reading.[47] For what could be more clichéd, after all, than our inherited monolithic conception of Womanhood?

✧ 6 ✧

Perspective in Tolstaya's
Wonderland of Art

*But, when the tide rises and sharks are around, His voice has a
timid and tremulous sound.*

Lewis Carroll, *Alice in Wonderland*

Exploring, in his *Lectures on Aesthetics*, the relationship between truth
and art, Hegel argues that the modern world no longer grants art the
importance it formerly enjoyed, particularly in the Middle Ages: "For us it
has lost genuine truth and life" (quoted in Harries, "Hegel on the Future of
Art," [677]).[1] Competing theories of aesthetics analyzing the nature and
role of art, which increased exponentially in the nineteenth century, continue to engage thinkers to this day. Artists themselves have contributed
extensively to this debate, in which they manifestly have a vested interest.
In this context, as in so many others, Russia, where Aleksandr Solzhenitsyn
has characterized literature as an "alternative government," is a special case.
A series of catastrophic historical developments and unexamined traditions
in Russia saddled its literature with functions that in freer and more enlight-
ened societies are normally fulfilled by religion, philosophy, and politics.
These conditions, perhaps inevitably, forged one of Russia's hardiest national myths—a myth that rescues art, and especially literature, from the
jaws of inconsequentiality by restoring it to its medieval stature:[2] that of
literature as a sacred phenomenon, of its production as epiphanic process
and voluntary self-abnegation, and of the writer as prophet, martyr, rebel,
and hero. The universality that this concept of art and its practitioners
enjoyed in the Soviet Union, curiously enough, did not deter writers from
tirelessly reformulating in their works the cornerstone dilemmas that the
concept purports to have resolved. Tolstaya's input in this immense fund of
fiction consists of the two stories "Fakir" and "Okkervil River."

The problematic nature of art and its relation to everyday life is succinctly encapsulated in the polysemous title of Tolstaya's "Fakir." The title invokes the three faces of the protagonist Filin highlighted at different stages in the narrative, which in turn reflect three alternate views of the artist conventionally entertained in Western culture: that of (1) magician or ascetic wonder-worker, (2) faker or artificer, and (3) mendicant. Each of these options automatically raises key questions: If art is magic, then surely it, like God, must operate in mysterious ways that defy human comprehension (prestidigitation as secularized miracle)? If art is a lie perpetrated by a faker, how can it lead to truth? If an artist is a beggar relying on the largesse of his society, are manipulation and pragmatism the mainspring of his activities, and is the indirect purchase of legislative powers the society's motivation for underwriting art? Periodic legal disputes in the United States over the censorship of art (e.g., the Mapplethorpe case), and particularly of works subsidized by public funds, illustrate the extent to which these are perennial and legitimate, if irresoluble, questions. Tolstaya's text, however—narrated in quasi-direct discourse from the viewpoint of Galia, a subjective, limited center of consciousness—starts by postulating rather than querying.

Through the mediating agency of Galia's awed wonder, the fakir Filin (literally, eagle owl)[3] enters the narrative he dominates as a superior, magical being endowed with extraordinary powers. Unlike the "ordinary" people to whom Galia ritually contrasts him ("what did he ever see in us ordinary people?" [156]/"chto on v nas, obyknovennykh, nashel?" [148]), Filin materializes miraculously in the story ("Filin—unexpectedly, as usual— *appeared* in the telephone receiver" [155, emphasis added]/"Filin—kak vsegda, neozhidanno—*voznik* v telefonnoi trubke" [147]), much like the music in his apartment, which floats "from somewhere up above" (157) ("otkuda-to sverkhu" [148]). His physical appearance and dress, like the apartment he occupies, are conspicuously exotic, opulent, and mysterious: endowed with Anatolian sooty eyes, a silvery beard, handsome expressive brows, and Mephistophelian eyes,[4] he sports a velvet jacket or raspberry robe with tassels, silver Mongolian slippers, and a Venetian ring or one fashioned from a Turkish (Antioch) coin. A rare individual with an impressive demeanor and highly cultivated tastes, Filin is an unrivaled master of the visual and gastronomical feast: he surrounds himself with choice, exquisite objects (blue and gold collector's cups, snuffboxes, Wedgwood, hothouse roses) and proffers resplendent food and drink (grapefruit with shrimp, patés, special pirozhki, pastries, imported cigarettes, English tea). That the apartment and its contents provide an enabling setting, a live theatre in which Filin orchestrates a program for his guests' delectation, is revealed in the story's opening paragraphs:

The evening's *program* was clear: a crisp white tablecloth, light, warmth, special puff-pastry pirozhki à la Tmutarakan, the nicest music coming from somewhere in the ceiling, and engrossing conversation. Dark blue curtains everywhere, showcases with his collections, beads hanging along the walls. The *new toys* might be a snuffbox with a portrait of a lady in transports over her own naked pink powderiness, a beaded purse, perhaps an Easter egg, or something else *useless but valuable*.

Certainly *plenty to look at*. (155–56, emphases added)

Programma vechera byla iasna: belaia khrustiashchaia skatert', svet, teplo, osobye sloenye pirozhki po-tmutarakanski, priiatneishaia muzyka otkuda-to s potolka, zakhvatyvaiushchie razgovory. Vsiudu sinie shtory, vitriny s kollektsiiami, po stenam razveshany busy. *Novye igrushki*— tabakerka li s portretom damy, upivaiushcheisia svoei rozovoi goloi napudrennost'iu, bisernyi koshelek, paskhal'noe, mozhet byt', iaitso ili zhe tak chto-nibud'—*nenuzhnoe, no tsennoe*.

Est', *est' na chto posmotret'*. (147)

Accordingly, when Galia and her down-to-earth husband Iura leave Filin's quarters, Galia notes that the sky directly above Filin's building is "a real Moscow, *theatrical-concert-hall* sky" (166, emphasis added) ("nastoiashchee moskovskoe, *teatral'no-kontsertnoe*" [157]). On the stage that he designs and manages, Filin directs performances by such dramatis personae as Matvei Matveich, with his gripping tales about the reign of Anna Ivanovna; Vlasov the Bard, with his repertoire of satiric songs; and the muzhik Valtasarov, a brilliant ventriloquist. As impresario, Filin "demonstrates" not only these personalities but also his women—such "collector's rarities" as the circus artiste and the ingenue who dabbles in watercolors, both, significantly, associated with glitter ("a circus performer [. . .] twisting on a trapeze, silvery scales *shimmering*" [156, emphasis added]/"tsirkachka [. . .] v'etsia na sheste, *blistaia* cheshuei" [147]; "a girl [. . .] of *dazzling whiteness* [. . .] , Filin [. . .] warning us to bring sunglasses to avoid snow blindness" [156, emphasis added]/"devochka [. . .] *belizny neobyknovennoi* [. . .] Filin [. . .] preduprezhdaet [. . .] prikhodite v chernykh ochkakh vo izbezhenie snezhnoi slepoty" [147]).

The luxurious items, esoteric comestibles, performers, and guests acquire their distinction through context: as Galia and Iura discover when they invite Matvei Matveich and the bard to their apartment, without Filin and the magical aura of his setting, the two become commonplace irritants. Filin's unique abilities enable him to transmute all aspects of life into something extraordinary: a querulous old bore into a fascinating raconteur; a disappointed, harried housewife like Galia into an eager participant in the process of individuation; the unremarkable Allochka into the evocatively named Alisa;[5] pirozhki into "tartaletki"; mundane occurrences into exciting, if improbable, events. Like Mephistopheles, whose eyes his resemble, Filin accomplishes feats of transformation ("she [. . .] stared at the all-powerful gentleman who with a wave of the hand, a flicker of an eyebrow, could *transform the world* to the point of unrecognizability" [165, emphasis added]/"ona [. . .] gliadit na vsesil'nogo gospodina, manoveniem ruki, dvizheniem brovei *preobrazhaiushchego mir* do neuznavaemosti" [156]). Although these metamorphoses depend in part on the mise-en-scène—the accouterments that create optimal conditions for an audience's empathetic engagement—they result primarily from Filin's command of language. Alisa's confession, "I'm always so sorry for the last of anything" (163) ("Mne vsegda tak zhalko bylo vsego poslednego" [153]), inspires Filin to launch a game of literary association hinging on the premonitory word "last" ("poslednii"). Filin's quote, "The last one, an accidental one" (163) ("Poslednii, sluchainyi" [153]), from a Bulat Okudzhava song,[6] prompts Galia's line from Pushkin, "The last scattered storm cloud" ("Posledniaia tucha rasseianoi buri"),[7] followed in turn by Iura's reference to James Fenimore Cooper's *The Last of the Mohicans* (154). Like Filin's staging of others' performances, however, this frivolous pastime demanding cultural recall and recycling barely hints at the depths of Filin's creative originality, the full expression of which requires another forum. Tapping the seemingly inexhaustible potential of language and his own imagination, Filin displays an unparalleled mastery of oral narrative, as attested by his fantastic stories about Pushkin, Kuzma, Ignatii Kirillych, and the ideal recipe for pirozhki (R152–53); about the dog who cooked meals for its owners (R155–56); about the partisan at whose feet a German pilot dropped Wedgwood china (R154–55); about the retired ballerina Doltseva-Elanskaia (née Sobakina!), who once stopped a ship with her leg (R160); about the explorer who froze his ears, which subsequently fell off (R166); and about Goethe and fish (R166–67). Not unlike the improviser in Pushkin's "Egyptian Nights,"[8] Filin treats any situation or comment as narratable material—a chance for flights and conversions of reality through the medium of words that cajole his guests into credulity, irrespective of logic and the laws of probability. In short, he offers them art.

Whether something qualifies as art depends largely on context, as illustrated by Marcel Duchamp's notorious example of the urinal. Whereas in a museum an exhibited urinal becomes an artistic object of contemplation, elsewhere it serves a purely utilitarian function as something into which to urinate.[9] Once detached from its function, this most practical and "base" piece of plumbing becomes available for "sudden elevation into art" (Culler, *Framing the Sign*, 179). Any article robbed of utility and framed for contemplation potentially belongs to an aesthetic category.[10] Likewise in "Fakir," Filin's stories rely on context for their status as art. That context is the enchanted sphere that Filin inhabits—a veritable Wonderland of beautiful but useless items ("nenuzhnoe, no tsennoe") with its resident Alice/Alisa, née Alla/Allochka. What obviously links Filin's apartment with the topsy-turvy world of Lewis Carroll's *Alice's Adventures in Wonderland* and *Through the Looking Glass* is the impression projected by both milieux that "anything can happen." The magical and fantastic is the rule, not the exception. On a more profound level, however, the common denominator between the two works is a fascination with the possibilities and limits of language.

In her excellent study of interartistic homologies, titled *The Colors of Rhetoric*, Wendy Steiner contends that illustration in Carroll's masterpiece of nonsense makes "the nonsensical hypothetically possible and, more generally, [. . . raises] the issue of correspondence between text and world, [. . . for] the Wonderland that [. . . Alice] enters is the text before us" (Steiner, 127). In the Queen of Hearts episode and elsewhere, Carroll explores the distinguishing features, norms, and violations of narrative as well as our expectations of it.

Mutatis mutandis, these are the overriding concerns of Tolstaya's story, which shares with Carroll's texts the conviction that language creates its own reality, however circumstantial. If the most memorable instance of discourse-driven presence in Carroll is the famous nonsense-poem "Jabberwocky" ("'Twas brillig, and the slithy toves/Did gyre and gimble in the wabe"),[11] the equivalent in "Fakir" are surely Filin's fanciful tales, patent fabrications that nonetheless sweep the listeners along by sheer narrative momentum generated through verbal means. Outside the context of Wonderland, "Jabberwocky" becomes rubbish, just as outside the special environment of Filin's theater/apartment his bold improvisations merely seem untruths.

Tolstaya lavishes considerable descriptive energy on the locus that vouchsafes the artistry of Filin's imaginative divagations. Through carefully selected details she gives a vivid impression of the apartment's interior, uses loaded metaphors for capturing the exterior of the building, then places the whole symbolically within the broader context of Moscow and its outskirts.[12] A haven of "warmth and light," "comfort and luxury," the apartment epitomizes affluent, refined taste. More suggestively, Tolstaya speaks of the apartment as a palace (R158) or tower— both images of centralized authority, power, and wealth. A poetic, densely instrumented passage registering Galia and Iura's arrival at the apartment explicitly emphasizes its aesthetic dimension and its fortress-like unassailability:

And they would float it, [. . .] into the warmth and light, the *sweet piano trills*, and proceed to the table where the *hothouse-reared roses* know nothing of frost, wind, and darkness that have besieged *Filin's impregnable tower*, powerless to penetrate within. (160, emphases added)

I vplyvut oni, [. . .] v teplo i svet, v *sladkie fortep'iannye rulady*, a proshestvuiut k stolu, gde *razmorennye rozy* znat' ne znaiut ni o kakom moroze, vetre, t'me, chto obstupili *nepristupnuiu Filinovu bashniu*, bessil'nye probrat'sia vnutr'. (151)

Moreover, the particularized description of the building's torte-like exterior highlights emblems of culture and power, in an occasionally archaic vocabulary that metonymically conjures up traditions and history:

Filin's palace nestled in the middle of the capital, a pink mountain, ornamented here and there in the most varied way—with all sorts of architectural doodads, thingamajigs, and whatnots: there were towers on the socles, crenels on the towers, and ribbons and wreaths between the crenellations, and out of the laurel garlands peeked a book, the source of knowledge, or a compass stuck out its pedagogic leg; or, if you looked, you'd see a puffy obelisk in the middle. [. . .] So you imagine that any moment trumpets will blare, someone somewhere will strike cymbals, and drums will play something governmental and heroic. (165–66)

Posredi stolitsy ugnezdalsia dvorets Filina, rozovaia gora, ukrashennaia semo i ovamo raznoobrazneishe,—so vsiakimi zodcheskimi edakostiami, shtukentsiiami i fintibriasami: na tsokoliakh—bashni, na bashniakh—zubtsy, promezh zubtsov lenty da venki, a iz lavrovykh girliand lezet kniga—istochnik znanii, ili vysovyvaet pedagogicheskuiu nozhku tsirkul', a to, gliadish', poseredke vspuchilsia obelisk. [. . .] Tak i chuditsia, chto seichas protrubiat kakie-to truby, gde-to udariat v tarelki i barabany sygraiut chto-nibud' gosudarstvennoe, geroicheskoe. (156)

Tolstaya intermittently reinforces this ornate image of impregnable strength, and through the whereabouts of the building within the larger panorama of urban existence intimates the centrality of art in society: Filin dwells at the heart of "living life" (i.e., the city center), whereas Galia, whose subjective perceptions guide our cognitive and responsive processes, resides on the periphery, her existence illuminated by occasional summonses to the "Source." Quite appropriately, whereas Carroll's Alice tumbles down into the Wonderland of her unconscious, Galia and her husband ascend to the "Palace of Art."[13] The visual and conceptual symbolism of the apartment's vertical placement ("Filin lived in a high-rise" [157]/"Filin zhivet v vysotnom dome" [148]; " 'We-e-e descend. From the co-o-onquered heights' " [160]/" 'I spuskaemsia my-y. S pak-karennykh vershin-n' " [151]), plus its central location, not only alludes to the semidivine, elevated nature of art, but also envisions it as the heart that pumps the lifeblood of culture to the remote and benighted areas of the social organism.[14]

The bulk of the story equates the areas outside the city limits with primitivism, deprivation, ceaseless struggle, and death: "Beyond [Filin's] apartment house the boundary road lay like a hoop of darkness where the frost and cold of uninhabited plains penetrated beneath your clothes, and the world for a second seemed as horrible as a graveyard" (157) ("Za domom [Filina] obruchem mraka lezhala okruzhnaia doroga, gde moroz, kholod bezliudnykh ravnin pronik pod odezhdu, mir na mig pokazalsia kladbishchenski strashnym" [148]).

If Filin's domicile is a repository of art, culture, and civilization, those far removed from its caressing lights dwell in the brutal darkness of ignorance. To convey the grim physical and spiritual circumstances of such an existence, Tolstaya aggregates details of darkness, cold, and isolation calculated to stress hardship and misery, climaxing in a desolate image:[15]

> It was impossible, unbearable to think that the thick darkness extended farther, over the fields that blended into a white roar, over badly constructed fences, over villages pressed into the cold earth where a doomed dull light quivers as if clenched in an indifferent fist, . . . and farther once again, the dark white cold, a crust of forest where the darkness is even thicker, where perhaps is forced to live the unfortunate wolf, who appears on the hill in his rough wool coat smelling of juniper and blood, wildness, disaster, and grimly gazes with disgust at the blind windy vistas, clumps of snow hardening between his cracked yellow claws, his teeth gritted in misery, and a frozen tear hangs like a stinking bead on his furry cheek, and everyone is the enemy and everyone is the killer. (167)

> Ved' nevozmozhno, nemyslimo dumat' o tom, chto eta glukhaia t'ma tianetsia i dal'she, nad poliami, slivaiushchimisia v belyi gul, nad koe-kak spletennymi izgorodiami, nad pridavlennymi k kholodnoi zemle derevniami, gde obrechenno drozhit tosklivyi ogonek, slovno zazhatyi v ravnodushnom kulake, . . . a dal'she vnov'—temno-belyi kholod, gorbushka lesa, gde t'ma eshche plotnei, gde, mozhet byt', vynuzhden zhit' neschastnyi volk,—on vykhodit na bugor v svoem zhestkom sherstianom pal'tishke, pakhnet mozhzhevel'nikom i krov'iu, dikost'iu, bedoi, khmuro, s otvrashcheniem smotrit v slepye vetrenye dali, snezhnye katyshi nabilis' mezhdu zheltykh potreskavshikhsia nogtei, i zuby stisnuty v pechali, i merzlaia sleza voniuchei businoi visit na sherstianoi shcheke, i vsiakii-to emu vrag, i vsiakii-to ubiitsa. (157–58)

This anthropomorphized figure of suffering and atavism, which evokes the saying "Man is a wolf to man,"[16] emblematizes the condition of humankind without culture's civilizing influence. Whatever Galia's romantic–sexual fantasies regarding Filin, her worship of him stems essentially from her yearning for culture; Iura, whose rough manners, empiricist bent, and cheerful insensitivity set him apart from his wife, explicitly "wasn't interested in culture" (173) ("iskusstvom ne zainteresovalsia" [163]). For Iura, a urinal, whether in a museum or a bathroom, would invariably serve the same practical function. That is why Iura finds the uneducated ventriloquist Valtasarov, who disturbs Galia, entertaining: "She sensed in Valtasarov the degree of noncivilization from which she and Iura were a stone's throw away—over the city's boundary line, beyond the ravine, to the other side" (168) ("V Valtasarove pomereshchilas' ei ta stepen' odichaniia, do kotoroi im s Iuroi rukoi podat'—cherez okruzhnuiu, za kanavu, na tu storonu" [158]).

Culture's professed capacity to sensitize, refine, and elevate[17] has habituated society at least since the Romantic period to venerate art as a lofty entity, enthroned above the sweat and push of everyday life and inaccessible to the average mortal.[18] Tolstaya's use of space in "Fakir" indicates her affinities with this tradition of aristocratic apotheosis. Filin's enchanted "palace of art" is symbolically perched high above the grocery store where Filin purchases some of his supplies. Tactile, material life, which feeds the body, is beneath—subordinate to—the realm of intangibles that nurture the mind and psyche.[19] Such a positioning, which visually installs hierarchy and discreteness,[20] also implies the imperfect or incomplete equivalence between words and the reality they purport to convey—an issue fundamental to the place of art in society.

The inseparability of artistic categories from context and the precariousness of art are spotlighted in a pivotal episode in the story when Galia unexpectedly glimpses Filin outside his habitual context. That moment inaugurates a revised image of the artist as fraud. Until then, Galia had perceived Filin through reverent, uncritical eyes as an omnipotent dispenser of largesse:

> Oh, Filin! Generous owner of golden fruit, he hands them out right and left, giving food to the hungry and drink to the thirsty; he waves his hand, and gardens bloom, women grow more beautiful, bores get inspired, and crows sing like nightingales. (169)

> O, Filin! Shchedryi vladelets zolotykh plodov, on razdaet ikh napravo i nalevo, nasyshchaet golodnykh i poit zhazhdushchikh, on makhnet rukoi—i rastsvetaiut sady, zhenshchiny khorosheiut, zanudy vdokhnovliaiutsia, a vorony poiut solov'iami. (159)

Divorced from his artistic laboratory, his theater, he suddenly appears to Galia in such a diminished light that for a second she fails to recognize him:

he passed her in the subway—*small, hurrying, careworn*—he went around her without noticing and just walked on, and it was too late to hail him! He walked *like an ordinary man, his small feet* [. . .] stepped on the spittle-covered bathroom tiles of the passageway, ran up the worn steps; *small fists* rummaged in pockets, located a handkerchief, hit his nose—boof! boof!—and back in the pocket; then he shook himself *like a dog*, adjusted his scarf, and went on [. . .] . He walked without looking back [. . .]—he leaped up *like a schoolboy*, glided onto the escalator— and was gone, vanished. (174–75, emphases added)

on proshel mimo nee v metro—*malen'kii, toroplivyi, ozabochennyi,*— minoval ee, ne zametiv, i idet sebe, i uzhe ne okliknut'! On idet, *kak obychnyi chelovek, malen'kie nogi ego* [. . .] stupaiut po zasharkannomu bannomu kafeliu perekhoda, vzbegaiut na ob''edennye stupeni; *malen'kie kulachki* shariat v karmanakh, nashli nosovoi platok, pnuli— buf! buf!—po nosu—i snova v karman; vot on striakhnulsia *kak sobaka*, popravil sharf —i dal'she [. . .] . On idet, ne oglianuvshis' [. . .]—vot podprygnul *kak shkol'nik*, skol'znul na eskalator—i proch', i skrylsia. (164–65)

In this dramatically reversed image, Filin shrinks in size and significance. Indistinguishable from the other "usual people" to whom he formerly was contrasted, he is further diminished by the lowering comparisons with a dog and a schoolboy and above all by the obliteration of his creative voice. The only sound to emerge from the inventive, mesmerizing manipulator of words is the commonplace trumpeting of a nose being blown. Decontextu- alized and deprived of his artistic medium, Filin, when uninspired, dwindles into banal averageness.[21]

With Alla's telephone call, this first, tentative step in Galia's disillusion- ment almost immediately solidifies into a definitive break with her earlier perceptions and attitudes as the narrative races to an accelerated conclusion. Both Alla and Galia denounce Filin as a pretender purely on the grounds of his having "rented his setting": that is, having sublet from a polar explorer the apartment everyone presumed belonged to him. As someone registered in the town of Domodedovo, Filin is exposed, in Galia's view, as "no better than they, he was just like them" ("nichem ne luchshe ikh, on takoi zhe")— a refugee from beyond the borders of civilization. Rushing to confront the "pathetic midget" ("zhalkii karlik") and "clown in a shah's robe" ("kloun v khalate padishakha" [165]), Galia cannot recapture her former faith in the "mendicant faker" and bids elegiac farewell to the "pink palace" of her dreams in an apostrophe constructed from a chain of revealing metaphors stressing transience, elusiveness, and ostentation: "Your tree with golden fruit has dried up and your words are just fireworks in the night, a moment's run of colored zephyrs, the hysteria of fiery roses in the darkness over our hair" (178) ("Tvoe derevo s zolotymi plodami zasokhlo, i rechi tvoi—lish' feiervork v nochi, minutnyi beg tsvetnogo vetra, isterika ognennykh roz vo t'me nad nashimi volosami" [167]). In her disappoint-ment, Galia sweepingly dismisses Filin as a liar. Indeed, he implicitly (but perhaps unwittingly?) has perpetuated lies through omission by allowing everyone to assume his ownership of the apartment and its contents. Yet Galia's bitterness blinds her to several details that complicate both the nature of lying and Filin's connection with lies.

That Filin genuinely loves beauty and art is emphasized not only during the social evenings he arranges in advance (when he could be accused of orchestrating the scene just for show), but metonymically even during Galia's impromptu visit at story's end, when she surprises Filin eating his dinner in solitude. Without an audience to appreciate the impact of the atmosphere, Filin nonetheless is listening to Brahms and has placed a vase of white carnations on a table. More importantly, Galia's challenging re-mark about the polar explorer instantly elicits from Filin a number of color-ful narratives. These tall tales in no way differ from those that previously enraptured Galia, yet now they merely intensify her anger at Filin. Why? Because while Filin and his authorial practices have remained unchanged, Galia's perspective has irrevocably altered, unavoidably affecting her re-ception of his work. Just how crucial perspective is to one's experience of art is an issue that Tolstaya tackles midway through the story in a scene that rehearses the final meeting between Galia and Filin as artist/faker.

Meditating on her life, Galia recalls an excruciating humiliation from her past that appears minor, yet supplies the story's major aesthetic insight. Delighted to have obtained a ticket to the Bolshoi Ballet, by the time she takes her seat Galia has lost the "golden atmosphere of the lofty and beauti-ful" (173) ("zolotuiu atmosferu vosvyshennogo" [163]) that she had plea-surably sensed within herself when leaving home. With that inimitable crassness familiar to anyone who has traveled in the Soviet Union, a woman in the ladies' room upbraids her for cleaning off her boots and dress, dirtied by the rain and mud Galia had battled en route to the Bolshoi. Vociferous abuse in public (the ugliness of harsh reality) destroys Galia's psychologi-cal readiness to enter the artistic world on stage (a self-enclosed domain of distillation). Much as Tolstoy in *War and Peace* shows Natasha Rostova viewing the first act of an opera through the estranged eyes of a naif uniniti-ated into the conventions of the genre,[22] so Tolstaya has Galia watch the ballet without the suspension of disbelief essential to any experience of art.[23] Now unwilling to surrender to any illusion, Galia supplants ballet conventions with her own painful knowledge, from which she authors a

melancholy scenario of the performers' real-life biographies that she super-
imposes on them:

> Galia flattened the dancers with her gaze without any pleasure, making
> out through her opera glasses their yellowish workers' faces, their labor-
> ing neck muscles, and severely, ruthlessly told herself that they weren't
> swans at all but union members, that their lives were like everyone
> else's—ingrown toenails, unfaithful husbands—and that as soon as they
> finished their dance, they would pull on warm knit pants and head for
> home, home: to icy Ziuzino, and puddly Korovino, and even to that most
> horrible boundary road. (173–74)

> Galia bez vsiakikh vostorgov davila tantsovshchits vzgliadom, razlichaia
> v binokl' ikh zheltovatye trudovye litsa, rabochie sheinye zhily, i surovo,
> bezzhalostno tverdila sebe, chto nikakie oni ne lebedi, a chleny prof-
> soiuza, chto vse u nikh kak u prostykh liudei—i vzrosshie nogti, i
> nevernye muzh'ia, chto vot seichas otpliashut oni skol'ko veleno,
> natianut teplye reituzy—i po domam, po domam: v ledianoe Ziuzino, v
> zhidkoe Korovino, a to i na samu strashnuiu okruzhnuiu dorogu. (163)

What the passage clarifies is the illusion inherent in art, and the latter's
dependence on subjectivity and suspension of disbelief. Art's reliance on
faith is hinted at earlier by Filin. After spinning his audacious yarn about
Wedgwood china dropped from an airplane, he answers Iura's boisterous
incredulity with the statement, "but, you know ... somehow, I prefer to
believe" (164) ("no, znaete ... kak-to ia predpochitaiu verit' " [155]). Faith
in the illusions he creates is, in fact, the price Filin tacitly exacts from his
audience. Just as her mood and the merciless opera glasses offer Galia a
new vantage point that militates against her acceptance of ballet conventions, so her newly discovered image of Filin as an inhabitant of Domodedovo instead of a sophisticated verbal magician precludes Galia's further
participation in his performances. The atomizing logic of *ostranenie* prevents a submission to art's lure.

Depending on the perspective from which one approaches art, its seams
can show. Art requires the voluntary collusion of its audience, just as religion can exist only if worshipers believe. That analogy, which has a robust
tradition in Russian letters, runs throughout the story and culminates in the
pointe summing up Galia's disenchantment: "our god is dead and his temple is
empty" (178) ("i bog nash mertv, i khram ego pust" [168]).[24] Galia's crisis
in faith brings her closer, in a sense, to Iura's level. Indeed, the comment
accompanying her last glance at the store beneath the fateful apartment,
"like a transparent worm, the store [. . .] had eaten away the foot of the
palace" (178) ("magazin [. . .] podtochil, kak prozrachnyi cherv', nogu

dvortsa" [167]), registers Galia's Iura-like deflation of Filin's soaring feats of legerdemain by humdrum, literalizing explanation.

What complicates the mechanism of Galia's disillusionment is the paradox that her unblinkered perception of the fictitious in art discloses her myopia regarding the falsity of another cultural convention that she accepts wholesale: the totalizing paradigm, which unquestioningly posits an unbroken continuity between artists as individuals, on the one hand, and the products of their artistry, on the other. In an afterword appended to "Fakir" in the collection *Poslednii etazh*, Tolstaya makes explicit her position on the confusion between writer and authored text:

> As an individual, a writer has nothing in common with the author of her books. An author may be a pale romantic youth, but the writer—fat, bald, short of breath, and fond of liver pirozhki. The entire romantic school assumes a priori cloaks, curls, daggers ... yet all you need to do is look at the writers' portraits: some wear glasses, some have three chins. [. . .] I don't consider myself answerable for readers' illusions, just as I don't consider that I owe them anything.

> Pisatel' kak lichnost' ne imeet nichego obshchego s avtorom svoikh knig. Avtor mozhet byt' romanticheskim, blednym iunoshei, a pisatel'-to tolstyi, lysyi, s odyshkoi i liubit pirozhki s liverom. Vsia romanticheskaia shkola predpolagaet kakie-to plashchi, kudri, kinzhaly ... a stoit posmotret' na portrety pisatelei: kto v ochkakh, kto s tremia podborodkami. [. . .] ia ne schitaiu sebia otvetstvennoi za illiuzii chitatelei, kak i ne schitaiu, chto ia im chto-nibud' dolzhna. (Kaledin, 146)

Galia conceives of art along the organic principles of a reductive Romanticism, whereby art, artist, and artistic object constitute an indissoluble whole that leaves no room for disjunctive contradiction or heterogeneity. That brand of thought leads to, and in turn derives affirmation from, the creation of cults, as the cases of Byron, Chopin, Pushkin, and a host of others testify. It forces the elimination of the artist as independent individual by absorbing him into an increasingly repressive role blueprinted by hegemonic audience expectations and desires. The process dictates that the artist adjust his life in conformity with his work as it is understood by the public, enabling that public to move unhampered between work and authorial life without differentiating between the two, as though they merely mark two stages in the kind of totalizing process that de Man fought to undo in textual readings.[25] Because Filin's identity as artist/magician is buttressed, narratively speaking, by his image as a fascinating man in his own right (an image constructed by Galia's romanticizing impulses), any deviation in that image causes the collapse of his perceived artistic persona and his creations. When the romantic aura haloing Filin's reputation evaporates, the artist/magician is demoted to fraud, though nothing in Tolstaya's text even hints at the slightest change in his authorial practices or his art. The temptation to read "Fakir" as Tolstaya's restatement of the problem raised by Pushkin's "Mozart and Saleri"—the (in)compatibility of villainy with art—should be resisted, given the total absence of villainous traits in Filin's portrait.[26] That is why even the reader who has trusted absolutely Galia's presentation of the materials up to the turning point in the story must dissociate herself at that juncture from Galia's viewpoint. For at the moment that Galia on illegitimate grounds exchanges one prefabricated myth for another the reader's sense of Galia's function in the story legitimately shifts: Galia's perceptions no longer steer us in interpreting the object of the narrative; instead they *become* that object. Her narration crosses the boundary into narrated element, compelling the reader's withdrawal from her perspective on events. As frequently happens in Tolstaya's prose, the story's final section further complicates the narration. In the penultimate paragraph, Galia's melancholy farewell to her dreams via quasi-direct discourse makes use of the collective "we" form (embracing Iura? the reader?). Since the last paragraph continues in the same mode, the voice one hears is presumably Galia's. If so, then the story has authentic, though unsatisfactory, closure, which registers Galia's unduly accelerated reconciliation with her loss and her totally unexpected preparedness to glorify the positive potential of that which earlier provoked only horror and rejection on her part—the bleak vista of the city's outlying regions:

> And now, home. A long way to go. Ahead is a new winter, new hopes, new songs. Well, let's sing the praises of the outskirts, the rains, the grayed houses, the long evenings on the threshold of darkness. Let's sing the praises of the deserted lots, the grayish grasses, the cold of the mud under cautious feet, let's sing the slow autumn dawn, the barking dogs amid aspens, the fragile gossamer webs, and the first ice, the first bluish ice in a deep imprint of someone else's foot. (178–79)

> A teper'—domoi. Put' ne blizkii. Vperedi—novaia zima, novye nadezhdy, novye pesni. Chto zh, vospoem okrainy, dozhdi, poserevshie doma, dolgie vechera na poroge t'my. Vospoem pustyri, burye travy, kholod zemlianykh plastov pod boiazlivoi nogoi, vospoem medlennuiu osenniuiu zariu, sobachii lai sredi osinovykh stvolov, khrupkuiu zolotuiu pautinu i pervyi led, pervyi sinevatyi led v glubokom otpechatke chuzhogo sleda. (168)

Yet, given the resentment of Galia's skepticism and her steadfast, categorical dismissal of the dreary areas fringing the city center, these intimations of a new beginning might more convincingly be attributed to an imposed authorial voice. Through the ancient trope of song as artistic creation ("Arma virumque cano"),[27] that voice implicitly posits two notions: that all aspects of life provide inexhaustible material for art and that perspective determines the presentation and reception of these materials (which corroborates one of the story's chief aperçus). Despite the appearance of a neat circular structure—insofar as "Fakir" closes with Galia's return to the wilderness beyond Moscow's Ring Road that she leaves as the story opens—the sheer ambiguity of the ending resists genuine closure.

Closure is a particularly fraught issue in "Fakir" because the specific genre of Filin's art raises questions about the nature and function of storytelling. The last two decades or so have witnessed a formidable array of studies, chiefly by French structuralists, tackling the knotty issue of narratology.[28] Some narratologists, notably Frank Kermode and Peter Brooks,[29] have theorized inventively about the significance of plot beginnings and ends. Inspired by Walter Benjamin's dictum that "Death is the sanction of everything that the storyteller can tell" (Benjamin, 94), Brooks has examined with admirable insight the Freudian implications of narrative as desire, an approach that gains considerable weight in the light of *The Thousand and One Nights*, where narration quite literally serves the purpose of warding off death. As Brooks argues, inasmuch as Shahrazad cures and prolongs the Shah's derailed erotic desire by narrativizing it, narration in the work is a life-giving force (Brooks, *Reading for the Plot*, 60–61).

If desire motivates and fuels narrative, and closure signals death, then Filin's stringing of one narrative after another on the slender thread of association may be seen as perpetual desire perpetually deferring death; indeed, his narratives "resurrect" Pushkin, Goethe and Ulrike, Eckerman, the old chef Kuzma and the younger Ignatii Kirillych, the German pilot, the ballerina Olga Sobakina, and so on. A seductive vitality, significantly, is shared by all Tolstaya's gifted narrators, who exercise an inexplicable hold over their audience: Tamila in "Rendezvous with a Bird," Pipka in "Fire and Dust" ("a new guest would [. . .] exclaim in joyous astonishment: 'Just listen to her! A thousand and one nights!' " [104]),[30] and, to a lesser degree, Korobeinikov in "Heavenly Flame" and the ancient Aleksandra Ernestovna in "Sweet Shura." What matters in narrative is the dynamics of a posited life, the force that drives the *siuzhet* along its digressive, unfettered course, until the exhaustion of psychic energy. And at each conclusion we await new beginnings—an eternal impulse to continuity within change[31] or cessation symbolized by the two-faced Roman god Janus, the ritualistic cry of "The King is dead! Long live the King!" the concept of dying and entering into another life, and so forth. As Benjamin astutely contends, "The idea of eternity has ever had its strongest source in death" (93). It is no coincidence that the author whom Filin claims to read to Sobakina during his visits is Laurence Sterne, the supreme master of narrative manipulation and of the insatiable narrative drive that defies closure. In a Brooksian vein, D.A. Miller's sophisticated examination of novelistic closure evocatively entitled *Narrative and Its Discontents* maintains that the narratable, "whether in its erotic or semiotic dimension, . . . inherently lacks finality. It may be suspended by a moral or ideological expediency, but it can never be properly brought to term. The tendency of a narrative would therefore be to *keep going*" (Miller, xi).[32] Indeed, propulsion energizes the conclusion of "Fakir," which gives every indication of tying up loose ends as Galia takes her leave of Filin, the city, the reader, and the narrative ("Farewell!"/"Proshchai!"), only to subvert our expectations in the following paragraph, with which the story stops. That final section blatantly lacks finality. As if polemicizing with the conventional envoi, it not only returns Galia and the reader to the beginning of the story just told (literally, to the initial locus of the city's outskirts) but gives promise of a new narrative in a different key: "Ahead is a new winter, new hopes, new songs. Well, let's sing the praises of the outskirts" (178).[33] One may infer from the structure of "Fakir," then, that the endings of narratives take us to new beginnings, with a revised perspective; art equips us either for new quests or for the same quest, but now transplanted to a different epistemological system.[34]

Problematized closure is only one among many features that "Fakir" shares with "Okkervil River," a companion piece that follows a parallel trajectory from worship to disillusionment as it wrestles with the same aesthetic dilemmas: the function of art and its relationship to the artist and to quotidian life in its visible manifestations.[35]

The saliency of setting in "Okkervil River" exceeds that in "Fakir," for Leningrad and its rivers trail behind them a plexus of cultural myths inseparably intertwined with Tolstaya's major concerns. In addition to relying on intertexts treating the Petersburg phenomenon (Pushkin's *Bronze Horseman*, Gogol's "Overcoat," Dostoevsky's *Crime and Punishment* [Prestuplenie i nakazanie], Bely's *Petersburg*),[36] Tolstaya makes use of Peter the Great's historical role as the city's founder to install her central theme of artistic creation. Through Peter's reification of an inspired idea, Tolstaya indirectly portrays the complex relationship between the imagination, on the one hand, and the tangible products of that faculty, on the other.

The story examines art through multiple practitioners who highlight different facets of a single comprehensive issue: Peter the Great, Vera Vasilevna,[37] and Simeonov, in descending order of empirical verification as concerns the significance of their creative activities. While Peter's fabled transformation of Russia's bleak northern swamps into the showcase of Petersburg raises the moral issue of the human cost at which this colossal achievement was accomplished,[38] the actual city nonetheless testifies concretely to Peter's status as artistic genius immortalized through a creation fusing beauty and usefulness (Horace's *utile et dulce*). Vera Vasilevna's contribution to art, more modest in scale and preserved in the more perishable form of gramophone records, lacks the pragmatic dimension and affects fewer lives. Tolstaya illuminates the discrepancy in their scope tropologically: Peter's maritime command of rivers and seas shrinks to Vera Vasilevna's domestic ablutions in Simeonov's bathtub. At a still further remove from Peter (approximating, in fact, the clerk Evgenii of Pushkin's *Bronze Horseman*), Simeonov's solipsistic creativity confines itself to the purely imaginative sphere, yielding nothing tangible and touching no one but himself. Can one lay legitimate claim to the status of artist if one's imagination, however fertile, never engenders anything concrete?

By invoking Pushkin's *Bronze Horseman*, Tolstaya unfolds the creative process of Peter's grandiose accomplishment as sequentiality along a continuum, whereby the originative concept *precedes* the palpable product into which it becomes translated instead of being contrasted with it. Inasmuch as Vera Vasilevna's art is performative, inspiration and actualization presumably coincide during her recording sessions. The two phases become oppositional, however, in Simeonov's instance; since his mental activity never begets anything apart from additional fantasies, the reader is hard put to determine whether he qualifies as an artist, an artist *manqué*, or simply an ineffectual dreamer at the mercy of far-fetched, unrealized yearnings who merely reshuffles or recycles ready-made materials as long as he can sustain his derivative flights of fancy:

> Let's have the light blue fog. The fog in place, Vera Vasilevna walks, her round heels clicking, *across the entire paved section sustained by Simeonov's imagination*, here's the edge of the scenery, *the director's run out of means*, he is powerless, and, weary, he releases the actors. (21, emphases added)

> Podat' goluboi tuman! Tuman podan, Vera Vasil'evna prokhodit, postukivaia kruglymi kablukami, *ves' spetsial'no prigotovlennyi, uderzhivaemyi simeonovskim voobrazheniem moshchenyi otrezok*, vot i granitsa dekoratsii, *u rezhissera konchilis' sredstva*, on obessilen, i, ustalyi, on raspuskaet akterov. (21)

The fluidity of the dividing line demarcating artistic inspiration from the unbridled play of unfulfilled erotic fantasies is transmitted in the story's presiding metaphor of the river, which, "flows, narrowing and widening feverishly, unable to select a permanent image for itself" (21–22) ("sudorozhno suzhaias' i rasshiriaias', techet i nikak ne mozhet vybrat' sebe ustoichivogo oblika" [21]). The protean amorphousness of a body of water, on the one hand, and its unique power to construct and annihilate ("as only rivers can"/"kak umeiut delat' tol'ko reki"), on the other, point to the paradoxical, contingent nature and function of art, which constantly redefine themselves through time. From Vera Vasilevna's art Simeonov derives both compensation for the dreariness of his existence and stimulation for his own imaginative exertions.

Although the relationship between artist and admirer in "Okkervil River" reverses the gender roles of "Fakir," Simeonov essentially duplicates Galia's assumptions and expectations regarding art. Likewise viewing the artwork as one with its creator, he interprets Vera Vasilevna's singing in terms of their imagined shared experience and entertains erotic fantasies about the singer as an attainable sexual partner. Tolstaya injects Simeonov's wishful dreams about the chanteuse with traditional fetishist insignia redolent of sexual arousal and voyeuristic possession: Simeonov and she "come together" in a *garden*; she appears in a *round* hat with a *veil*, in long gloves that she pulls on and off, and in black shoes with *"apple-round" high heels*, on which she minces and teeters unsteadily.[39] Tolstaya inscribes the confusion between profession and person in a powerfully suggestive synecdoche of displacement, whereby Simeonov's placing a record of the diva's performance on the gramophone becomes his laying the actual woman on her back, impaled by the (phallic?) needle of the equipment: "where are you now, Vera Vasilevna? Where are your white bones now? And, *turning her over on her back, he placed the needle*" (19, emphasis added) ("gde vy teper', Vera Vasil'evna? Gde teper' vashi belye kostochki? I, *perevernuv ee na spinu, ustanavlival iglu*" [18]); "skipping, creaking, and hissing, *Vera Vasilevna quickly spun under the needle*" (18, emphasis added) ("podskakivaia, potreskivaia i shipia, *bystro vertelas' pod igloi Vera Vasil'evna*" [16]). Whereas the diva's grotesque physical attributes have little relevance for someone enamored exclusively of her vocal skills, they certainly trammel the scope of erotic imaginings harbored by anyone who, like Simeonov, extrapolates from her public artistic self (voice) onto her private physical person (body) as an object of desire.

If in "Fakir" decontextualization triggers Galia's disillusionment, in "Okkervil River" Simeonov's is effected through materialization. Empirical reality in the form of Verunchik's asexual bulk, her greed, and her boisterous vulgarity crushes the intangible visions apotheosizing a delicate, desirable beloved. Faced with the alternatives of visiting the real Okkervil River or mentally fabricating a more poetic version of it, Simeonov opts for the incorporeal imagined. When confronted with two similarly antithetical Vera Vasilevnas, however, Simeonov modifies his initial disavowal of both as mutual erasures into what Tolstaya ambiguously portrays as a possible synthesis of the polarities.[40]

The story's ending lacks closure to a greater degree than that of "Fakir" because it leaves open a greater number of interrelated questions. One can only speculate whether Simeonov is striving for a potential reconciliation, based on some kind of accommodation, between the idealized projection of his dreams and the (very) corporeal Vera Vasilevna noisily lumbering in his bathtub; whether he will handle the dualism discretely, continuing to fantasize about her on the basis of her voice while separately tolerating her immediate physical presence; whether the juxtaposition of the two will sensitize him to paradoxical aspects of art that earlier escaped his notice. On the one hand, the conclusion stresses repugnant details of the singer's brute physicality that militate against her poeticized persona:

> Despite himself, Simeonov kept listening to the creaks and splashes of Vera Vasilevna's heavy body in the cramped tub, to her soft, heavy, full hip pulling away from the side of the damp tub with a slurp and smack, to [. . .] how a red parboiled Vera Vasilevna emerged in a robe [. . .] and Simeonov [. . .] went to rinse off after Vera Vasilevna, to use the flexible shower hose to wash off the gray pellets of skin from the tub's drying walls, to scoop the white hairs from the drain. (28–29)

> Simeonov protiv voli prislushivalsia, kak kriakhtit i kolyshetsia v tesnom vannom koryte gruznoe telo Very Vasil'evny, kak s khliupom i chmokan'em otstaet ee nezhnyi, tuchnyi, nalitoi bok ot stenki vlazhnoi vanny, kak [. . .] vykhodit v khalate krasnaia, rasparennaia Vera Vasil'evna [. . .] a Simeonov [. . .] shel opolaskivat' posle Very Vasil'evny, smyvat' gibkim dushem serye okatyshi s podsokhshikh stenok vanny, vykolupyvat' sedye volosy iz slivnogo otverstviia. (27–28)

On the other hand, Simeonov is described as "brought up short, smiling" ("zatormozhennyi, ulybaiushchiisia"), and once Potseluev switches on the gramophone, the transcendant sounds of Vera Vasilevna's voice float both above her body and "above Simeonov bent in his lifelong obedience" (29) ("nad sugnuvshimsia v svoem pozhiznennom poslushanii Simeonovym" [28]) —which implies a hierarchy privileging the elusive aesthetic over the immediate corporeal. The ending is nonetheless ambiguous and, moreover, hints at a potential new beginning of a narratable interaction along altered lines between Simeonov and Vera Vasilevna, Simeonov and art. Tolstaya withholds summative statements, literalizes her organizing trope of the river, and leaves the reader suspended in uncertainty.

Developing along parallel lines that periodically intersect, the two narratives confront a single insoluble problem: the connection between art and everyday life. At the height of the modernist movement in Europe, José Ortega y Gasset in his landmark essay, *The Dehumanization of Art* (1925), argued that "Perception of 'lived' reality and perception of artistic form [. . .] are essentially incompatible because they call for a different adjustment of our perceptive apparatus" (25). An object of art, in fact, "is artistic only in so far as it is not real" (10), and modern art specifically is inhuman "not only because it contains no things human, but also because it is an explicit act of dehumanization" (22). That disjunction between the human and the aesthetic is inscribed variously in Tolstaya's texts as the dynamic tension between multiple dichotomies: the outlying regions and the heart of the city; Filin's tower and the store below; the actual Okkervil River and the one situated solely in Simeonov's mind; Vera Vasilevna's body as gross matter and her voice as artistic force, and so on. As Tolstoy demonstrated in *War and Peace*, the atomizing process of *ostranenie*, which does away with the "adjustment of our perceptive apparatus" essential to an aesthetic apperception, prevents one from yielding to art, just as skepticism and rationality deter one from succumbing to religious belief. Terry Eagleton rightly states that religion's "ultimate truths, like those mediated by the literary symbol, are conveniently closed to rational demonstration, and thus absolute in their claims" (23). Within the spatial symbolism of religious thought, unbelief or a refusal to accredit anything not subject to empirical verification belongs to lower spheres (the store that feeds the body), whereas the spiritual or disembodied eternal moves heavenward, like Filin's tower and the soaring notes of Vera Vasilevna's voice above the city, where the heart and spirit presumably receive succour. Within the domain of language, this gravitation in opposite directions may be seen as the difference between metaphor—which Ortega y Gasset, significantly, dubs "the most radical instrument of dehumanization" whose "efficacy verges on magic" (35, 33)—and literalization. If for the major part of "Fakir" Galia as acolyte ascends to Filin's plateau, by story's end she falls to Iura's level of pragmatic skepticism: "like a transparent worm, the store had eaten away the foot of the palace."

In an interview some years ago, Tolstaya singled out the traditional Russian proclivity to view art as religion (with mixed consequences):

> In our country literature in a certain sense occupies the position of religion. People expect prophecy from a writer. They expect definite elucidation from literature, not in the sense of "education," but in the sense of "enlightenment." This came about historically [. . .] . As a result of tradition,

intellectual reasoning is secondary in our country, the primary capacity being a kind of spiritual emotion.

> Literatura u nas, v kakom-to smysle, zanimaet polozhenie religii. Ot pisatelia zhdut prorochestva. Ot literatury zhdut kakogo-to opre-delennogo prosvetleniia, ne v smysle "education," a v smysle "enlighten-ment." Eto slozhilos' istoricheski [. . .] . Traditsiia porabotala takim obrazom, chto razum u nas zanimaet vtoroe mesto, a kakaia-to dushevnaia emotsiia—pervoe mesto. (Barta, 268)

Tolstaya basically dissociates herself from the zealot's insistence that art serve a divine purpose, a view dogmatically espoused by Gogol in his "Portrait" and *Selected Passages from Correspondence with Friends* (Vybrannye mesta iz perepiski s druz'iami), by Leo Tolstoy in *What Is Art?* (Chto takoe iskusstvo?) and his postcrisis writings, and subsequently revived by such Symbolists as Andrei Bely and Viacheslav Ivanov. The binarism of Tolstaya's tropes (which tend to pit matter against spirit), however, and her poeticized treatment of the imagination prompt her reader to associate art with a transcendent dimension of human experience, even though her deflationary irony destabilizes any statements that ignore subjectivity, context, process, and pluralism. Tolstaya's fiction proposes no answers to how the transcendent dimension fits in with the mundane, practical aspects of existence. Her emphasis on the primacy of language in literary creation, on the dissociation of the aesthetic from the human within the artist herself, and on the disjunction between the artist and the artistic product aligns her perhaps most intimately with Pushkin, who also spoke matter-of-factly about divine inspiration while in the same breath, in forthrightly prosaic terms, dissecting a writer's technical difficulties and treating finished texts as negotiable commodities. Unlike philosophy, literature operates not by compelling argumentation but by seductive example, and in that sense Tolstaya's "Fakir" and "Okkervil River," by virtue of their impact on the reader, make the case for art without conclusively defining its function. For Tolstaya, like Pushkin, makes her readers luxuriate in "the pleasure of the text,"[41] immerse themselves in "the exuberant dance of language, delighting in the texture of words themselves" (Eagleton, 82–83), transferring the act of reading from the laboratory, as Eagleton felicitously puts it, to the boudoir—a wonderland in its own right and in Tolstaya's writing.

✧ 7 ✧

Fantasy and Fatality:
Narrative as Creative and Killing Strategy

The publication in 1965 of Jerzy Kosinski's first novel, *The Painted Bird*, provoked passions on account of its relentlessly violent, physiologically explicit exposé of Poland's anti-Semitism during World War II. It simultaneously sanctified Kosinski as a martyred survivor of the Holocaust who inscribed his gruesome ordeals in what critics unanimously hailed as a courageous autobiography. Almost thirty years later, the late Kosinski and his novel are themselves the subjects of a "scandalous" exposé, as a result of the Polish journalist Joanna Siedlicka's revelation—corroborated by James Park Sloan[1]—that Kosinski "had profoundly falsified his wartime experiences" (Sloan, 46). Weighing the indignation of readers who feel cheated in learning that the novel's atrocities originated in Kosinski's imagination instead of having been inflicted on his body, Sloan ironically observes: "Now all must profess to be shocked—shocked—that a practitioner of the liar's profession, a man who survived the war by living a lie, told lies" (53).

Unlike those who feel "betrayed" by Kosinski, Tolstaya, as a fellow-practitioner of *that* profession, readily acknowledges that "to tell stories" is to tell lies, to fashion captivating untruths. Yet not all untruths are alike, and their effects also decisively differ. Those differences manifestly intrigue Tolstaya, for at least five of her narratives—almost a quarter of her prose fiction—explore from a variety of perspectives the nature, reception, and consequences of fictions: "Fire and Dust" ("Ogon' i pyl'"), "Sonia," "Fakir," "Heavenly Flame" (Plamen' nebesnyi" [1987]), and "Sweet Dreams, Son" ("Spi spokoino, synok" [1986]).

Having discussed the first three in earlier chapters, I shall merely note here that in "Fire and Dust" Pipka as an ambulatory treasure trove of fantastic tales embodies Tolstaya's identification of narrative momentum with the life force;[2] that equation also operates in "Sonia," where a playfully sadistic lie paradoxically irradiates one life and ultimately saves another, through a redemptive faith that makes "a lie come true"; in "Fakir," the tale-spinner Filin similarly infuses magic into the daily existence of his "audience," as long as they suspend their disbelief. While that pivotal qualification adumbrates Tolstaya's shift to a more alloyed perspective, lies as artistic/narrative inspiration in "Fakir" nonetheless not only inspire the seduced listeners but also seduce the reader.

These meta-works credit colorful fictions that blatantly defy all logic with the ability to expand one's universe through extending the realm of possibilities; by constructing counterworlds, fictions compensate for, and liberate one from, the limitations of this one. Their truths rely on visions and epiphanies not susceptible to immediate empirical verification (the word *narrative* derives via the Latin *gnarus*, meaning "knowing," from the Sanskrit root *gna*, meaning "know").[3] Whereas that Romantic/Symbolist concept of art as a special category of knowing informs the other three stories in question, "Heavenly Flame" and "Sweet Dreams, Son" cast a darker glance at the motivation for and the specific form and consequences of narrating lives or perpetuating lies.

"Heavenly Flame" is a narrative of classical simplicity with vaguely Turgenevian overtones, inasmuch as it boasts three male characters constellated around a focal female; a hospitable dacha as the locus of action; and a radical shift in human relations owing to a single, decisive moment of moral betrayal.[4] The plot recounts how the frequent, welcome visits of Korobeinikov, a patient with ulcers at a neighboring sanatorium, to the dacha of Olga Mikhailovna and her (unnamed) husband become a source of irritation after their acquaintance Dmitrii Ilich falsely informs them that, during his stint in a Siberian camp, his acquaintance Korobeinikov appropriated and published his poems, passing them off as his own (i.e., *The Quiet Don* [Tikhii Don] revisited). Despite Dmitrii Ilich's subsequent admission that he fabricated the entire episode, his hosts' altered attitude toward the unsuspecting Korobeinikov degenerates into active hostility that in all likelihood will terminate their relations.

Like the majority of Tolstaya's stories, "Heavenly Flame" essentially pits spirit against matter, or, more specifically here, one kind of lie against another. Olga Mikhailovna, the self-conscious object of male desire, and her nameless cypher of a husband are flanked by Korobeinikov and Dmitrii Ilich in the implicit roles of rivals and foils. Tolstaya, in fact, parallels the two antagonists so as to underscore more effectively the contrasts between them: both have physical weaknesses, Korobeinikov an ulcer, Dmitrii Ilich a limp; both are impassioned raconteurs; the dacha, for different reasons, draws both. Korobeinikov is, metaphorically speaking, the heavenly flame of the title because of his moral purity, his appreciation of intangibles (he derives more benefit from warm human contact than from medication), and his fascination with transcendent, inexplicable phenomena associated with cosmic or celestial forces: aliens, flying saucers, the descent of a heavenly flame, and the like.[5] Valuing human fellowship, through his tales he attempts to plumb the enigma of others' experiences. Tolstaya allies him consistently with mystery, nature ("carrying a bit of nature"/"neset kusok prirody"), and illumination, crystallizing his inner qualities in the light his torch casts in the darkness ("then nothing can be seen in the night but a white star where Korobeinikov had been standing" [81]/"togda nichego uzh ne vidno v nochi, tol'ko belaia zvezda na tom meste, gde stoial Korobeinikov" [132]).[6] In short, he, like Pipka and Filin, is the "good narrator"—or the "righteous man" as delineated in Walter Benjamin's article on Leskov, titled "The Storyteller" (108–9).

Korobeinikov's counterpart, Dmitrii Ilich, an urban acquaintance of Olga Mikhailovna's, affects bohemianism and destroys nature by slashing leaves with the cane he carries. The mainspring for Dmitrii Ilich's visits is vanity, to be satisfied primarily by an illicit, unconsummated romance with Olga Mikhailovna; his earthbound stories incline toward gossip and reveal people in a negative light, while aggrandizing him as an authority and a fascinating, sophisticated man of the world. If childlike authenticity is Korobeinikov's trademark, Dmitrii Ilich favors the theatricality of the preening poseur. Whereas Korobeinikov naively interprets their dacha activities as an honest contest in narrative skill and sifts his memory for more absorbing tales, Dmitrii Ilich resorts, ironically, to the kind of compromised tactics that in another context would land his rival in Siberia—blackening his reputation out of envy with nary a twinge of remorse. When his ploy succeeds, he minimizes the weighty consequences of his lies about Korobeinikov by flatteringly claiming jest and jealousy as his self-exculpatory motives.

Tolstaya structures the narrative through two interwoven devices: (1) a steady pattern of tales, spun alternately by Korobeinikov and Dmitrii Ilich, which provide the stable background against which to project the other device; (2) the incremental infusion of hostility into the hosts' treatment of Korobeinikov, hence the rapid modulation in narrative tone. This technique serves to emphasize both the subjective nature of perception and its totalizing proclivities, which seek the psychological security (1) of discriminating (once and for all) between "ours" (*svoi*) and "not ours" (*chuzhie*)[7] and (2) of positing a continuity between story and storyteller (text and author).

Narratively speaking, the transition from welcome to contempt that Olga Mikhailovna's household shows Korobeinikov vividly attests to the saliency of a subject in the presentation of materials—and here Kosinski rears his inanimate head. Although Korobeinikov's conduct and habits remain unchanged throughout the story, Dmitrii Ilich's false revelations mark the division between the two polarized images of Korobeinikov as a likable friend and a villainous irritant ("Fakir" contains a parallel shift in perception, hence reception). Initially, Olga Mikhailovna's announcement, "Here comes Korobeinikov, he's got a mushroom" (78) ("Vot Korobeinikov idet, grib neset" [130]), instantly produces a positive atmosphere:

> And her words made everyone feel good, kind of peaceful, as in childhood: the sun shines serenely; the seasons slip by serenely; serenely, with no shouting or panic, autumn draws near. A nice man is coming, carrying a bit of nature. How sweet. (78)

> I ot etikh ee slov vsem khorosho stanovilos', spokoino, kak v detstve: tikho svetit solntse, tikho skol'ziat vremena goda, tikho, bez krika i paniki, podstupaet osen'. Idet milyi chelovek, neset kusochek prirody. Simpatichno. (130)

Until the reversal, Korobeinikov inspires the solicitude and affection of his hostess, who praises his entertaining, fantastic stories. Immediately following Dmitrii Ilich's mendacious revelation, the tone and lexicon (of the double-voiced narrative, which reflects chiefly Olga Mikhailovna's point of view) construct an antithetical image of Korobeinikov: "[from the woods] comes the vile Korobeinikov, carrying his foul toadstool" (84) ("idet gnusnyi Korobeinikov, neset svoi poganyi grib" [135]); his stories are now "nonsense about miracles" ("chush' pro chudesa"), his ashtray full of cigarette butts "as if measured the guilt of an unclean man" (86) ("slovno mera viny nechistogo cheloveka" [136]), about whom "everyone [. . .] thinks hostile thoughts" (84) ("kazhdyi [. . .] dumaet chto-nibud' nepriiaznennoe" [135–36]). What does this story suggest about how we generate and absorb narratives/untruths?

Both Korobeinikov and Dmitrii Ilich fabricate scenarios of what never happened, and their success as fabulists depends not only on their skill but also on the receptivity of their audience.[8] Yet the lies disseminated by Korobeinikov result from the fictionist's unavoidable need for the verbal embodiment that by definition violates strict principles of truth telling, even if it does so to make accessible an otherwise inexpressible larger truth or insight.[9] In an absolute sense, form inescapably compromises essence; or, to invoke Hayden White's concise formulation, narrativizing discourse—whereby "the narrator feigns to make the world speak itself [. . .] *as a story*" (White, 6–7)—precludes narration. Yet, if the reader/listener accepts the tacit contract between storyteller and audience, these lies are utterly free of destructiveness and relatively free of self-interest.[10] They service a perceived truth, the significance of which, presumably, outweighs the compromise of sacrificing literal fidelity to empirical data.

Dmitrii Ilich, the liar as pseudofictionist, however, is driven by a cruder and narrower teleology—of self-promotion and/or belittlement of others—with a view to immediate personal gain. His lies serve not truthfulness but ruthlessness (i.e., expediency, not experience). Above all, "Heavenly Flame" reveals (1) the primacy of listener or reader response, (2) the complex psychology that determines the degree to which we collude in the fictionist's manipulation of our credulity,[11] and (3) the predisposition to demand an unwavering line of seamless continuity between authors and their fictions (the current Kosinski dilemma, to which I shall return later).

"Sweet Dreams, Son" presents a similarly complex notion of narrative bifurcated along two plotlines. The story offers a glimpse into the life of Sergei, orphaned during World War II, who, driven by a search for his "lost" identity, married into a bourgeois family attached to possessions: the watery, insubstantial Lenochka, her vulgarian mother Maria Maksimovna, and the late pater familias, Pavel Antonovich, a military doctor. Characteristically, Tolstaya interweaves two distinct but related threads (two incommensurate losses—of origins and object) that, once again, contrast two modes of make-believe: Sergei's unarticulated wishful fantasies (conveyed through inner monologue) as to the probable identity of the mother he never knew, and Maria Maksimovna's vocal slanderous insistence that the theft of her furcoat at a flea market was orchestrated by Pania, the family's cleaning woman. It gradually becomes clear that the accusation displaces onto the disempowered Pania the arrogant Pavel Antonovich's criminal act: *he* originally stole the furcoat in Germany during the war.

If Sergei's speculative flights evidence the indispensability not only of origins but also of narrative for structuring our identities, the discrepancy in Maria Maksimovna's presentation of Pavel Antonovich's undisputed action, on the one hand, and Pania's arbitrarily posited one, on the other, testifies to (1) totalizing strategies in narrative, and (2) the power of words to reorganize, according to psychological expediency, our perception and memory of what happened. Crudely put, it suits Maria Maksimovna's unacknowledged emotional needs to present her husband not as a dishonest, obsessive failure and tyrant but as an exemplar of self-abnegating courage, just as blaming her servant Pania for the theft of the furcoat is necessitated by Pavel Antonovich's successful prosecution of Pania for the "crime."

"Sweet Dreams, Son" illustrates how an event early in a narrative may circumscribe narrative options at a later juncture. Both Maria Maksimovna's and Sergei's narratives are fueled by desire rooted in a sense of self, but whereas his moves centrifugally so as to explore and discover, hers operates centripetally to shore up a self-image that she guards no less tenaciously than she does her material possessions. As in "Heavenly Flame," the story demonstrates the destructive potential of creation—of "telling stories"—and simultaneously, our universal psychological dependency on narratives.

What is at issue here is the ethics of narrative production and consumption. As Robert Scholes has noted, "a literary text [. . .] is important to us because it can enter the textual web that constitutes each of its readers and play a role in that reader's construction of his or her own narrative, the text we each make that convinces us we are living a 'life' (10). Or, to rephrase it, our production and reception of narrative is endlessly mediated by our own experiences and self-image. Hence come the concepts of the implied author and the involuntarily confessional reader. Through Dmitrii Ilich and Maria Maksimovna, Tolstaya illustrates a failure in the ethics of authoring, which demands self-knowledge and allegiance to its revelations. They violate that ethics, insofar as theirs are not the inevitable lies of narrativizing but the voluntary untruths of character assassination. And through Olga Mikhailovna and Lenochka, who ally themselves with whatever proceeds most flatteringly or requires no moral effort, Tolstaya analogously problematizes the ethics of reading (or audience). In a passage from *Middlemarch* cited by Scholes, George Eliot marvelously captures the syndrome of the unethical reader: "In warming himself at French social theories he had brought away no smell of scorching. We may handle even extreme opinions with impunity while our furniture, our dinner-giving, and preference for armorial bearings in our own case, link us indissolubly with the established order."[12]

What is particularly intriguing about "Heavenly Flame" and "Sweet Dreams, Son" within the context of Tolstaya's oeuvre is their implicit polemic with other Tolstayan narratives—specifically "Fakir" and "Fire and Dust"—and what they reveal about Tolstaya's authorial approach to questions that preoccupy her. All four texts metaphorize the storyteller's vivid power as incandescent warmth and flame, but whereas "Fakir and "Fire and Dust" conceive of narrative energy as life-transforming élan, in "Heavenly Flame" and "Sweet Dreams, Son" that momentum carries elements of fatality, for it can create in order to eliminate. In that sense "Heavenly Flame" and "Sweet Dreams, Son" provide, if not a corrective to the sunnier view of the other two stories, then a counterperspective.

That perspectivism manifests itself in kindred juxtapositions familiar from other Tolstayan texts. For example, " 'On the Golden Porch' " and "Rendezvous with a Bird," which envision childhood as a radiant paradise, contrast with "Loves Me—Loves Me Not" and "Night," which convey the fearsome horrors to which the vulnerable psyche of a child is hostage. Such alternate viewpoints in Tolstaya's works should discourage readers from reductively finalizing her as a writer driven by a single stable angle on the world. Or, to put it bluntly, Tolstaya is a fabulous and inconsistent "liar," whose passion for storytelling seeps into her conversations, journalism, and all genres even remotely receptive not to the historical discourse that narrates but to the discourse that narrativizes.

If we circle back to Jerzy Kosinski's posthumous reputation with that distinction in mind, we find it difficult, I think, to disagree with Sloan's rebuttal that "abstracted from its archival pretensions, [*The Painted Bird*] gains in stature as an achievement of the novelistic imagination" (Sloan, 53). That imagination, in turn, depends on ours for bridging the space between an experienced truth and its externalization via a narrative that must lie so as to recreate that truth for us.

Tolstaya's fiction does not openly engage political and social issues, for which some Russian critics took her to task during the exposé phase of glasnost. Yet the playful and poetic aspect of her prose, and her emphatic focus on language, on stylistic effects, should not obscure her concern for metaphysical and philosophical questions. The dilemma of lies has a particular edge in the Russian context. The specific course of Soviet history has made it difficult not to read these two stories within the framework of ethical issues to which the fabrication of stories is fundamental.

Betrayals and accusations in a country where people's lives have been abruptly curtailed because of a finger pointed at them carry a special, potentially fatal, weight. Perhaps because Soviet and Russian history seems to have evolved in a steady rhythm of denunciations and punishments, of treachery and recriminations, Soviet literature teems with narratives in an accusatory and confessional mode.[13] The Soviet and especially Stalinist era, with its orgy of paranoid vigilance and system of flushing out enemies, transformed even casual comments about individuals or groups into unwitting sentences of doom, as Solzhenitsyn's novels repeatedly illustrate. Although Tolstaya's fiction does not engage in unmediated political statement, she does explore the mechanism of accusation—one patently mendacious, the other probably erroneous—in these two otherwise rather dissimilar stories. In each case the apportioning of blame affords immeasurably more insight into the accuser than the accused; the beneficiary of the accusation is intended to gain in stature but achieves the reverse; and the accusatory act is curiously implicated in the habit of storytelling, of narrating lives.

If such is the case, then Tolstaya's own passion for narrative may explain her fascination with the lure of storytelling. While conscious of the perils land mining the fabulist's storehouse of ploys and devices, even in her journalism and interviews Tolstaya repeatedly yields to the seduction of narrative—a paradox to which I return in the Conclusion.

✧ **8** ✧

Tolstayan Times:
Traversals and Transfers

Time, which is the author of authors.

Francis Bacon, *Advancement of Learning*

Time travels in divers paces with divers persons.

William Shakespeare, *As You Like It*

During one of his habitual meditations on history, Iurii Trifonov reportedly stated, "Time imposes its frame on a man, but it is within a man's power to widen the frame, if only slightly."[1] In her prose, Tolstaya not only widens the frame but packs within it an assortment of experiences that insistently push against the restraining contours and, on occasion, actually extend our vision beyond the frame. The multilayered apperception of time in Tolstaya's fictional universe assimilates manifold temporal concepts, variously designated as folkloric or mythic; "monumental" (Ricoeur);[2] "pure" or "experienced" (Bergson);[3] and "great" (Bakhtin).[4] Tolstaya's highly complex handling of time originates in her syncretism—her propensity to condense elements from disparate sources into maximally compressed texts that usually narrate metonymical lives illustrative of timeless configurations.

Implicitly conceived by Tolstaya as a collective singular,[5] time, like most phenomena and conditions in her created universe, hinges chiefly on individual perception (Ricoeur's "soul, mind, consciousness") and derives only secondarily from external data (Ricoeur's "world").[6] Consequently, temporal categories and one's experience of them vary not only according to changing circumstances but also, and primarily, in relation to age, cast of mind, and psychological states. Roughly speaking, the three broad phases of inner development determining temporal consciousness in Tolstaya's fictional world coincide with the three stages of human life charted by the Sphinx's famous riddle in Sophocles's *Oedipus the King*: childhood, adulthood (or maturity), and old age.

According to Trifonov, "Every writer has 'an emergency ration' or [. . .] a treasure to which he resorts sooner or later: childhood" (147). Tolstaya began sooner rather than later, excavating her treasure with her first story, " 'On the Golden Porch' " (1985), which identifies childhood with mythic time, that is, the timelessness of the eternal present. There and in several subsequent works, Tolstaya spatializes childhood time through the chronotope of the Edenic garden: "In the beginning was the garden. Childhood was a garden. Without end or limit, without borders and fences" (41) ("Vnachale byl sad. Detstvo bylo sadom. Bez kontsa i kraia, bez granits i zaborov" [40]). During this innocent or unconscious phase of life, only seasonal or diurnal markers organize the temporal flow in an iterative pattern. This profoundly cyclic life, as in folklore,[7] consists predominantly of mornings, days, evenings, and nights against a background of springs, summers, autumns, and winters, with no hours or years (what Bergson calls "physical" and Ricoeur "cosmological" time) impinging on a child's mythic sense of her/his surroundings: "The day was boring: they waited for lunch and then waited for dinner. Grandfather ate a hard-boiled egg. It rained again at night" ("Rendezvous with a Bird" [128]) ("Den' proshel skuchno: zhdali obeda, potom zhdali uzhina. Dedushka s''el krutoe iaitso. Noch'iu opiat' poshel dozhd' " [122]).

As noted in Chapter 2, numerous autobiographies, including Rousseau's *Confessions*, Mary McCarthy's *Memories of a Catholic Girlhood*, Nabokov's *Speak, Memory*, and Kathleen Raine's *Farewell Happy Fields*, have conventionalized the garden as a metaphor for childhood or a setting associated with light, fruit, water, abundance, order, and, above all, timelessness.[8] Musing on this *topos* in his own *Autobiography*, Edwin Muir tellingly remarks, "It was as if, while I lay watching that beam of light, time had not yet begun" (18). Nabokov likewise remembers "the harmonious world of a perfect childhood" as a "veritable Eden of visual and tactile sensations" in a "free world of timelessness" (E17, R14). A major component in this early idyll of boundless joys, then, is a sense of plenitude and security paradoxically combined with freedom from temporal linearity: that is, from chronology, large-scale cause and effect, and teleology.

Years as such have little meaning in a child's universe. Hence children's frequent recourse, in Tolstaya's fiction, to those maximal (or "otherworldly") formulations discredited by Leo Tolstoy like "never," "forever," and "always"; hence also their penchant for fantastic, inconceivable temporal hyperbole as well as anachronistic conflation of time frames.[9] Characteristically, the child narrator in " 'On the Golden Porch' " alludes to a period "When we graduate (in a hundred years) to the eighth grade" (42) ("Kogda [cherez sto let] my pereidem v vos'moi klass" [40]); young Petia in "Rendezvous with a Bird" has no difficulty believing that Tamila is seven thousand years old (R115); and the recalcitrant girl narrator of "Loves Me—Loves Me Not" declares of her beloved old nurse Grusha, "Pushkin loved her very much too, and wrote about her, calling her 'my decrepit little dove.' But he didn't write anything about Marivanna" (4) ("Pushkin ee tozhe ochen' liubil i pisal pro nee: 'Golubka driakhlaia moia!' A pro Mar'ivannu on nichego ne sochinil" [3–4]).

In its most radical expression this timelessness or the incapacity to conceive of temporal movement as gradual change or progression (instead of cyclic repetition) manifests itself in a rejection of death. Reminiscing about her old governess Zhenechka, the adult narrator in "Most Beloved" explicitly recalls that in childhood "to tell the truth, we were certain of her immortality—as we were of our own" (92) ("my, po pravde govoria, byli uvereny v ee bessmertii—a zaodno i v svoem" [93]). Collapsing the distinction between the dead and the living, the narrator of "Loves Me—Loves Me Not" observes, "High up, in the window, nose pressed against the dark glass, the hanged uncle waits, running his hands over the glass, peering out" (13) ("Vysoko, v okne, pripliusnuv nos k temnomu steklu rukami, brezzhit poveshennyi diadia, vodit po steklu rukami, vsmatrivaetsia" [12]), while her counterpart in " 'On the Golden Porch' " announces: "Life is eternal. Only birds die" (42) ("Zhizn' vechna. Umiraiut tol'ko ptitsy" [41]). When Petia, in "Rendezvous with a Bird," gains knowledge of mortality through his grandfather's death, he cannot return to the prelapsarian perpetual present of his childhood Eden but must enter the more problematic and differentiated sphere of maturity.[10]

The loss of timeless harmony and immortality as one falls into the adult world of chaos, pain, death, and darkness inevitably marks, for Tolstaya, a new perception of, and relationship to, time (Lifson, 50). Whereas immersion in the present, in the immediacy of presence, characterizes childhood, Tolstaya portrays adulthood contrastively in terms that recall Aristotle's "before and after."[11]

Aristotle defines time as "the number of motion in respect of 'before' and 'after,' " his "instant" requiring that "the mind make a break in the continuity of movement, insofar as the latter is countable. This break can be made anywhere. Any instant at all is worthy of being the present. The Augustinian present,[12] however, [. . .] is any instant designated by a speaker as the 'now' of his utterance."[13] The connection between movement and time on which Aristotle insists is most palpable during this middle stage of existence, wherein adults experience time primarily as mutability and respond to it in Augustinian terms: with memories of the past and expectations of the future.

The underlying sameness of these modes of temporal perception, despite their ostensibly diametrically opposed impetus, is dramatized in Lewis Carroll's *Through the Looking Glass*, where the White Queen argues for a two-directional memory: "It's a poor sort of memory that only works backwards" (254). Memory of the past, in other words, determines expectations of the future and acts, in a sense, as its arbitrary arbiter. Frank Kermode recognizes as much, offering two persuasive (if homespun and small-scale) illustrations in his assertion that "there is [. . .] a kind of forward memory, familiar from spoonerisms and typing errors which are caused by anticipation, the mind working on an expected future" (53). Although antithetically oriented, retrospection (what Genette labels narrative analepsis) and prospection (Genette's narrative prolepsis) may be said to participate in a common mental activity along a single continuum and, narratively, to invoke the same device of anachrony—of reaching into the past or future.[14]

Narratively speaking, for Tolstaya the retrospective stance of adulthood accomplishes a twofold effect. Since it registers the deprivation of an earlier, carefree state born of a transforming uncorrupted vision, its diachronic cast emphasizes, *within the narrative itself* (or, to borrow Genette's vocabulary, on the level of *story*), the "devouring" nature of temporal flow; hence the "ubi sunt?" elegiac nature of backward glances.[15] Yet retrospection potentially offers the reader (i.e., on the level of narrative) a synchronic, bifocal view of a given phenomenon in which clinical powers of mature observation are textually juxtaposed with a child's vivid imagination, impervious to time's passage.[16] Here, as elsewhere, Tolstaya relies on a strategy that simultaneously achieves two contradictory ends: on the one hand, it separates temporal units in the participant's biography, while, on the other, it narratively draws those phases together for the reader in a proximity that urges analysis. In " 'On the Golden Porch' " only two pages separate a poetic, trope-laden paean to the magical contents of Uncle Pasha's attic as viewed through the child narrator's eyes from the prosaic dismissal of the same phenomena by her adult self, which, however, deliberately engages (for contrast's sake) the earlier, irrevocable perspective (R47–48). What the collocation underscores is the unifying or narrative aspect of memory, analogous to the narrative cast of one's reading practices and of one's approach to history.[17]

To establish the seemingly definitive break (creating a "now") between a golden past and the lackluster, contingent present, Tolstaya employs developed metaphors that highlight physical, spatial barriers (separation), yet are embedded in a context of immediacy (identification). To examine several eloquent examples: the adult narrator in " 'On the Golden Porch' " reminisces, "looking back once, with unbelieving fingers we felt the *smoked glass behind which* our garden waved a hankie before sinking to the bottom for the last time" (49, emphasis added) ("oglianuvshis' odnazhdy, neodumevaiushchimi pal'tsami my oshchupali *dymchatoe steklo, za kotorym*, prezhde chem uiti na dno, v poslednii raz pakhnul platkom nash sad" [47]); in "Sweet Shura,"

Thousands of years, thousands of days, thousands of translucent *impenetrable curtains* fell from the heavens, thickened, *turned into solid walls, blocked roads*, and kept Aleksandra Ernestovna from going to her beloved, lost in time. He remained there, on the other side of the years, alone on the dusty, dusty station [. . .] Time passes, and *the invisible layers of years get thicker*, and the rails get rusty, and the roads get overgrown. (37, emphases added)

Tysiachi let, tysiachi dnei, tysiachi prozrachnykh *nepronitsaemykh zanavesei* pali s nebes, sgustilis', *somknulis' plotnymi stenami, zavalili dorogi*, ne puskaiut Aleksandru Ernestovnu k ee zateriannomu v vekakh vozliublennomu. On ostalsia tam, po tu storonu let, odin, na pyl'noi stantsii [. . .] Vremia idet, i *nevidimye tolshchi let vse plotnee*, rzhaveiut rel'sy, i zarastaiut dorogi. (35)

In "The Circle," Tolstaya resorts to zeugma to concretize insuperable temporal occlusion through the photographs of the black-market female dwarf in her youth, in which "the young speculator waved *through the glass, through time, through a lifetime*" (72, emphasis added) ("makhala ruchkoi iunaia spekuliantka *cherez steklo, cherez vremia, cherez proshedshuiu zhizn'* " [69]).[18] Nostalgia for an irretrievable past and yearning for a projected future pull adults away from the present moment—a deflection partly reinforced by their submission to clock (cosmological) time (e.g., the adult narrator in " 'On the Golden Porch' " calculates, "I have five minutes to spare" [49]/"U menia est' eshche piat' minut" [47]). Soul time and cosmological or clock time operate according to different if occasionally intersecting principles. Since clocks represent an effort at physical (external) tabulation of temporal flow, it is no accident that Tolstaya announces the moment of her characters' physical (tangible) deaths through the traditional metaphor of the striking hour (in "The Circle," for Vasilii Mikhailovich "the hour of departure had struck" [76]/"probil chas ukhodit' "[72]); in " 'On the Golden Porch,' " one of two figures on a clock who represent "the masters of Time" ("khoziaeva Vremeni"), "the golden Lady of Time, having drained the goblet of life, will strike a final midnight on the table for Uncle Pasha" (50) ("zolotaia Dama Vremeni, vypiv do dna kubok zhizni, prostuchit po stolu dlia diadi Pashi posledniuiu polnoch' " [48]). The present of adulthood, then, derives essentially from the past and the future, which jostle each other in one "heterochronous" (Bakhtin's "multi-temporal")[19] Tolstayan story after another as they dialogize a multiplicity of chronotopes to convey the diversity of human experience through "great time."

In her treatment of memory, Tolstaya, not unlike Husserl, draws a distinction, on the one hand, between retention or primary remembrance, which more or less parallels Kermode's "immediate memory," defined as "the registration of impressions we fail to 'take in,' but can recover a little later by introspection" (Kermode, 53); and, on the other hand, recollection or secondary remembrance, located at a greater remove from the recalled event (Ricoeur, *Time and Narrative, III*, 26). Adulthood in Tolstaya's universe feeds off both and relies on both for future projections. With advancing age, however, primary remembrance fades, ceding to recollection, which increasingly dominates.

In old age, according to Tolstaya, the future orientation weakens or disappears entirely, edged out by the impulse to sum up, to evaluate the past. Memories rule old age and in a sense return the individual to childhood, with its undifferentiated approach to the world. Facts, fantasies, lived experience, hopes, possibilities, and so forth all occupy the same psychic level for Tolstaya's aged characters, for they are all equally distant (or proximate). Stories such as "Sweet Shura" and "Most Beloved" dramatize this disregard for boundaries, which Tolstaya's narrative technique intensifies. One might summarize this period of one's life as the Augustinian phase, in which "soul" time preponderates, while "world" time recedes to the periphery. In effect, what various critics have singled out as Tolstaya's predilection for portraying childhood and old age can more precisely be explained as her fascination with the dictates of one's inner being, as opposed to the demands of an external, objective reality and its corollary—cosmological time.

The three eras roughly mapped out above in no way mean to imply clear-cut temporal divisions on the narrative level in Tolstaya's fiction. On the contrary, perhaps the most distinctive feature of Tolstaya's style—and one that lends it a unique rhythm—consists of her proclivity to sabotage temporal distinctions or to render them ambiguous through the violation of traditional boundaries. Admittedly, Tolstaya does refer to seasons, to years, and to periods labeled "before," "after," and "later," but these ostensibly precise signposts dissolve—lose their ability to signify—for lack of grounding in a meaningful context. In "Most Beloved," for instance, the reader learns that the comment, "Good tea, Evgeniia Ivanovna. It's hot" (104) ("Khoroshii chai, Evgeniia Ivanovna. Goriachii" [101]), invariably elicits an emotional reaction from Zhenechka because those words were uttered by the historian who represents the sole love interest ("perhaps for a week, perhaps for her whole life" [104]/"mozhet byt' na nedeliu, mozhet byt', na vsiu zhizn' " [101]) in her experience: "That's what someone said to her at three o'clock on one prewar February afternoon, in a warm wooden building" (104) ("Tak ei skazali dnem, v tri chasa, v dovoennom fevrale, v teplom derevenskom dome"). Rather than conveying valuable information, however, the specificity of the hour and month underscores the *lack* of more general temporal indicators (such as the year, the length of their acquaintance, etc.), the presence of which would locate the event in some sort of sequence, thereby eliminating the grotesqueness of this excessive, almost Gogolian, precision.[20]

Moreover, Tolstaya often makes it impossible to gauge the correspondence between narrative and narrated time, and on those rare occasions when she does provide conditions for such a calculation, it becomes instantly apparent that the ratio is lopsided and in any case prone to uncertainty, for those conditions alter. Tolstaya's dazzling succession of mimetic and diegetic, of scenic and summative, of iterative and durative, of chronological and analeptic or proleptic defies any attempt to categorize her narrative mode except by individual sentences—a unit insufficiently comprehensive to lead to meaningful generalizations about Tolstaya's treatment of time. Perhaps the one tenable observation to be made about her temporal orchestration on a larger scale is that she opts for diffusion through uncommon diversity.

Why, one may ask, does Tolstaya load her short stories with multiple, swiftly alternating chronotopes? Because she wishes to compress as much as possible on the horizontal axis of linear time and space and the vertical axis of psychological time and space into a brief narrative. To create the illusion of presenting an entire life (extensive narrated time) within a dozen pages (minimal narrative time) necessitates extraordinary omission and a condensation that can only be achieved by rapid, unorthodox transfers instead of the leisurely or unobtrusive modulations that a longer narrative traditionally permits. Tolstaya's bold trespass of conventional borders in the interests of diffusing time takes several forms: (1) manipulation of verb aspect and tense; (2) purposely enigmatic use of narrative voice; (3) symbiotic interplay between extended metaphor and metonymy; and (4) subjectivization or humanizing of objects.

Verb Aspect and Tense

Analyzing Proust's innovative treatment of time, Genette raises the rarely confronted issue of frequency, that is, the relationship of repetition between the narrative and the diegesis. Germane to frequency is the distinction Genette makes between the singulative narrative (whereby a verb indicates a single completed action—equivalent to the Russian perfective) and the iterative (whereby a verb signals a habitual action in a way that verges on the descriptive—a feature of the Russian imperfective) (Genette, *Narrative Discourse*, 113–14). Genette concludes that iterative and singulative forms in Proust's *A la Recherche du temps perdu* "are entangled in a way that leaves the verbal aspect in utter irresolution" (147). That deliberate mixture of aspect in order to disperse time is likewise a major trait of Tolstaya's narratives, which regularly interweave single-action verbs with iteratives that economically establish a way of life. As a result, what is habitual and what is singular becomes equivocal. If one adds to the dimension of frequency that of duration, which in Russian is also carried by the imperfective aspect, then one can appreciate how Tolstaya's alternation of imperfective and perfective raises several unanswerable questions.

To complicate the picture further, Tolstaya has a penchant for showing the past spilling over into the present, which she transmits by a scrambling of tenses. The legitimate and customary use of the present tense in Russian within a narrative passage in the past tense so as to increase the flavor of immediacy expands in Tolstaya's hands into a stratagem for condensing "all time" into a single time. Furthermore, the ability of the Russian future tense to denote repeated actions in the past or present enables Tolstaya to convince the reader throughout several paragraphs that what is a wish or a waking dream actually took place, and likely more than once. Tolstaya's compression of these devices into a relatively small space manifests itself most effectively in the profoundly retrospective story "Most Beloved."

Within the subsuming realm of reminiscences, the narrator of "Most Beloved" moves back and forth on the temporal axis with a stunning rapidity and ostensible arbitrariness that play havoc with conventional notions of narrative chronology. Characteristically, most of Tolstaya's emphatically precise details work against verifiable facts. As elsewhere (e.g., "The Circle"), she takes pains to leave open to conjecture whether the story's heroine is even alive at the point where narrative and narrated intersect. Zhenechka's death is intimated, in a typical Tolstayan paradox, through repeated references to her immortality: "she meant to live forever" (92) ("Ona sobiralas' zhit' vechno" [93]); "And we thought Zhenechka was immortal" (106) ("A my-to dumali, chto Zhenechka bessmertna" [103]); "and we believed that Zhenechka was immortal" (114) ("i my poverili, chto Zhenechka bessmertna" [108]); recollections of an era, "Long, long ago [. . .] [when] Zhenechka was alive" (92) ("Davnym-davno [. . .] [kogda] byla zhivaia Zhenechka" [93]); and the elegiac observation: "she is no more, she's a shadow now, and the night wind will blow away her ramshackle dwelling" (115) ("ee bol'she net, ona stala ten'iu, i vetkhoe ee zhilishche razveet nochnoi veter" [109]). No clue is provided as to the cause or time of Zhenechka's (probable) death.

The story's extensive time-recording lexicon renders supremely palpable the passage of time, while steadily blocking the reader's access to the story's sequence of events. Countless references to seasons nonetheless give no idea whether these are separated by a few years, a decade, or more. Many of the story's effects are achieved primarily by Tolstaya's loops and leaps from one period to another, as she sums up an unspecified but undoubtedly long interval through the single summative (perfective) sentence "Time passed, and we became adults" (111) ("Vremia proshlo, i my stali vzroslymi" [106]), yet details in five paragraphs a single episode that could have lasted just a few minutes but *never* occurred: the section opening with "We'll choose a day" (114) ("My vyberem den'" [108]) and the following paragraph, both couched in the future tense, modulate to the present in the third paragraph ("We wade through the grass" [115]/"My idem cherez travu vbrod" [109]), which remains in effect until the close of the fifth paragraph. That ending, however, erases the contents of the entire section with the simple words, "it's not true, no one will come, there is no one to come, she's gone, she's a shadow" (115) ("nepravda, nikto ne priedet, nekomu priekhat', ee bol'she net, ona stala ten'iu" [109]). Having just exposed that stretch of narrative as fantasy through the implied confirmation of her heroine's death,[21] in the paragraph that immediately follows Tolstaya proceeds to resurrect Zhenechka, narratively speaking, as she backpedals with no warning to an imprecisely identified earlier moment when Zhenechka was awaiting a letter. Although the reader can deduce that this moment comes late in Zhenechka's life because the parodistically ludicrous letter that finally arrives expresses misgivings that Zhenechka may die in her relatives' home (presumably of old age), once again the exact temporal relationship of this incident to previous and subsequent ones remains enigmatic.

What renders the treatment of time in this story more complex, perhaps, than is customary in Tolstaya's fiction is its extraordinary structure: Tolstaya essentially moves over what is presumably the same general terrain twice, bringing the narration up to the immediate present at least three times.[22] Framed in two lyrical passages that install the central locus of the family dacha (a rough analogue for Zhenechka's biography: "our dacha is aging, collapsing on one side" [92]/"stareet, zavalivaetsia nabok nasha dacha" [93]), the narrative first sketches out in the present and future tenses (so as to signal iterative actions) Zhenechka's arrival at the dacha and the children's behavior with her (R93–95); it then backtracks to her introduction into the household, tracing her characteristic pattern over the years via illustrative incidents (R95–99); it moves still further back in time to her youth and her putative love (R99–101), after which, in an extended reprisal of the story's opening ("the dacha quietly ages" [106]/"tikho stareet dacha" [102–3]), it effects a transition to the second portion of the narrative. After its initial temporal regression, that section for the most part observes chronology, though in an uneven rhythm of detailed close-up alternating with a summarizing panoramic perspective (R104–8; 109–10). The second half of the story approximately retraces the first, not only complementing and paralleling it (often in reverse, for its progress is sequential, whereas that of the first part is predominantly refluent), but also relying on readers' recall of the texture of earlier portions to seduce them into credulity in the subsequent segments. Thus the passage starting with "We'll choose a day" (114) ("My vyberem den' " [109–10]) acquires the illusory aura of a refrain accurately designating repetition of a formerly enacted ritual because its tense, mood, and tone deliberately echo the earlier evocations of the dacha (R93–94, 102–3). Only with "it's not true" ("nepravda") in the final sentence does the imaginary (exclusively interior) nature of the activities (convincingly exteriorized through physical minutiae) become apparent. In brief, we are cajoled into acceptance on the basis of precedent. Here and elsewhere in Tolstaya, verb aspect and tense tend to supply elusive and misleading clues, enlisted in the interests of obfuscating rather than illuminating temporal demarcations.

Voice

Part of the complexity of Tolstaya's texts also arises from the reader's inability to anchor the narrative in a single voice or to pinpoint who precisely is speaking at a given moment. Tolstayan stories of childhood proceed chiefly through quasi-direct discourse, but even within that category, the voice may be located at any stage of the narrator's life. Tolstaya represents that life with an unpredictably irregular selectivity in which the ratio between narrated time and narrative time (Genette's duration [*Narrative Discourse*, 93]) varies so pronouncedly that a given scene of several minutes may occupy several pages, while a single synoptic sentence may encapsulate whole decades. If, as Genette claims, Proustian narrative "tends to become increasingly discontinuous, syncopated, built of enormous scenes separated by immense gaps and thus tends to deviate more and more from the hypothetical 'norm' of narrative isochrony" (93), Tolstaya's brief, maximally compressed narratives push that discontinuity to its limit. Within such unevenly spotlighted or incarnated segments of an individual biography one is hard put to determine with any accuracy not only the precise period of a given existence that the text is bringing to life but also the temporal standpoint from which the narrative emanates, that is, the maturity of the voice. For instance, in " 'On the Golden Porch,' " the implied bifocal presentation of material not only becomes explicitly bifocal (with the posterior prevailing, without fully eliminating the anterior), but at several junctures defies differentiation, for example, "And from over there, beyond the distant horizon, waving a motley flag, full of laughter and noise, already came running the green summer with ants and daisies" (46) ("A ottuda, iz-za dalekogo gorizonta, uzhe bezhalo, smeias' i shumia, razmakhivaia pestrym flagom, zelenoe leto s murav'iami i romashkami" [44]). Through a synthesis of what arguably conveys a typical child's focus ("with ants and daisies") and an adult's tropological formulation (the green summer waving a motley flag), Tolstaya leaves the reader suspended in uncertainty regarding the narrating voice's temporal distance from reported events.

That lack of fixity also characterizes the narrative apostrophes scattered throughout Tolstaya's fiction. Close to the conclusion of " 'On the Golden Porch,' " a seasonal metaphor (which continues the child's mode of organizing time's flow that the first half of the story installs) announces Uncle Pasha's sudden (?) aging and attendant enervation of physical powers: "Autumn came into Uncle Pasha's house and hit him on the face. Autumn, what do you want? Wait, surely you're kidding?" (49) ("Osen' voshla k diade Pashe i udarila ego po litsu. Osen', chto tebe nado? Postoi, ty chto zhe, vser'ez?" [47]). The apostrophe to autumn, unlike the subsequent one to life ("What silly jokes you play, life!" [49]/"Kak glupo ty shutish', zhizn'!" [48]), may seem sufficiently ingenuous for us to assign the temporal perspective of this paragraph to the narrator's childhood. Yet within that very paragraph the narrator notes: "How adult we've become" (49) ("Kak my vyrosli" [47]), and in the next paragraph, with no signal of an abrupt break or extended temporal lapse, "It's so long since I was here! I'm getting old!" (49) ("Kak davno ia zdes' ne byla. Kakaia zhe ia staraia!" [47]). If, indeed, the narrator has reached old age, then whom does she apostrophize in the paragraph's opening: "What are you bustling about for? You want to show me your treasures?" (49) ("Chto ty tak suetish'sia? Ty khochesh' pokazat' mne svoi sokrovishcha?" [47]). Presumably Uncle Pasha, who was fifty years old when the narrator was still a child (R42), but who now may be anywhere between seventy and a hundred, depending on one's subjective notion of what constitutes old age.

Through such contradictory pseudodating, Tolstaya thwarts any efforts to establish at story's end even the approximate age of the narrating "I" and other central characters: at some point during the narrator's childhood Uncle Pasha's first wife, Veronika (young, but of unspecified age), dies; roughly in that same period, her younger stepsister, Margarita, moves in with Uncle Pasha; an unknowable number of years later, when the narrator is (or feels) old, Uncle Pasha ages noticeably; after an equally unspecified interval of days? months? years? he dies. How does one reconcile the narrator's lament at this juncture about her senescence with the yellow dog bought to guard Veronika's property? After her death he languishes in a trunk with mothballs (R44), yet survives to close Uncle Pasha's eyes before departing (R48)—a fantastic, ambulatory advertisement for canine longevity that violates all biological and narrative logic! The by now wizened Margarita urges her middle-aged daughter ("pozhilaia" [48]) to bury Uncle Pasha's remains, now reduced to "dust" ("prakh" [48]) stored in a can in the chicken coop. Unless Uncle Pasha underwent cremation (never mentioned), how many years must have elapsed for his body to have disintegrated into dust? Despite the wealth of Tolstaya's temporal signals, the reader's sense of the duration inscribed in the text—thirty years? forty? fifty?—remains purely conjectural.

Various devices at first may distract the reader from the uneven pacing of the narrative, whereby the major portion of the story's narrated timespan is packed into the last two pages of the nine-page narrative, as the past iterative virtually disappears, ceding to the multifunctional present tense and the terse singulative past. The concluding paragraphs differ from the remainder of the story, for they unmistakably register a mature consciousness whose philosophical ruminations and omissive summation set this coda somewhat apart. This is not to deny that earlier sections of the story absorb aspects of the adult point of view. When the enraptured child narrator exclaims at the contents of Uncle Pasha's attic, "O room! O childhood dreams!" (47) ("O komnata! O detskie sny!" [45]), the adjective "detskie" instantly bespeaks a retrospective vantage point, for only an adult awareness could classify those dreams as specifically childlike. But that awareness ousts the child's mentality, which has filtered the majority of experiences and thus determined much of the narrative's discourse, strikingly late in the story. Moreover, that displacement leaves unresolved a host of questions about narrative and narrated time.

The startling apostrophe to Uncle Pasha, "Hey, wake up, Uncle Pasha! Veronika is going to die soon" (45) ("Ei, prosnis', diadia Pasha! Veronika-to skoro umret" [44]), which belongs to the domain of Genette's (originally Tsvetan Todorov's) " 'predictive' narrative" (*Narrative Discourses*, 216), likewise presents the reader with a number of problems. Cast *in the future tense*, it launches a prophetic glimpse into Uncle Pasha's imminent way of life that acquires the status of exposition:

> You'll wander around the empty house without a thought in your head, and then you'll straighten out, bloom, look around, remember, push away memories and desire, and bring—to help with the housekeeping—Veronika's younger sister, Margarita, just as pale, large, and beautiful. And in June she'll be laughing in the bright window, bending over the rain barrel, passing among the maples on the sunny lake.
> *Oh, how in our declining years . . .* (45)

> Ty pobrodish' bez myslei po opustevshemu domu, a potom vosprianesh', rastsvetesh', ogliadish'sia, vspomnish', otgonish' vospominaniia, vozzhazhdesh' i privezesh'—dlia pomoshchi po khoziaistvu—Veronikinu mladshuiu sestru, Margaritu, takuiu zhe beluiu, bol'shuiu i

krasivuiu. I eto ona v iiune [of what year? —H.G.] budet smeiat'sia v svetlom okne, skloniat'sia nad dozhdevoi bochkoi, mel'kat' sredi klenov na solnechnom ozere.

O kak na sklone nashikh let . . . (44)

This is manifestly not a child's discourse, although the narrated time in question represents a phase in the narrator's childhood. Even ignoring the flagrant inconsistency of proleptic omniscience in a narrator who doubles as narrated participant in the story's diegetic and thus has limited knowledge, the reader cannot assign the passage to a reasonably specific time frame. Nor can s/he be certain that the same voice at the identical stage of development is responsible for the truncated citation from Tiutchev's lyric, which, through its grammatical timelessness, enables the story to overtake the narrating in the next paragraph.[23] If ascription is more nakedly problematic here than in other Tolstayan stories, it merely underscores what may be partially camouflaged elsewhere: Tolstaya's jumbling of temporal categories for the sake of metonymical compression.

Metaphors and Metonymies

Tolstaya's skillful fusion of metaphor and metonymy likewise helps her to manipulate narrative time in a distinctive manner. Contrary to Aristotle and subsequent rhetoricians and critics who regard metonymy and synecdoche as a subspecies of metaphor, Roman Jakobson conceives of them as antithetical because they are generated according to opposite principles. Whereas metaphor belongs to the selection axis of language, metonymy belongs to its combination axis. If one accepts as accurate the structuralist law of language whereby all linguistic units provide context for simpler linguistic units and find their own context from more complex ones, then metonymies become condensations of contexture, produced by deleting one or more items from a natural combination.[24] Both Jakobson and more recent theorists of narratology such as Peter Brooks characterize prose as "forwarded essentially by contiguity" (Jakobson, 96), thus predominantly metonymical. If metonymy as a trope results from the process of combination and nonlogical deletion, the selected details comprising the trope are, as E.B. Greenwood has reasoned, "surrogates [. . .] for the mass of observed detail which would have been there in actuality" but has been deleted (341–42). In such cases, then, "the appropriate critical response to the metonymic text would seem to be an attempt to restore the deleted detail, to put the text back into the total context from which it derives" (Lodge, 93). Thus, theoretically at least, metonymy propels narrative along the horizontal axis while concurrently inviting the reader to insert all the material that has been deleted en route. That task of insertion or completion retards movement forward and potentially reorients the reader to the vertical axis, the axis of metaphor.[25] It is precisely through the interpenetration of metaphor and metonymy, through a tilting of the two axes and a bold exploitation of hybrids that Tolstaya creates temporal and spatial disjunctions in order to inflate and scramble her fictional time and space.

An exemplary text for analysis in this regard is "Okkervil River." If the narrative driven by contiguity (the preponderently metonymical mode recording Simeonov's meeting with the singer he has long worshiped) may be represented by a continuous horizontal line, Tolstaya constantly halts, retards, or reverses that movement through metaphors. Particularly the matrix metaphor of the river, which swells into a mini-universe representing the emotional state into which Vera Vasilevna's singing plunges Simeonov, occupies substantial narrative time while, conversely, embodying what is essentially narrated timelessness, for that universe exists outside of time. The lushly poeticized world verbally installed by the metaphor contributes vertical content or depth without pushing the narrative along. What "action" transpires does so in Simeonov's fantasies, that is, along the vertical axis:

> [He] listened once more, longingly, about the once-faded, pshsts, chrysanthemums in the garden, pshts, where they had met, and once again, gathering underwater pressure, throwing off dust, laces, and years, Vera Vasilevna creaked and appeared as a languorous naiad—an unathletic, slightly plump turn-of-the-century naiad—O sweet pear, guitar, hourglass, slope-hipped champagne bottle! (19)

> [On] snova slushal, tomias', ob ottsvetshikh davno, shchshchshch, khrizantemakh v sadu, shchshchshch, gde oni s neiu vstretilis', i vnov', narastaia podvodnym potokom, sbrasyvaia pyl', kruzheva i gody, potreskivala Vera Vasil'evna i predstavala tomnoi naiadoi—nesportivnoi, slegka polnoi naiadoi nachala veka—o sladkaia grusha, gitara, pokataia shampanskaia butyl'! (18)

In Bakhtinian terms, Tolstaya resorts here to the chronotope of the miraculous world, with "an emotional, subjective distortion of space, which is in part symbolic," a world that is stretched out along the vertical axis so that everything coexists "in sheer simultaneity" (as in Dante) and "time is utterly excluded from the action." These units, in other words, synchronize diachrony.[26] After its first, establishing evocation, Tolstaya metonymically conjures up this atemporal world existing wholly in Simeonov's imagination[27] by simply referring selectively to aspects of it (e.g., the river bank, Vera Vasilevna's round heels, the chrysanthemums) as the need arises or by extending the metaphor through additional details. In fact, the links that hold her narrative together are located not on the horizontal plane of diegesis but rather in the echoes between these deflective metaphors that expand into trope-saturated limbos. These limbos enable Tolstaya to move back and forth temporally and spatially without essentially disturbing, but by suspending, the linear narrative activity in which the tenor of her metaphor is embedded.

Moreover, by expanding or taking far afield the vehicle of her metaphor,[28] Tolstaya achieves two goals: she deflects her readers from the prosaic forward motion, dissuading them from a clear-cut chronology or sequentiality; and through reverberations between her metaphorical structures she is able to provide a sense of coherence (operating largely on a figurative level) that diverts one from the very issue of temporal and spatial markers. In other words, the erection of such a multidirectional framework allows her to move freely along both planes (backward and forward, up and down), while the repetition of motifs from those structures of metaphor, judiciously implanted at intervals, establishes a verbal rhythm that creates the illusion of unity. What we have, in a sense, is subversion regularized. An invaluable benefit of such a staggeringly daring disregard for conventional narrative practices is the reader's conviction that s/he has witnessed the key moments, or been privy to the primary aspects, of a given character's life and can deduce the rest—that is, the reader responds appropriately to the metonymy of a life exposed largely in metaphorical terms. By exploding a standard unfolding of time and space, Tolstaya abstracts the enormous gaps in the narrative of that biography and merely provides several highly charged details from which to extrapolate and fill in the spaces. Since intensity of impact must compensate for lack of comprehensiveness, those details incline toward dramatic contrast, establishing either poles between which our input may function or a concentration of one or two traits that we may generalize into a recognizable type. That is why some Tolstayan portraits, for example, in "Sonia," "Peters," "Most Beloved," "Fire and Dust," and "Sweet Shura," smack of caricature if divorced from the metaphors where the revelatory nuances reside.

Of all Tolstayan texts, "Okkervil River" explores that technique most thoroughly, but it also affects narrated and narrative temporality in such metaphor-laden stories as "Rendezvous with a Bird," "Fire and Dust," "The Circle," "Night," and "Sleepwalker in a Fog," where the rhythm is regulated by metonymical implantation at various junctures of an overarching metaphor that intimates a miraculous or transcendent world. Although elaborated on a more modest scale, the lost continent of Atlantis ("Rendezvous with a Bird"), the lure of sirens on distant shores ("Fire and Dust"), the voyage ("The Circle"), the mysterious dark night ("Night"), and fog

("Sleepwalker in a Fog") fulfill a function parallel to that of the river in "Okkervil River." In all instances, the rhythmic undulation of motifs from these time-free metaphors serves to disperse time, thereby facilitating quintessentially Tolstayan temporal leaps and transfers that resist measurement.

Objects and Memory

As several commentators have noted, Tolstaya's stories teem with objects crowded densely into rooms, thoughts, and paragraphs. The vivid, indeed, aggressive presence of examples from every conceivable category of material phenomena (furniture, cutlery, flora and fauna, clothing, printed matter, etc.) asserts itself frequently through colorful, extended metaphors or personifications that transmute inert matter into living beings: fruits and cheeses sleep, dresses tuck up their knees, bathing suits squint in anticipation, a sewing box sleeps belly-up with paws in the air, and so on. Objects in Tolstaya's fictional universe fulfill three functions that, generally speaking, cannot be divorced from the inner lives of her characters. In that sense they corroborate Kant's notion of time as the form of our "inner" and space as the form of our "outer" experience, and the inescapably symbiotic nature of their intersection, which Bakhtin's concept of the chronotope presupposes.

If one divides Tolstaya's cast of characters rather crudely, as some critics have done, into two contrasting groups—of idealists or spiritual beings, on the one hand, and pragmatists, on the other, one sees that the latter, such as Rimma in "Fire and Dust" and Maria Maksimovna in "Sweet Dreams, Son," tend to overvalue material possessions, dream of additional acquisitions, and, within the narrative, appear framed in object-packed settings. At their simplest, these objects exteriorize internal hierarchies—they straightforwardly attest to the characters' subordination of spiritual values to material comfort.

Apart from serving as an index of a character's acquisitiveness, objects also function as trappings reflecting characters' tastes, powers of self-presentation, or assumptions about social status. Thus in the story "Fakir" Filin's talent for conjuring up delicious food served in exquisite dishes amidst elegant surroundings haloes him with an aura of refinement and uniqueness, even though he objectifies his guests by assimilating them into his artistically arranged backdrop. Since the fraudulent social status implied by the specifics of his mise-en-scène has extraordinary significance for him, for his current amour Alisa, and above all for the recording center of consciousness, Galia, the concrete items reveal the psychological frailties of all three.

From a contemporary standpoint, however, these are rather tired techniques, enervated by regular deployment in nineteenth- and twentieth-century fiction (e.g., Dickens, Balzac, Flaubert, La Fontaine, James, Trifonov). More original and complex is Tolstaya's third use of objects: as a means of extending the temporal framework of her narratives and situating that extension in a moral context. Tolstaya's device of linking objects with human history, memory, and conscience plays a crucial part in her strategy of temporal displacement.

Pushkin, as we know, had a penchant for studding his works, and particularly his narrative poems, with lists (e.g., *Ruslan and Liudmila, Eugene Onegin, Poltava, Count Nulin*), and in this regard Tolstaya may be considered his true, if profligate, descendant. Story after Tolstayan story swells entire paragraphs with inventories of objects that, tellingly, tend to be heaped in an attic (e.g., " 'On the Golden Porch' "), a bazaar, or a market ("Loves Me—Loves Me Not," "The Circle," "Sweet Dreams, Son"), and thus have a past, a history of previous ownership that documents human experience. Objects embedded in such eloquent contexts become so thoroughly integrated into their owners' lives as to appear inseparable from them. Although Tolstaya most frequently presents those items as fallen into desuetude, after they have been wrenched from the original context that conferred meaning upon them,[29] the articles, when recontextualized, acquire what we normally consider human qualities—consciousness, emotions, and the like. Metonymically they preserve, if only *in potentia* (for those insignias must be acknowledged for the preservation to become actualized), aspects of the lives they formerly inhabited. This susceptibility of objects to participation in human life may be seen in "Loves Me—Loves Me Not," for instance, where the five-year-old protagonist says of the lampshade that she and her father purchase at the flea market:

> The lampshade is young and skittish, it isn't used to me yet [. . . .] Papa has the lampshade, still dark and silent, but already a member of the family; it's ours now, one of us, we'll come to love it. And it waited quietly: where was it being taken? It didn't know that time would pass and it, once the favorite, would be mocked, cast down, discarded, exiled, and a new favorite would take its place: a fashionable white five-petaled "shorty." And then, insulted, mutilated, betrayed, it would go through the last mortification: it would serve as a crinoline in a children's play and then plunge forever into wastebin oblivion. *Sic transit gloria mundi.* (9)

> Abazhur molodoi, puglivyi, on ko mne eshche ne privyk [. . . .] Papa [idet] s abazhurom, eshche temnym, molchalivym, no uzhe priniatym v sem'iu: teper' on nash, on svoi, my evo poliubim. I on zamer, zhdet: kuda-to ego nesut? On eshche ne znaet, chto proidet vremia—i on, nekogda liubimyi, budet osmeian, nizvergnut, sorvan, soslan, a na ego mesto s likovaniem vzletit novaia favoritka: modnaia belaia piati-lopastnaia raskoriaka. A potom, obizhennyi, izurodovannyi, predannyi, on

perezhivet poslednee glumlenie: posluzhit krinolinom v detskom spektakle i navsegda kanet v pomoechnoe nebytie. *Sic transit gloria mundi.* (8)[30]

In this anthropomorphized image, the item's projected history (Genette's prolepsis) approximates human fate, as the case of the governess Marivanna in "Loves Me—Loves Me Not" and stories like "Sweet Shura" and "Sleepwalker in a Fog" illustrate: in advanced age those who formerly held center stage in the human drama become relegated to the proproom and forgotten. For the material world, to which humankind at least partly belongs, is selectively subject to the forces of time—to mutability, dissolution, and, ultimately, oblivion. Yet, as the narrator in "Most Beloved" comments,

> Time's meat grinder readily destroys big, solid, cumbersome objects—cabinets, pianos, people—while all manner of fragile odds and ends that appeared on God's earth to gibes and raised eyebrows—all those little porcelain dogs, miniature cups, miniscule vases, rings, drawings, snapshots, boxes, notes, knickknacks, thingamajigs, and whatchamacallits—pass through unscathed. (98)

> Miasorubka vremeni okhotno sukrushaet krupnye, gromozdkie, plotnye predmety—shkafy, roiali, liudei,—a vsiakaia khrupkaia meloch', kotoraia i na bozhii-to svet poiavilas', soprovozhdaemaia nasmeshkami i prishchurom glaz, vse eti farforovye sobachki, chashechki, vazochki, kolechki, risunochki, fotokartochki, korobochki, zapisochki, fintifliushki, pupunchiki i mumunchiki—prokhodiat cherez nee netronutymi. (97)[31]

Typically for Tolstaya, the tiny, ostensibly insignificant item preserved from the past can prove most revelatory if invested with human experience and can kindle our memory not only of bygone days but also of those beings whose lives overlapped, however briefly, with our own. Recent scholarship on rubbish (*sic*) has arrived at a number of conclusions relevant to Tolstaya's memorializing proclivities. In his essay entitled "Rubbish Theory," Jonathan Culler rightly maintains that relics and representations that have no use value "or any value in an economic system of exchange" have the "signifying function of a marker [in Tolstaya's case, a life]," and while "its very inferiority to what it marks makes it rubbish," we firmly believe that "if we throw out this junk we are being disrespectful to the past it memorializes, as though our discarding decreed that it was not authentic." It is precisely the "transient" (Tolstaya's "khrupkaia meloch' ") degraded to rubbish that "has a chance of being discovered and suddenly transformed into a durable"[32]—the various photographs, old letters, and hideous little knickknacks in which Tolstaya's stories abound.

In the era of glasnost, remembering acquired the dimension of a national cause, as Soviets strived to recuperate previously unacknowledged or inaccessible portions of their history. Even before glasnost, however, such chroniclers as Solzhenitsyn valorized memory for enabling the holy mission of preserving historical truth.[33] Writers as dissimilar as Varlam Shalamov, Nadezhda Mandelshtam, and Lidiia Chukovskaia likewise have struggled to immortalize a record of human experience that they fear will otherwise escape human memory. Uninitiated into the deconstructionist skepticism of the new historicism, Russians unanimously assume that an "objective" history lies waiting to be reclaimed and shared on a national scale. Little though Tolstaya has in common with these writers, her preoccupation with time's passage and particularly its effect on perception and memory has led at least one critic to conclude: "Time *is* T. Tolstaya's chief heroine. It is what makes us pay attention to old age, old women, old letters, old records, forgotten feelings" ("Vremia i est' glavnaia geroinia T. Tolstoi. Ona odariaet vnimaniem starost', starykh zhenshchin, starye pis'ma, starye plastinki, zabytye chuvstva" [Shishkova, 399]).[34] Time in Tolstaya's universe yields somewhat less readily to repossession than in Proust, either involuntarily or through conscious effort. Recollection inevitably entails subjectivity and stresses loss, for the interdependence of a specific moment in time with a given human perspective and set of circumstances makes it impossible for either to be regained completely,[35] as Heraclitus's famous maxim "You cannot step into the same river twice" asserts and as the narrator in " 'On the Golden Porch' " discovers when she returns to the attic housing the mysterious objects that enthralled her in childhood:

> So that's it, this is what enchanted us? All this secondhand rubbish, these chipped painted night tables, crude oil paintings, lopsided plant stands, worn plush velvet, darned lace, clumsy fakes from the peasant market, cheap beads? And this sang and glittered, burned, and beckoned? What mean jokes you play, life! Dust, ashes, rot. Surfacing from the magical seabed of childhood [. . .] , what have we brought up with us besides sand? But, just as a quarter of a century ago, Uncle Pasha winds the golden clock with trembling hands. Above the clockface, in the glass room, the little inhabitants huddle—the Lady and the Chevalier, masters of Time. (49)

> Chto zhe, vse eto i bylo tem, pleniavshim? Vsia eta vetosh' i rukhliad', obsharpannye krashenye komodki, topornye kleenchatye kartinki, kolchenogie zhardin'erki, vytertyi pliush, shtopannyi tiul', rynochnye koriavye podelki, deshevye stekliashki? I eto pelo i perelivalos', gorelo i zvalo? Kak glupo ty shutish', zhizn'! Pyl', prakh, tlen. Vynurnuv s volshebnogo dna detstva [. . .] , chto, krome gorsti syrogo peska, unesli

my s soboi? No, slovno chetvert' veka nazad, drozhashchimi rukami diadia Pasha zavodit zolotye chasy. Nad tsiferblatom, v stekliannoi komnatke, s''ezhilis' malen'kie zhiteli—Dama i Kavaler, khoziaeva Vremeni. (47–48)

Yet articles such as those inventoried above stimulate memory (however approximate) or speculation (however inaccurate) about times past and become potential links in the endless chain of human existence. "Le présent," as Leibniz observed, "est chargé du passé, et gros de l'avenir."[36] In the specific example just cited, the seemingly random bric-à-brac, not unlike a grave marker, which, while registering death, brings memories to life, raises to the surface the luminous image of Uncle Pasha sedimented in the narrator's psyche.

Especially objects manifestly associated with temporal continuity, and appearing singly rather than as entries in a catalogue, filter the past into Tolstaya's present. Photographs, portraits, old letters, and poems enable Tolstaya's personae to regain and retain memories of bygone days. Worn snapshots in "Sweet Shura," "Most Beloved," " 'On the Golden Porch' "; portraits of now-dead relatives in "Peters" and "Sweet Dreams, Son"; correspondence yellowed with age in "Sonia" and "Sweet Shura"; and poems (composed by authentic and would-be poets now dead) in "Loves Me— Loves Me Not" and "The Circle" all insinuate the past into the present. These visual and verbal *memento mori* not only activate memory but in a sense resuscitate the dead, whose participation is enlisted in the narrative's present through two favorite Tolstayan devices that dissolve temporal and spatial boundaries. A passage from "Sweet Shura" offers a superb instance of Tolstaya's technique. During the narrator's visit to the story's eponymous octogenarian protagonist (surrounded, significantly, by "bric-à-brac, oval frames, dried flowers" [31]/"bezdelushki, oval'nye ramki, sukhie tsvety" [30]), in the midst of the latter's excursus into the past, the narrator discerns a young version of the old woman in the photographs on the wall. Instead of referring to the photographs, Tolstaya bypasses mention of mediating representation so as to evoke the young Shura's presence in the room directly: "on the peeling wallpaper smiles, muses, and pouts a charming beauty—sweet Shura, Aleksandrovna Ernestovna. Yes, yes, that's me! In a hat, and without a hat" (32) ("na otstavshikh oboiakh ulybaetsia, zadumyvaetsia, kapriznichaet upoitel'naia krasavitsa—milaia Shura, Aleksandra Ernestovna. Da, da, eto ia! I v shliape, i bez shliapy" [30]). Since no formal punctuation marks set off the old Shura's confirmation of her younger identity, the two merge and, moreover, ease the transition to talk of Ivan Nikolaevich, her lover of sixty years ago, whose image, like Shura's, remains intact: "he's crammed into the album, spread-eagled in four slits in the cardboard, squashed by a lady in a bustle, crushed by some short-lived white lapdogs that died before the Russo-Japanese War" (32) ("on stisnut v al'bome, raspialen v chetyrekh kartonnykh proreziakh, prikhlopnut damoi v turnire, zadavlen kakimi-to nedolgovechnymi belymi sobachkami, podokhshimi eshche do iaponskoi voiny" [30]). Because Aleksandra Ernestova's memories of Ivan Nikolaevich and her ancient decision not to run away with him have not diminished in relevance or vitality over six decades, and, with the aid of photographs, become shared by the narrator in the present, Tolstaya re-creates the moment of decision also in the present, oscillating unobtrusively not only between external and internal discourse but also, as one can in Russian, between past tense and the dramatic present:

> She's made up her mind. Here he is—right next to you—just reach out! Here, take him in your hands, hold him, here he is, flat, cold, shiny, with a gold border, slightly yellowed: Ivan Nikolaevich! Hey, you hear?— she's decided, yes, she's coming, meet her, she's stopped hesitating, she's made up her mind, hey, where are you, yoo-hoo! (37)

> Da ona uzhe reshilas'. Vot on—riadom,—ruku protiani! Vot, voz'mi ego v ruki, derzhi, vot on, ploskii, kholodnyi, gliantsevyi, s zolotym obrezom, chut' pozheltevshii Ivan Nikolaevich! Ei, vy slyshite, ona reshilas', da, ona edet, vstrechaite, vse, ona bol'she ne kolebletsia, vstrechaite, gde vy, au! (35)

Here, Ivan Nikolaevich, like Shura, exists concurrently in several forms and dimensions: as young in the photograph that, however, shows signs of age; as alive to hear the news, but actually dead; and, finally, as revealing his thoughts and speaking to those holding his photograph, who are nevertheless fully aware that he no longer exists. The same devices of moving freely and unpredictably between past, present, and future tenses so as to efface all temporal distinctions; and of handling representational media like portraits, photographs, letters, and poems as though they were the actual subjects of representation, so as to resuscitate the subject temporarily— these devices are applied to the grandfather in "Peters," the father-in-law in "Sweet Dreams, Son," Izolda in "The Circle," and other figures from the past who play such prominent parts in Tolstaya's fiction.

To grasp the exact time of events, comments, or thoughts in Tolstaya's stories is often impossible because temporal distinctions collapse when the past seeps into the present, feeding and infusing it with a prior perspective. With time reconstituted through recollection and absorbed into the narrative present with the aid of animated metonymical objects, the text keeps the dead narratively alive. These metonyms[37] are enlisted in the service of a moral imperative in Tolstaya's universe: to discover and preserve the significance of an individual life through memory. According to Tolstaya, a life may be evaluated only posthumously, a conviction that dovetails with Walter Benjamin's argument for the retrospectivity of narrative in general: "Death is the sanction of everything that the storyteller can tell" (94). Because a retrospective vantage point is a prerequisite for the appreciation of a given individual's contribution to the total sum of human existence, anyone concerned with values must necessarily keep looking back, engaging in the complex ideational process of recognition, identification, and appraisal.[38] Hence the salient role in Tolstaya's fiction of the "creative and constructive" process that we call memory (Cassirer, 74), and the proliferation of dreams (both waking and sleeping) in which the past surfaces to confront and invade the present. The process explodes what Paul Ricoeur, following Nietzsche, calls monumental time (*Time and Narrative*, II, 106), the claims of which Tolstaya recognizes but subordinates to the nuanced complexities of "soul" time.

The Tolstayan story that most passionately articulates the urge to remember is "Sleepwalker in a Fog."[39] There that impulse manifests itself through two highly dissimilar characters: the middle-aged protagonist Denisov, whose subjective point of view dominates throughout, and his fiancée Lora's father, Vasilii Vasilevich, whose nocturnal antics identify him literally with the story's title. Both try to make sense of the world and its order—Denisov spatially by altering the disposition of oceans and continents on the map in his room, the retired old zoologist taxonomically, by summarizing in the simplest terms possible (i.e., for children) the defining features of various animals and the seasons. Both are troubled by memory. The older man during his sleepwalking rampages through the apartment incessantly repeats, "I knew, but I forgot" (33) ("Ia znal, no zabyl" [22]). While Tolstaya keeps pregnantly imprecise the object of his forgetfulness, clearly his memory has lost hold of something from the past. By contrast, Denisov's lapse in memory is fully and painfully clarified within the larger framework of his obsession with immortality.

From the very opening, Denisov's personal anxiety supplies the key to the story's universal concern that human destiny may be reduced to an impermanence synonymous with nonexistence: "dying and being forgotten, being erased from human memory, dissolving in the air without a trace" (5) ("umeret' i byt' zabytym, steret'sia iz liudskoi pamiati, bessledno rasseiat'sia v vozdukhe" [9]). In the course of the narrative, Denisov's thirst to be perpetually acknowledged after death as a significant individual instance in the continuum of humanity ("he dreams [. . .] of fame, memory, immortality" [9]/"mechtaet [. . .] o slave, o pamiati, o bessmertii" [10]) develops into an awareness that the dead in general deserve some affirmation of their existence from the living. That realization is triggered in a revelatory dream in which three figures appear before Denisov, presumably during the time of the blockade, demanding that he give them some of the bread he has just bought. His selfish reluctance to do so, within the dream, leads him, upon wakening, to lacerating self-justification that retraces his steps to a period thirty-five years earlier (in which, so to speak, the dream comes true). During those grim years, his aunt Rita, whom he recognizes as one of his three dream phantoms, perished in the blockade. Characteristically for Tolstaya's fiction, Rita, then a young woman on the verge of marrying, left behind a concrete object as a *memento mori*—a powder compact that the boy Denisov exchanged for a penknife, causing his mother to beat him and burst into tears.[40] The remaining two-thirds of the story is a pilgrimage of penance, tracing Denisov's frantic efforts to salve his conscience and compensate for having forgotten and thus, in a sense, betrayed his aunt. His conscience-stricken enterprise assumes the form of a ludicrous substitution. Appointing himself the "emissary of the dead" ("poslanets mertvykh"), he resolves to immortalize an unremarkable schoolmate of Lora's called Makov, who froze in the mountains during an expedition. No one, including Makov's family, harbors any enthusiasm for Denisov's cause, which degenerates into a Marx Brothers farce as he agitates to obtain a wardrobe for Makov's sister, ostensibly as a gesture of respect for the dear departed.

Denisov's efforts, like all his pangs of impotent sympathy for human sufferers, come to naught. For he, along with the rest of Tolstaya's Strindbergian cast living under the metaphor of the story's title, represents modern humanity: roaming in a fog of metaphysical uncertainty, groping for clues that will shed light on the meaning and goal of life. These spiritually dispossessed include Denisov, the seeker who queries, "What will remain of us?" (23) ("Chto ostanetsia ot nas?" [17]) and desperately insists that a life should leave behind traces that will have meaning for others; Rita, the narrative's representative of the dead, who, according to Denisov's subjective surmise, yearns to have her existence actively incorporated into the general fund of human experience, "otherwise why infiltrate our dreams, reach out your hand, ask for alms—bread, or, perhaps, simply memory?" (22) ("inache zachem pronikat' v nashi sny, protiagivat' ruku, prosit' podaianiia—khleba, ili, mozhet byt', prosto pamiati?" [17]); the enigmatic naval captain who occupies the apartment above him and plays out his fantasies by floating paper boats in the tub that overflows into Denisov's apartment, before the "men in white" take him away; Lora, who

> also wanders haphazardly, arms outstretched, groping at ledges and fissures, tripping in the fog; she shudders and twitches in her sleep, reaches for

will-o'-the wisps, her graceless fingers grasp at the reflection of candles;
she grabs ripples on the water's surface, lunges after smoke shadows
(18);

tozhe bredet naugad, vytianuv ruki, obsharivaia vystupy i rasseliny,
spotykaias' v tumane, ona vzdragivaet i ezhitsia vo sne, ona tianetsia k
bluzhdaiushchim ogniam, lovit pal'chikami otrazheniia svechei, khvataet
krugi na vode, brosaetsia za ten'iu dyma (14–15);

and Lora's widowed father, who stumbles about in his daughter's apartment, seeking to retrieve what he has forgotten. At the story's ambiguous,
open-ended conclusion, he breaks free of his customary pattern to run out
into the dark unknown of the night:

The sleepwalker is running along impassable paths, eyelids closed, arms
outstretched, a quiet smile on his lips, as though he sees what the seeing
cannot, as though he knows what they have forgotten, as though at night
he grasps what is lost during the day. He runs along the dewy grass,
through patches of moonlight and deep black shadows [. . .] .
   Surely he'll reach the light? (43)

Somnambula bezhit po bezdorozh'iu, smezhiv vezhdy, vytianuv ruki, s
tikhoi ulybkoi, slovno znaet to, chto oni zabyli, lovit noch'iu to, chto
poteriano dnem. On bezhit po rosistoi trave, po lunnym piatnam i
chernym teniam [. . .] .
   Neuzheli on ne dobezhit do sveta? (26)

The moral imperative of memory as a safeguard to continuity and preservation of culture accounts for the regular excursions into the past found in
Tolstaya's works. These internal retrogressive journeys across diverse strata or
categories of time represent attempts to recuperate not only past experiences
but also the epistemological stance that enabled them. For in Tolstaya, as in
Bergson, memories interlace perceptions and, conversely, become actual by
being embodied in some perception. That convergence accounts for the "subjectivity" of perceptual images (objects perceived). Thus objects potentially
afford their perceivers the opportunity to recover, however imperfectly, former
viewpoints, that is, times past, and to integrate them into the present. That
insight is inscribed in Tolstaya's own texts, for the dense intertextuality of her
prose and its temporal diffusions stylistically convey the enrichment vouchsafed by keeping alive those cultural practices to which a vigilant memory
and a receptive imagination offer access.

Tolstayan Tropes:
Perils, Pleasures, and Epiphanies

*What is called "rhetorical," as the devices of a conscious art, is
present as a device of unconscious art in language and its
development. [. . .] No such thing as unrhetorical, "natural"
language exists that could be used as a point of reference:
language is itself the result of purely rhetorical tricks and
devices.*

Friedrich Nietzsche, *Course Notes*

The last two decades' fundamental revision in critical and theoretical
assumptions, stimulated partially by deconstructionist forces, invites a
reassessment of the traditional, though by no means unproblematic and
clear-cut, distinction between poetics and rhetoric.[1] Whereas poetics,
mainly through its ostensibly elevated teleology (the service of Art), early
established itself as the aloof aristocrat of verbal theory and praxis, rhetoric,
as "the art of using language for persuasion" (Cuddon), has, in the twentieth
century, struggled for recognition on the fringes of respectability, less of a
kissing cousin to poetics than its illegitimate sibling—a declassé pragmatist.
In ancient Greece and Rome, where rhetoric's concern with ethics[2] lent it
greater esteem than it has since commanded, only a minority (notably Plato)
denigrated rhetoric as a sham art that could have no true subject matter,
given its exclusive preoccupation with appearance or illusion (i.e., decep-
tion) instead of truth.[3] Aristotle, who conceptualized the fields of poetics
and rhetoric, saw no contradiction between rhetoric's practical aspects and
its concurrent status as an art—a status defined by its capacity to be organized according to a system. Indeed, he institutionalized rhetoric from the
standpoint of philosophy.[4] Determining whether the disappearance of rhetoric

as a discrete discipline in the nineteenth century resulted from or, on the contrary, led to the degeneration in rhetoric's reputation requires a separate and detailed study. Paul de Man, who ascribes the preceding century's devaluation of traditional rhetorical forms to the advent of a subjectivistic critical vocabulary, has noted and promoted the recent revival of rhetoric, not as the normative or descriptive but as the pervasive condition of language, critical to the issue of intentionality.[5] No one would deny, however, that whereas poetics has consistently maintained its lofty perch in this century, rhetoric has yet to recover fully from its loss of prestige within the scholarly community. Perhaps common parlance best illustrates the valorizing implications of the two rubrics for the (hypothetical?) average reader or speaker in modern times: whereas the reaction, "That's just rhetoric!" suffices to dismiss a statement as pyrotechnics without substance, the potentially analogous observation, "That's just poetics!" is more likely to flatter and certainly to bemuse the addressee. Moreover, since the word "poetics" registers the phenomenon's proper sphere of address as the genre of poetry, its modern extension breeds such oxymoronic formulations as "the poetics of prose" or such neologisms as Saul Morson's Bakhtin-inspired "prosaics."

Commentators have characterized the "poetic prose" of Rimbaud, Joyce, and Woolf as prose that "approximates to verse in the use of rhythm, perhaps even a kind of meter [. . .] , in the elaborate and ornate use of language, and especially in the use of figurative devices like onomatopoeia, assonance and metaphor" (Cuddon, 520). In Russia, somewhat less contentiously labeled "ornamental prose,"[6] it has been associated with the morganatic authorial practices of Gogol, Bely, Remizov, Babel, Sokolov, and Tolstaya. Benefiting from the partial rehabilitation of rhetoric by I.A. Richards, Kenneth Burke, Wayne Booth, and de Man,[7] I treat those features often called poetic as rhetorical devices conflating insight with their own mediated brand of persuasion.[8] In accord with Burke's conviction that "the notion of persuasion to *attitude* would permit the application of rhetorical terms to purely poetic structures" (Burke, 50), my usage categorically rejects the Platonic and populist view of rhetorical devices as cosmetic or culinary—the Estée Lauder or Julia Child of discourse.

Tolstaya's Rhetorical Devices

Tolstaya's prodigal reliance on rhetorical devices that the vast majority of prosaists invoke sparingly seems, indeed, not only to legitimate but to encourage a critical approach to her fiction that formerly was reserved for readings of verse. In fact, Tolstaya isolates the capacity of modern prose to assimilate forms and devices typical of poetry as its single most distinctive feature. No one familiar with her prose will be surprised to learn that listening to the music of Mozart and Bach quickens her impulse to write, for to varying degrees, her own twenty-one stories exploit the full panoply of auditory devices: alliteration, assonance, onomatopoeia, anaphora, rhyme, and rhythm. Moreover, Tolstaya has a penchant for lavishly combining several of these effects, as in the following passage taken randomly from "The Moon Came Out" ("Vyshel mesiats iz tumana"), which, if rearranged on the page, instantly reveals its susceptibility to poetic scansion:

I nado vsem v vyshine	-/--'/--'
prostiralsia mir vzroslykh—	--'/-'/'-
shumiashchikh, gudiashchikh	-'-/-'-
vysoko vverkhu, kak sosny	--'/-'/-'-
v nenast'e. (33)	-'-

The alliteration of v-s-z, plus the internal rhyme of "prostiralsia/mir," "shumiashchikh/gudiashchikh," the approximate rhyme of "gudiashchikh/nenast'e," and the rustling suggested by the onomatopoeic "sosny v nenast'e" instantly engage the reader's sensual responses and urge deceleration. Just a few paragraphs later, Tolstaya orchestrates a comparable passage:

A zemlia chernaia, plotnaia	--'/'--/'--
a trava syraia, gustaia,	--'/-'-/-'-
i pod kazhdym kustom	--'/--'
tverdym kuskom	'/--'
lezhit lilovaia ten'.	-'/-'/--'
Syro, gusto, tenisto,	'/-'-/-'-
Sad zapushchen. (34)	'/-'-

The approximate or full rhyme of the epithets "chernaia/plotnaia," "syraia/gustaia," of the nouns "kustom/kuskom," and of the truncated and predicative adjectives "gusto/zapushchen" fortifies the rhythm of the unit, which brims with sibilants. On a smaller scale, both rhythm and alliteration within shorter sentences impart emotional coloration to such summative, loaded statements as, for example, the ominous "The sky was silent, the earth died" (55) ("Nebo molchalo, zemlia umerla" ['/--'/--'/--'] [34]) or "The black skulls of electric meters huddled together" (59) ("Sbilis' v kuchu chernye cherepa elektricheskikh schetchikov" [34]), where through auditory means Tolstaya forces the reader to pause and pay special attention to emblems of doom.

Within the same story, anaphora likewise creates rhythmic patterns, while simultaneously accentuating the psychologized details of a stunted, lonely life: "*beyond* the speckled blue casserole, *beyond* the heavy smell of fermentation, *beyond* the tearstained glass, another person's wall darkens and swells with autumnal anguish" (61, emphases added) ("za sinei riabovatoi kastriul'koi, za tiazhelym dukhom kvashen'ia, za zaplakannym steklom temneet i nabukhaet osennei toskoi chuzhaia stena" [35]). Numerous instances of anaphora in the interests of emphasis and accretion, on the one hand, and of regulated pacing, on the other, occur in "The Circle" ("Krug" [R66, E69]), "Fire and Dust" ("Ogon' i pyl' " [R97, E102]), "Peters" (R169, E181), "Sleepwalker in a Fog" ("Somnambula v tumane" [R9, E5]), " 'On the Golden Porch' " (" 'Na zolotom kryl'tse sideli . . . ' " [R45, E47]), "Most Beloved" ("Samaia liubimaia" [R108, E114]), and others. Frequently, syntactic parallelism strengthens the rhythm produced by such repetitions.

Auditory effects of this kind operate in tandem with devices encountered only occasionally in prose. Each Tolstayan text comprises a dense network of *accumulatio*, hyperbole, irony, paradox, maxims, zeugma, oxymoron, periphrasis, apostrophe, rhetorical questions, personification, synecdoche, metonymy, and so on. To cite but a few vivid, representative examples:[9] "Grisha—custodian, poet, genius, saint!"/"Grisha, dvornik, poet, genii, sviatoi!"—Derzhavin-like *gradatio* in "The Poet and the Muse" (120/116); "To shout to her through the years and misfortunes"/"Kriknut' ei cherez gody i nevzgody"—zeugma plus internal rhyme in "Okkervil River" (24/23); "What are you, life?"/"Chto zhe ty takoe, zhizn'?"—apostrophe, rhetorical question, and personification in "Peters" (195/184); "oblivion blossoms everywhere"/"i vse zatsvetaet zabveniem"—oxymoron/paradox in "Most Beloved" (110/105); "And the disappointed Izolda wandered on [. . .] past the galoshes and plywood crates, past the tattered magazines and wire brooms, past the drunkard [. . .] , past the young fellow [. . .] , past and past"/"I bredet razocharovannaia Izol'da proch' [. . .] mimo galosh i fanernykh iashchikov, mimo zamusolennykh zhurnalov i provolochnykh mochalok, mimo p'ianitsy [. . .] , mimo parnia [. . .] , mimo i mimo"—anaphora in "The Circle" (69/66); "the moonlit, lilac scent of the divine music"/"lunnyi, sirenevyi aromat bozhestvennoi muzyki"—synesthesia in " 'On the Golden Porch' " (47/46); "they [. . .] proceeded to the table, where the hothouse roses know nothing of any frost"/"oni [. . .] proshestvuiut k stolu, gde razmorennye rozy znat' ne znaiut ni o kakom moroze"—assonance with partial rhyme in "Fakir" (160/151); "it would even have been quite a nice-looking face if it hadn't taken forever to get from the nose to the upper lip"/"dazhe vpolne milovidnoe bylo by litso, esli by ot nosa do verkhnei guby ne nado bylo ekhat' tri goda"—grotesque hyperbole in "Most Beloved" (97/96); and finally, "A sickeningly beautiful woman with tragically undisciplined hair was wringing her hands over the dying man"/"Nad umiraiushchim zalamyvala ruki omerzitel'no krasivaia zhenshchina s tragicheski raspushchennymi volosami"—oxymoron in "The Poet and the Muse" (120/114).

Accumulatio especially appeals to Tolstaya as an opportunity for both verbal virtuosity and succinctness. She unfurls catalogues, full of Leporello-like panache, to convey plenitude, chaos, or claustrophobia, depending on the context. Usually interpolated in descriptions of rooms, bazaars, attics, and other repositories of physical objects aggregated over time, *accumulatio* enables Tolstaya to capture in one laden sentence an immediacy, a vivid sense of subjectively perceived place or atmosphere. For instance, in "Loves Me—Loves Me Not," the little girl's excitement at the hubbub of the flea-market stalls, with their seemingly limitless piles of enticing items, finds economic expression in a series of verbs and nouns:

> And they all gabbled and bustled, and shook blue diagonal remnants in front of Papa's face, and shoved sturdy black felt boots under his nose. [. . .] He should have bought up everything: vases and saucers and flowered scarves, stuffed owls and porcelain pigs and rag rugs! We could have used the pussycat banks, and whistles and paper flowers—poppies with inked cotton in their centers—and paper fans, red and green trembling jabots on two sticks. (8)

> I vse oni gorlanili, i suetilis', i triasli pered papinym litsom sinimi diagonalevymi otrezami, i sovali v nos krepkie chernye valenki. [. . .] nado bylo na kupit' vsego-vsego: i vazochek, i bliudechek, i tsvetastykh platkov, i sovinykh chuchel, i farforovykh svinei, i lentochnykh kovrikov! Prigodilis' by i koshki-kopilki, i dudelki, i sviristelki, i bumazhnye tsvety—maki s chernil'nymi vatkami v serdtsevinkakh, i bumazhnye krasno-zelenye drozhashchie zhabo na dvukh palochkakh. (7)

The polysyndeton intensifies the impression of breathless multiplication, of additions that potentially stretch into infinity.

Elsewhere, by blending zeugma with *accumulatio* that proceeds through asyndeton, Tolstaya implies an undifferentiated perception of phenomena, more often than not colored by a psychological state ranging from revulsion or paranoia, at the one extreme, to wonder or bliss, at the other:[10]

> with a light rattle, the trolleys, books, processed cheeses, wet sidewalks, bird calls, Tamaras, cups, nameless women, passing years, and the perishables of the world fell away in all directions. (24)

> melkim grokhotom posypalis' v raznye storony tramvai, knigi, plavlennye syrki, mokrye mostovye, ptich'i kriki, Tamary, chashki, bezymennye zhenshchiny, ukhodiashchie goda, vsia brennost' mira. (23)

Or, as in the inventory of various plague-carrying rats and other rodents against which Pal Antonych waged his heroic battle in "Sweet Dreams, Son," Tolstaya injects irony through double-voicing:

Domestic, attic, ship, sewer, migrant, and field [rats]. Moreover, all those innocent-looking bunnies, gophers, even little mice . . . Gerbils, hamsters, moles! (137)

Domashnie, cherdachnye, korabel'nye, kanalizatsionnye, brodiachie, polevye. Bol'she togo, vse eti s vidu nevinnye zaichiki, susliki, dazhe malen'kie myshki . . . Tushkanchiki, khor'ki, zemleroiki! (130)

Not only the double-voicing and the unwarranted, tongue-in-cheek taxonomical breakdown into genus and species, but the rhyming diminutives that cap off the list undercut Maria Maksimovna's hyperbolic claims, exposing their absurdity. Whatever their specific function within the immediate context of a given narrative, the items and actions that Tolstaya packs into a single sentence or paragraph transmit the materiality of existence, the obtrusiveness of things, and the physicality of gesture.

One of the few rhetorical devices Tolstaya rarely enlists is the simile, encountered no more than thirty to forty times in her entire output. The lyrically retrospective story "Most Beloved" contains by far the highest index of similes, almost a third of the total within her fiction: "she comes [. . .] , in her hand the first bouquet of dill raised like a torch"/"ona idet [. . .] , podniav, kak fakel, pervyi buket ukropa" (92/93); "With both hands, strong as a sailor's, she'll pull [. . .] branches of lilac"/"Ona [. . .] obeimi rukami, sil'no, kak matros, pritianet vetvi sireni" (93/94); "her voice [. . .] like a blissful June day"/"ee golos [. . .] , kak blazhennyi iun'skii den' " (95/95); "Zhenechka's soul was built rather like a smooth pipe"/"Zhenechkina dusha predstavliala soboi podobie gladkoi truby" (97/96); "ladies [. . .] snort like eager fairy-tale stallions"/"damy [. . .] vydykhaiut nozdriami, slovno skazochnye retivye koni" (99/98); "blue ones like a mousse of whisked sky tinged with smoky thunderheads"/"golubovatye, kak vzbityi nebesnyi muss s dymnym otbleskom grozovykh tuch" (108/104); "Zhenechka dreamed of a genuine red rose, pure and deep, like the sound of a cello"/"Zhenechka mechtala o nastoiashchei krasnoi roze, chistoi i glubokoi, kak zvuk violoncheli" (108/104); "the pale, wide russulas that crumbled like shortbread"/"rassypaiushchiesia, kak pesochnoe pechen'e, blednye shirokie syroezhki" (109/104); "a lady with eyebrows black like a fallen angel's"/"dama s broviami chernymi, kak u pavshego angela" (112/107).[11] By and large, however, a simile neither moves quickly or energetically enough for Tolstaya's purposes, nor carries the dramatic transgressive impact she achieves through other, more frugal, means. Presumably that is why the similes she does introduce tend to rely on the instrumental case instead of the additional preposition "like" ("kak" or "slovno").[12] As Paul Ricoeur puts it, "direct attribution causes surprise, whereas simile dissipates the surprise" (*The Rule of Metaphor*, 47). To couch it in Marxist terms, investment in a simile would not yield the surplus value accrued by Tolstaya's favorite figure, the metaphor[13]—that "direct attribution" admired as "the most beautiful of tropes" by Quintilian, who rather fulsomely credited it with accomplishing "the supremely difficult task of providing a name for everything."[14]

Aristotle, who codified the usage of metaphor in both his *Poetics* and his *Rhetoric*, explicitly conceived of the trope as cognitive rather than semantic: "it is a metaphor which most produces knowledge" (*Rhetoric*, Book III).[15] In what is essentially an extension of the Aristotelian notion of metaphor, Richards contends that, although throughout the history of rhetoric metaphor has been regarded as an ornament or "*added* power of language, not its constitutive form," it is, nonetheless, "fundamentally [. . .] a borrowing between and intercourse of *thoughts*, a transaction between contexts. *Thought* is metaphoric, and proceeds by comparison, and the metaphors of language derive therefrom" (Richards, 90, 94). Whether metaphors have cognitive properties or merely semantic value remains a controversial topic among critics and philosophers,[16] who nevertheless tacitly concur that lack of cognitive value would render metaphors inconsequential.[17]

Inevitably, perhaps, literary scholars' disputes over metaphor have been apt to overlook a feature of the trope highlighted by Wendy Steiner in her *Colors of Rhetoric*, a cross-disciplinary study of interartistic tropes, and specifically those bridging literature and painting. Rhetoric in the seventeeth century, Steiner emphasizes, was a means of "presenting knowledge vividly, so as to be experienced in its truth rather than merely referred to." She rightly defines metaphor as the paradigmatic case of the evidentiary devices comprising that rhetoric (141). Ideally, the pictorial dimension of metaphor cooperates with its conceptual aspect to make its "truth" more palpable, more accessible to the senses.

Tolstaya's Metaphors

> *The greatest thing by far is to be a master of metaphor. It is the one thing that cannot be learnt from others; and it is also a sign of genius, since a good metaphor implies an intuitive perception of the similarity in dissimilars.*
>
> Aristotle, *Poetics*

> *Language is vitally metaphorical.*
>
> Shelley, "Defence of Poetry"

As Jonathan Culler has observed, the recent proliferation of conferences and publications on the nature of metaphor attests to its extraordinary current ascendancy.[18] Formerly just one trope among many, it has become the trope of tropes, or, in Culler's words, "a figure for figurality" (*The Pursuit of Signs*, 189). In that regard, Tolstaya's fiction converges with contemporary critical emphases, for not only its major effects but in some instances its capacity to signify are rooted in metaphor. Bold, original, and multifunctional, Tolstaya's metaphors range from implicit, embedded, and nominal to full-fledged and so thoroughly sustained and projected as to verge on allegory. With familiar metaphors that repetition has practically drained of figurality (e.g., the death of nature and the march of time—metaphorically labeled "dead metaphors"),[19] Tolstaya commingles less commonplace substitutions that often engage all the senses, cluster in complex combinations, and develop at startling length. For instance, in "Loves Me—Loves Me Not," a series of interlaced implied metaphors generated by likeness of sound, which encapsulate the sensations of fever, occupy an entire paragraph:

> Many times, 104-degree flus would scream and bang at my ears, pounding on red drums, surrounding me from eight sides and, swirling wildly, project a delirious film, always the same: a wooden honeycomb filling up with three-digit numbers; more numbers, louder noise, more urgent drums—all the cells will be filled now, just a little time left! My heart can't take any more, it'll burst—but it's been postponed, I've been released, forgiven, the honeycomb taken away, a round loaf of bread with a nasty smile runs along an airfield on spindly legs—and it grows quiet . . . except for tiny planes like dots of bugs that scurry along the pink sky, carrying away the black cloak of fever in their claws. It's passed. (7)

> Ne raz i ne dva sorokagradusnye grippy zakrichat, zastuchat v ushi, zab'iut v krasnye barabany, obstupiat s vos'mi storon i, besheno krutia, pokazhut kinofil'm breda, vsegda odin i tot zhe: dereviannye soty zapolniaiutsia trekhznachnymi tsiframi; chisla bol'she, grokhot gromche, barabany toroplivei,—seichas vse iacheiki budut zapolneny, vot ostalos' sovsem nemnogo! vot eshche chut'-chut'! serdtse ne vyderzhit, lopnet,— no otmenili, prostili, soty ubrali, probezhal s nekhoroshei ulybkoi kruglyi khleb na tonkikh nozhkakh po aerodromnonu poliu—i zatikhlo . . . tol'ko samolety bulashechnymi tochkami ubegaiut po rozovomu nebu i unosiat v kogotkakh chernyi plashch likhoradki. Oboshlos'. (7)

The drums, the honeycomb, and the airplanes (linked through the common denominator of a steady hum or buzz) all operate on the auditory level, mutually reinforcing and intensifying each other. Further abetted by the tactile and visual images interwoven with them, they collectively communicate the physical and psychological discomfort, pain, and disorientation of delirium. Tolstaya deploys a similar technique in "Night" to convey how the retarded Aleksei Petrovich perceives the ritual of his mother's dressing. The accretion of individual simple metaphors with a one-to-one correspondence—trumpets, columns, zenith, casing, edifice, rear formations, service stairs, and emergency exits—culminates in the metaphorical encapsulation: "The palace has been erected" (68) ("Dvorets vozdvignut" [95]). This nodal metaphor not only conjoins and constellates the disparate preceding metaphors, thereby modifying them, but also reinforces Aleksei Petrovich's awed sense of his mother's protective strength. Whatever its grotesqueness, her "estranged" bulky body is his fortress against the menacing "labyrinths of the incomprehensible, unnavigable world" (70) ("labirinty neponiatnogo, neprokhodimogo mira" [96]), with rules that lie forever beyond his circumscribed mental grasp. Or, in the story's dominant metaphor, she is the guiding star ("putevodnaia zvezda") illuminating his way through the night that constitutes his inarticulate existence.

Metaphor clusters of this bravura type, which most frequently convey physical appearance, atmosphere, or transitory states, reticulate throughout Tolstaya's fiction, yet are localized. That is, they do not resurface metonymically later in the same narrative. Their scope and burden are more modest than those of Tolstaya's matrix metaphors, which number fewer but predicate the tropological specifics of the text in which they occur. Such subsuming metaphors include the garden in " 'On the Golden Porch,' " the celestial in "Serafim," the ornithological in "Rendezvous with a Bird," the wooly mammoth in "Hunting the Wooly Mammoth," the circle in "The Circle," and rivers in "Okkervil River."[20] These conceptual metaphors not only afford fundamental insights through analogy and substitution, as all proper metaphors must,[21] but simultaneously spawn subsets of related metaphors that perform their function within the framework of the originating master trope. Of all Tolstaya's texts, "Okkervil River" exemplifies the rich revelations attendant upon such multifaceted, elaborated metaphors, even as it potentially questions its own processes.

The matrix metaphor of the river in "Okkervil River" collaborates with metonymy and intertexts to problematize the uncertain and shifting relations both between material and incorporeal and between the stuff of life and its transformation in art (an issue as old as literature itself). That relationship is articulated through three artists: Vera Vasilevna, Simeonov, and Tolstaya—all rehearsed in the historical figure of Peter the Great as city creator. All are implicated in the literary myth of Petersburg/Leningrad—the literal site of the story, but, as in Bitov's *Pushkin House*, also the trope for Russian culture. Immortalized concretely through the capital he founded and metaphorically through Pushkin's *Bronze Horseman*, Peter provides the paradigm for subsequent historical/mythic artists/creators:[22] that is, Vera Vasilevna, the singer captured forever, within the narrative, through the disks recorded for posterity, who extratextually continues the "historically accurate" cultural myth of Anna Akhmatova (AA—VV);[23] Simeonov, who, while amplifying the long line of pen-pushing Evgeniis and Akakii Akakievichs welded to the city's anatomy, at the same time engages in those transforming gestures customarily associated with art; and Tolstaya, who contributes her version to the tradition of city fictions dating at least from Pushkin through Gogol, Dostoevsky, and Bely to, most recently, Bitov (*Pushkin House*). Thus *The Bronze Horseman*, installed as an intertext in the first paragraphs of "Okkervil River," functions as the matrix metaphor for the story's overarching theme and its exemplifications.

Through its unequal adversaries, Pushkin's *poema* raises two related problems equally critical to metaphor, to Simeonov's existential condition, and to Tolstaya's fictional practices: (1) in the figure of Peter, the connection between mental and empirical categories, and (2) in the person of Evgenii, the vexed issue of real versus imagined (e.g., pursuit by Peter's statue). Pushkin's *poema* opens with the unforgettable lines:

> On the shore of the desolate waves
> He stood, full of great thoughts,
> And gazed into the distance.
>
> Na beregu pustynnykh voln,
> Stoial on, dum velikikh poln
> I vdal' gliadel.

"Into the distance" ("Vdal' ") here has temporal as well as spatial connotations, both relevant to anticipated embodiment. One might recall that, according to Kant and common sense, time and space are the two a priori conditions requisite for an experience of being—categories inherent in the transfers or displacements entailed in metaphor. Indeed, some lines and years later, "thought" ("duma") *is* the city of Petersburg in which Pushkin's (and now Tolstaya's modern) antihero nurtures his dreams and fantasies. Mental in *The Bronze Horseman* thus *precedes* empirical along a temporal continuum instead of contrasting with it; tangible phenomena incarnate the visions to which they owe their birth. In other words, through her metaphor/intertext, Tolstaya confers (literary) authority of sorts on the activity of her ironized synthetic protagonist (a conflation of Evgenii and Peter) as he mentally constructs *his* city on the banks of *his* river, having rejected the Okkervil River that actually runs north of the city. To augment that authority, Tolstaya erects in the magical sphere of Simeonov's Okkervil precisely those association-saturated motifs and objects that demonstrably belong to the tangible, nonfictional Leningrad environment—an environment that Tolstaya particularizes minimally apart from the brief introductory passage that opens the story. Her thematic concerns amply motivate the omission: for the waters, bridges, gates, granite embankments, fog, and murky skies familiar to anyone conversant with Russian culture have become canonized not through the city as empirical entity but through the Petersburg myth originating with Pushkin's artistic creation. Pushkin's relationship to that myth parallels Peter's relationship to the city; thus the narrative posits, and validates on analogic grounds, the myth's claim to ontological status (analogy being one of rhetoric's and philosophy's most prized principles, as well as metaphor's mechanism). Peter, Pushkin, Simeonov, and Tolstaya all participate in the same process: they transform raw materials into miniworlds according to the dictates of an inner vision that becomes reified.

If, as Culler contends, metaphors evidence a writer's "creativity and authenticity" as "artistic inventions grounded in perceptions of relations in the world," and illuminate "a higher imaginative truth," then metaphor may be said to carry the incalculable responsibility of validating literature as a human enterprise (*Pursuit*, 191, 192). In these circumstances, Simeonov's profession of translator acquires eloquent significance; for the Greek etymology of metaphor is *meta* + *phorein*—to carry over, or, in Latin, to translate, that is, substitute; likewise, *übersetzen* in German.[24] Contrary to what several analysts of the trope have asserted, substitution is not a mechanical replacement, at odds with Richards's theory of the interdependence and interanimation of words; rather, it originates in exactly such an understanding of discourse as contextualized utterance, ineluctably trailing behind it what Bakhtin calls memories or vestiges of earlier usage.[25] The cultural context of discourse colors all language conceptually; a substitution that is *purely* verbal, devoid of concept and associative elements, can occur only hypothetically. Accordingly, Simeonov the translator and artist generates linguistic and conceptual substitutions as long as his imaginative energies endure, preferring, like Gogol's anchorite artist in "The Portrait," the solitary life of the muse's devotee to the creature comforts vouchsafed by the domestic, earthbound Tamara. The literal (instead of the literary) substitution (i.e., fleshly Tamara for an incorporeal Vera Vasilevna) inevitably proves compromising—which explains Simeonov's sense that he perhaps has betrayed his Vera (faith, R25, E26).[26]

Throughout her narrative, then, Tolstaya in multiple ways contrasts art with the tangible experience of everyday reality as two antithetical, largely incompatible realms: "how restlessly the transparent, tamed shadows of our imagination scurry when the noises and smells of real life penetrate into their cool, foggy world" (23) ("kak bespokoino mechutsia prozrachnye, priruchennye teni nashego voobrazheniia, kogda sopenie i zapakhi zhivoi

zhizni pronikaiut v ikh prokhladnyi, tymannyi mir!" [22]). Their disparate-
ness acquires an additional dimension in Simeonov's meeting with the now
aged, grotesque-looking singer, through which Tolstaya evokes the myth of
the artist as an extension of her/his art—a myth roundly debunked by Vera
Vasilevna's crude manner and physical grossness (her greed, bulk, mus-
tache, large nose, skin pellets and pubic hair in the bathtub, etc.)[27] In the
person of Vera Vasilevna, in fact, Tolstaya dramatizes the paradox that
John Keats explored in his "Ode on a Grecian Urn": art's ultimate separation from the very life into which it purportedly offers insight. Whereas art
strives for universality and permanence, life deals in particulars and its
inescapable primary condition is mutability. Is accommodation of any sort
possible between timelessness and the time-bound? Tolstaya problematizes
her validation of art within her own text through irresolution via metaphor.
She opts for hierarchy over reconciliation in a summative, extended ana-
phoric metaphor that provides the narrative's closure:

> Potseluev [Kissov] wound up the gramophone, and the divine stormy
> voice, gaining strength, rose in a crescendo from the depths, spread its
> wings, soared above the world, above the steamy body of little old Vera
> drinking tea from the saucer, above Simeonov bent in his lifelong obedi-
> ence, above warm, domestic Tamara, above everyone beyond help, above
> the approaching sunset, the gathering rain, the wind, the nameless rivers
> flowing backward, overflowing their banks, raging and flooding the city
> as only rivers can. (29)

> Potseluev zavodil grammofon, slyshen byl divnyi, narastaiushchii,
> grozovoi golos, vosstaiushchii iz glubin, raspravliaiushchii kryl'ia,
> vzmyvaiushchii nad mirom, nad rasparennym telom Verunchika,
> p'iushchego chai s bliudechka, nad sognuvshimsia v svoem pozhiz-
> nennom poslushanii Simeonovym, nad teploi, kukhonnoi Tamaroi, nad
> vsem, chemu nel'zia pomoch', nad podstupaiushchim zakatom, nad
> sobiraiushchimsia dozhdem, nad vetrom, nad bezymiannymi rekami,
> tekushchimi vspiat', vykhodiashchimi iz beregov, bushuiushchimi i
> zatopliaiushchimi gorod, kak umeiut delat' tol'ko reki. (28)

The metaphor, redolent of Blok,[28] makes claims through the wings and
the repeated preposition "above" ("nad") for the transcendent nature of art,
emphatically divorced from earthly phenomena, the materiality of which
Tolstaya stresses here, as throughout. If Simeonov's case may be deemed
representative, one can serve art obediently only without fully understanding its nature and its role in one's existence. As in religion, one submits
without comprehension. Rather than resolving the story's central question,
Tolstaya seems to silence it through assertion, an assertion, moreover,

couched in metaphor—the rhetorical figure that consistently has substituted for art, one of the two key categories in question and *under* question. If I read this passage correctly, Tolstaya's strategy at this juncture exposes the process whereby, in Paul de Man's words, "Metaphor gives itself the totality which it then claims to define, but it is in fact the tautology of its own position" ("Epistemology," 15).[29] Tolstaya here not only forestalls the potential hermeticism of her verbal gestures but achieves a truly Keatsian irresolution through partial defiguration. The master trope of the Okkervil River dissolves in the concluding literalization of rivers, which, one might say, are brought down to earth. The defiguration performs the revelatory function that de Man, borrowing from Walter Benjamin, ascribes to "disfiguration." According to a de Manian reading, Tolstaya's awareness of the rhetoricity of language, which here registers the insufficiency or inefficacy of metaphor to "mediate the gulf between mortality and redemption" (timelessness) (Waters, lv) in a text that proceeds through tropological development, deconstructs her own narrative. The pressure brought to bear on the figurative dimension of language may be adumbrated by a pregnant statement midway through the narrative located *within* the matrix metaphor: "and only the Okkervil River flows on, narrowing and widening feverishly, unable to select a permanent image for itself" (22) ("i tol'ko reka Okkervil', sudorozhno suzhaias' i rasshiriaias', techet i nikak ne mozhet vybrat' sebe ustoichivogo oblika" [21]). That statement itself, however, instantiates the very problem of tropology. And at story's end, the master trope is potentially demoted from heuristic to tactical and provisional.

The concluding paragraph of "Okkervil River," then, opens up the text to the dilemma currently vexing specialists in literary and historical studies: namely, the status of metaphor and language itself as referential and consequently capable of representation, of the mimesis codified by Aristotle; or, on the contrary, as pure presence, a material entity pointing to nothing outside itself, having no *telos* in reality; or, in de Man's view, language as the repository of cognitive elements that, independently of the author, reveals its rhetoricity and thereby affirms the inevitability of misreading (Leitch, 186–87). Mark Lipovetskii, a Bakhtin-inspired critic sensitive to textual matters, has interpreted the endings of Tolstaya's stories as confessional dialogues with the self ("osobye ispovedal'nye *dialogi* avtora s samim soboi—cherez geroev, cherez metafory, akkumuliruiushchie dukhovnyi opyt kul'tury").[30] Yet the majority of Tolstaya's other stories, far from highlighting this quandary, seem to presuppose confidently the heuristic properties of metaphor. Given Tolstaya's metaphysical orientation, it is no coincidence that, her subversive ironic stratagems notwithstanding, her metaphors of the Edenic garden, the dust of mortality, the light of transcendence or spirituality, and so on, draw heavily on the Bible, especially Genesis, Ecclesiastes, the Book of John, and Revelations.[31] While "Okkervil River" postulates the metaphysics of art, it also appears to subject to doubt and possibly dissolution Tolstaya's most productive trope.

Metaphor, Transcendence, and the Ontological Dimension

> *In the beginning was the Word, and the Word was with God [. . .]*
> *And the Word was made flesh, and dwelt among us, [. . .] full of*
> *grace and truth.*
>
> John 1:1, 14

> *the things which are seen are temporal but the things which are*
> *not seen are eternal.*
>
> 2 Corinthians 4:18

The status of metaphor in Tolstaya's fiction is critical not so much because some critics have complained that she abuses the trope by allowing it to slip off the leash and run uncontrolled,[32] as because its major role among its multiple functions is its power to signify in the overarching binary opposition that presides over her oeuvre: the oppositional forces of noumena waging battle against phenomena. If one remembers that noumena, as a ground of phenomena unknowable by the senses but conceivable by reason, derives etymologically from the Greek *noumenon*—thing thought,[33] one can appreciate why writers preoccupied with noumenal forces might exploit to the maximum the potential of metaphor.

Whereas the empirical nature of objects automatically assures their ontological (i.e., extramental, noncontingent) status, the nonempirical nature of noumena, of the ontological sphere in the sense of spiritual, complicates the task of representing them as existing outside of mental or psychological projections. Faced with this very dilemma, the Symbolists opted for the paradoxical reversal of a neo-Platonic dialectic, which relegated the visible, verifiable everyday world of experience to mere semblance. This degraded reflection reified an imperfect apprehension of the ideal and immutable that comprises the higher sphere of true Forms, adumbrated in Plato's *Symposium* (post-371 B.C.) and later elaborated in the *Phaedo* (367 B.C.). Hence the Symbolists' concept of art as a displaced version of religion, with the artist as seer, and their symbols' primary function of intimating, however inadequately, the infinite possibilities of the transcendent world. Transcendent here embraces the Kantian notion of residing beyond the limits of all possible experience and knowledge, as well as the traditional meaning of extending beyond the limit of ordinary experience and a fortiori beyond the universe of material existence. Such a categorically dichotomous essentialization as the Symbolists' calls for an absolutist stance incompatible with Tolstayan epistemology. For, while abhorring materialists, Tolstaya fully acknowledges the material world rejected wholesale by the Symbolists, who downgraded it to the rank of shadows. Yet in grappling with the problem of verbally (i.e., fictionally) embodying transcendent categories, Tolstaya, *mutatis mutandis*, similarly opts for a tropological or figurative solution.

A writer intent on inscribing in a work of fiction the ontological status of the transcendent, which is, by definition, incorporeal, has limited methodological choices. An authoritative source within a given text may provide an omniscient commentary that either argues for the spiritual dimension in life or simply presupposes it as an a priori given and treats it as such (e.g., Lermontov, Tolstoy). Or one may dramatize events that by their nature defy logical explanation and thereby implicitly posit a higher agency: in other words, cast one's authorial lot with the depiction of what ultimately, through a strategically rhetorical process of elimination, proves to be the miraculous (an option understandably favored, for example, by such Catholic writers as Graham Greene and François Mauriac). Or, like the Symbolists, one may embed in realia a grid of symbols that collectively suggest spheres beyond the one represented and, more significantly, beyond the resources of actual representation itself. These are all heavily trafficked routes that Tolstaya's narratives take into account through the intertext and synthesis characterizing her multifaceted treatment of what have long been labeled "eternal questions."

In her first published stories, " 'On the Golden Porch' " and "Rendezvous with a Bird," Tolstaya invokes the metaphor of the lapsarian myth and the animism of folklore to establish quickly and economically the felt presence of transcendence. The Edenic garden, the fall from grace through knowledge of the flesh (which, of course, metaphorically encapsulates the problematics of incarnating transcendence), and the consequent lapse into mortality, on the one hand, together with the mythic symbols of crystal, egg, mountain, and dragon, on the other, provide the concretely grounded metaphysical underpinnings of the poles to which the mysterious objects, events, and tropes of the two stories gravitate. Although Tolstaya's later works move away from the metaphor of cosmic myth as narrative algorithm, they nevertheless interpolate universal religious motifs that constitute a part of every educated person's fund of reflexive cultural associations. Emblems of spiritual life, such as dove, butterfly, light, stars, heavens, fire, river, sun and moon, wings, ascension, and the colors blue and gold (canonized through icons and religious art in general) confront their polar antitheses of snake, food, drink, flesh, clothes, darkness, ice, dust, and crawling. Codified through repetition in Genesis, Ecclesiastes, and elsewhere, these pairings illustrate the extent to which all major religions are grounded in certain root metaphors (Tracy, 89–104). To adduce a few typical examples: the dove, butterly, dragonfly, and upward gaze, associated with the symbolically named Sonia in the story by that name, struggle against the attractively packaged, snakelike elegance of Ada Adolfovna; in like manner, the light and the "discussions of mysterious phenomena" (78) ("besedy o tain- stvennom" [131]) that accompany the ulcer-ridden Korobeinikov in "Heav- enly Flame" contrast tellingly with the fleshly appeal of Olga Mikhailovna, who coquettishly dispenses food, clothes, and noncommittal sexual favors. Tolstaya's wording at various junctures in the pointedly entitled "Heavenly Flame" leaves little doubt as to the domain metonymically represented by the physically ailing but spiritually endowed Korobeinikov:

> Korobeinikov directs the beam to the skies, but the weak light scatters and the skies remain just as dark as ever, only the top branches and the crows' nests are lit for a moment. Playful, he turns the flashlight back toward the porch, and then nothing can be seen in the night but a white star where Korobeinikov had been standing. (81)

> Korobeinikov napravliaet luch v nebesa, no slabyi svet rasseivaetsia, i nebesa ostaiutsia takimi zhe temnymi, kak i byli, razve tol'ko verkhnie vetvi da voron'i gnezda osveshchaiutsia na mig; baluias', on napravliaet fonar' k kryl'tsu, i togda nichego uzh ne vidno v nochi, tol'ko belaia zvezda na tom meste, gde stoial Korobeinikov. (132)

Kindred dualistic formulations are at the heart of "Fire and Dust," "Serafim," "The Circle," and "Sleepwalker in a Fog."

Such series of binary oppositions frequently accompany Tolstaya's evo- cation of psycho-physical states that traditionally have been deemed propi- tious for communication with otherworldly or noumenal sources, such as dreams and fantasies. These methods of narratively installing transcendence through mythic symbols of dream emanations have slighter claims to origi- nality or frequency than Tolstaya's device of the extended metaphor (as metonymy) that unobtrusively transports the reader to other worlds. By virtue of originating in the authorial imagination, these condensed identifi- cations recall, in a sense, Descartes's ontological argument for the existence of God, which posited a divinity on the basis of the human capacity to conceive of such an entity. Since authorial means authoritative, insofar as the author is the supreme or, tropologically speaking, divine creator of her text (the Word is with God),[34] the narratively grounded metaphor, like the divine Word, resides beyond analysis and challenge, that is, it seems to inhere in the world of the created fiction as one of its givens. Tolstaya encourages readers' faith in the ontological dimension of her developed metaphors, such as Simeonov's imagined Okkervil River, through the extraordinarily concrete details that, fictionally, lend them greater empirical solidity than that assigned to blatantly material phenomena, as, for example, Simeonov's apartment and the indefatigably amorous Tamara.

After the initial introduction of a matrix metaphor, Tolstaya at selective intervals draws metonymically or synecdochically on some of its aspects, which she extends through minute descriptive particulars. Gradually the vehicle of her metaphor emancipates itself from the tenor, almost completely displacing it.[35] Although the metaphor at such moments no longer has its *telos* in empiric reality, its exfoliation relies on the specificity and detail that we demand of art and associate with material phenomena. Thus the rhetorical device of *topothesia* ("description of a place") temporarily cedes to densely particularized *loxi positio* ("description of imaginary, nonexistent places") (Lanham, 100), or, to borrow Karsten Harries's formulation, "The [poet's] metaphor[s] promise a plenitude that temporal existence has to withhold [. . . ;] they gesture towards an elusive eternity, metaphors of a transcendence that is nothing other than the place left vacant by the dead God."[36] Yet the familiar practice of particularizing, I would argue, attempts fictionally to empiricize that counterworld, just as the inosculation of tenor and vehicle posits the interaction between noumenal and phenomenal. The installation of Vera Vasilevna's voice as an elemental riparian force in "Okkervil River" exemplifies Tolstaya's method:

> Vera Vasilevna skipped, creaking and hissing, quickly spinning under the needle; the hiss, creak, and spin formed a black tunnel that widened into the gramophone horn, and triumphant in its victory over Simeonov, out of the festooned orchid emerged her voice, divine, low, dark, lacy, and dusty at first, and then throbbing with underwater pressure, rising up from the depths, transforming, trembling on the water like flames—pshsts-pshsts-pshsts, pshsts-pshsts-pshsts—filling like a sail, getting louder, breaking hawsers, speeding unrestrained pshsts-pshsts-pshsts a caravel over the noctural waters splashing flames—stronger—spreading its wings, gathering speed, smoothly tearing away from the remaining bulk of the flow that had given birth to it. (18)

> podskakivaia, potreskivaia i shipia, bystro vertelas' pod igloi Vera Vasil'evna; shipenie, tresk i kruzhenie zavivalis' chernoi voronkoi, rasshirialis' grammofonnoi truboi, i, torzhestvuia pobedu nad Simeonovym, nessia iz festonchatoi orkhidei bozhestvennyi, temnyi, nizkii, snachala kruzhevnoi i pyl'nyi, potom nabukhaiushchii podvodnym

naporom, vosstaiushii iz glubin, preobrazhaiushiisia, ogniami na vode kolykhaiushchiisia, —pshch-pshch-pshch, pshch-pshch-pshch,—parusom naduvaiushchiisia golos—vse gromche,—obryvaiushchii kanaty, neuderzhimo nesushchiisia, pshch-pshch-pshch, karavelloi po bryzzhushchei ogniami nochnoi vode—vse sil'nei,—raspravliaiushchii kryl'ia, nabiraiushchii skorost', plavno otryvaiushchiisia ot otstavshei tolshchi porodivshego ego potoka. (16–18)

The sheer length and weight of such metaphors, with their accumulation of tangible minutiae, all attached to the metaphor's imagination-bred vehicle, inspire the reader to credit the existence and transcendent nature of an entity whose empirical status resists verification. As Harries puts it, "What metaphor names may transcend human understanding so that our language cannot capture it" (*Metaphor and Transcedence*, 72), but the rhetorical skill an author invests in a metaphor may inveigle a reader into an acceptance of that which resides beyond language yet is intimated by it. Tolstaya's metaphors summon readers to faith in the ontological existence of the incorporeal, the invisible, and the ineffable: spirit, beauty, *agape*, and imagination. Whereas her simpler metaphors range freely, her developed and matrix metaphors tend to draw on conventional associations with water, voyages, sirens, gardens, circles, fire, and so on. She reanimates and vivifies these somewhat worn tropes, however, both through the lush details of her elaborations and through her heretical synthesis of metaphor and metonymy.

The Heterodoxy of Hybrids: Transtroping
Metaphor and Metonymy

In a characteristically disputatious article on a passage from Proust's *Du Côté de chez Swann*, Paul de Man undertakes a refutation of Gerard Genette's claim that the intermingling of metonymy and metaphor in Proust makes for a felicitous cooperation.[37] Responses to de Man's piece, which draws rather sweeping conclusions based on a narrowly focused analysis of a single passage in a multivolume work, have not contested his assertions through a counter-reading of Proust's or any other writer's prose.[38] Yet an interpenetration of metaphor and metonymy not only moves Tolstaya's narratives in distinctive fashion but also distributes the elements of her matrix metaphors in patterns that lead to the insight de Man so prizes and finds lacking in metonymy.

For better or worse, the majority of discussions about metaphor and metonymy still take as their point of departure Roman Jakobson's classic article of over thirty years ago, "The Metaphoric and Metonymic Poles" (1956), neatly summarized, modified, and extrapolated in David Lodge's

Modes of Modern Writing.[39] According to the Saussurean structuralist principle of language as a twofold sign system operating by selection and combination, the process for generating metaphor is selection, for it involves the perception of similarity and implies the possibility of substitution. This substitution based on similarity, however, does not suppress awareness of difference, as the terms *tenor* and *vehicle* coined by Richards to designate the two components of a metaphor tacitly assume (A "holds" firm [tenor: Latin *tenere*], as one "travels" to B [vehicle]) and as Richards himself explicitly emphasized: "We must not suppose [. . .] that the interaction of tenor and vehicle are [*sic*] to be confined to their resemblances. [. . .] Some similarity will commonly be the ostensive ground of the shift, but the peculiar modification of the tenor which the vehicle brings about is even more the work of their unlikenesses than of their likenesses" (127).

Contrary to Aristotle and subsequent rhetoricians and critics who consider metonymy (and synecdoche, which often is collapsed with metonymy) a subspecies of metaphor, Jakobson conceives of them as antithetical. Whereas metaphor, according to his schema, belongs to the selection axis of language and depends on similarity, metonymy belongs to the combination axis and operates by contiguity. If metaphor stresses selection, metonymy necessitates deletion, for according to the structuralist model of language, which dictates that all linguistic units provide context for simpler units and acquire their context from more complex ones, metonymies are condensations of contexture resulting from the deletion of one or more items from a natural combination. Such a definition, which assigns metaphors verticality (paradigm) and metonymy horizontality (syntagm), naturally leads both Jakobson and such recent theorists of narratology as Peter Brooks to characterize prose as "forwarded essentially by contiguity," thus predominantly metonymical (Jakobson, 96).

Yet, if metonymy as a trope results from the process of combination and non-logical deletion, the selected details comprising the trope are, as E.B. Greenwood has reasoned, "surrogates [. . .] for the mass of observed detail which would have been there in actuality" but has been deleted (341–42). In such cases, then, "the appropriate critical response to the metonymic text would seem to be an attempt to restore the deleted detail, to put the text back into the total context from which it derives" (Lodge, 93). Therefore, theoretically, at least, even as metonymy propels narrative along the horizontal axis, it simultaneously invites the reader to insert all the material that has been deleted en route. That task of completion via insertion retards movement forward and potentially reorients the reader toward the vertical axis, the axis of metaphor.[40]

De Man faults Genette's reading of Proust chiefly on the grounds that

Proust's claimed aperçu, which properly should originate in the metaphor that purportedly apperceives essences, instead depends on a metonymy, which is an accidental connection. As de Man forcefully objects: "In a passage that abounds in successful and seductive metaphors and which, moreover, asserts the superior efficacy of metaphor over that of metonymy, persuasion is achieved by a figural play in which contingent figures of chance masquerade deceptively as figures of necessity" (*Allegories of Reading*, 67). Contingency here is the crux of de Man's argument. Given his programmatic rejection of organicism, of what he, his disciples, and his epigones label totalizing systems, contiguity by definition cannot participate meaningfully in establishing essence and value. That function remains the province of metaphor. Such a categorical separation unaccountably ignores the rich metonymic potential of metaphor in general and certain types of metaphor in particular. For instance, the metaphor "she is a leopard" presents the reader with the possibility of extending insights through the restoration of the context that the metaphor *automatically* implies: jungle, rapacity, physical grace combined with power, and so forth. Would a subsequent reference to jungle behavior or sinuous movement in a text that introduces the leopard metaphor be a "figure of chance"? No—on the contrary, surely such an implicitly metaphorical usage, like the original, and presumably tactically selected, metaphor to which the jungle reference is allied metonymically, springs from a "necessity" that may be both imaginative and empirically grounded in realia. Even Barbara Johnson, a stalwart advocate of de Man's methods, who, nevertheless, avoids direct confrontation with his overstated conclusions, acknowledges that "in any attempt to apply the metaphor/metonymy distinction [. . .] it is often very hard to tell the two apart."[41] De Man's argument presupposes the invariably fortuitous nature of context, whereas a writer may be motivated to generate a metaphor precisely for the context that s/he may deem crucial to an insight. How essential a crown is to kinghood or a prow to a ship (the most frequent examples of metonymy and synecdoche conventionally cited in handbooks of critical terms) depends on one's perspective and level of address. Whether a text that invokes such a metaphor subsequently develops the trope metonymically through reference to any associative features says a great deal about the centrality of the metaphor to the given work and its significance within it. In this regard, some vehicles will obviously be more productive than others. Such Tolstayan metaphors as the Edenic garden in "Rendezvous with a Bird" and the river in "Okkervil River," in fact, have been selected partly because their comprehensiveness facilitates the manifold metonymical references to the vehicle that Tolstaya weaves throughout both narratives for purposes that are by no means frivolous. The organizing river metaphor in "Okkervil River" constructs an entire world of bridges, chains, embankments, fog, and Vera Vasilevna's apple-round heels. These elements spill into the narrative individually and in clusters at those junctures where Simeonov's embattled imagination declares itself.

That de Man's fundamental skepticism regarding the symbiosis of metaphor and metonymy springs directly from his rejection of "coherent," "unitary," or "totalizing" readings in favor of "rupture," "blindness," and "disfiguration" finds curious corroboration in those Tolstayan texts where unity of structure and posited meaning actually rely on the interaction of metaphor and metonymy. In "Rendezvous with a Bird," for example, the regnant metaphor of Eden links the metonymically installed experiences of knowledge, sexuality, and mortality in a meaningful metaphysical pattern; without such mutual reinforcement, the metaphoric profundity and resonance as well as the metonymic signifying power would be diminished to the point of extinction. It is the metaphor of childhood as paradisiacal garden, in other words, that endows Petia's shattering second-hand knowledge simultaneously of flesh and death with the philosophical weight of the lapsarian myth and its multiple cultural resonances. Once the complex metaphor asserts its dominant role, Tolstaya needs only to refer metonymically to any of the panoply of motifs, objects, and so on, culturally embedded in that myth to evoke all of the concomitant elements. Any reader acquainted with the Bible, Western art, numerous illustrations or earlier literary versions of the myth (e.g., Milton's *Paradise Lost*) will succumb to the temptation of treating the tree under which Petia crouches at story's end as a metonym colluding with the story's presiding Edenic metaphor.

Many of Tolstaya's stories display a penchant for constantly halting, retarding, or reversing the forward motion of plot/narrative propelled by contiguity (the preponderantly metonymical mode) through metaphor or combination of metaphor and metonymy. These tropes, which occasionally expand into mini-universes, swell or distend time, giving it depth or vertical content. Moreover, the links holding her narratives together are located not on the horizontal plane of plot but rather in echoes between these seemingly deflective metaphors or trope-saturated excrescences that enable her to move back and forth spatially and temporally, suspending, but not essentially disturbing, the linear narrative activity in which the tenor of her metaphor is located. By taking the vehicle of her metaphor far afield, Tolstaya achieves several ends: she deflects her readers from the prosaic forward motion, dissuading them from a clear-cut chronology or sequentiality; she intimates the primacy of processes over actions; and through reverberations between her metaphorical structures, she provides a sense of coherence (operating largely on a figurative level) that distracts one from the very issue of temporal and spatial markers. In other words, the erection of her multidirectional framework allows her to move freely along both planes (backward and forward, up and down), while the ingemination of motifs from those structures of metaphor, judiciously implanted at intervals, establishes a verbal rhythm that creates the illusion of unity. What we have, in a sense, is subversion regularized.

An invaluable benefit of such a staggeringly bold disregard for narrative practices is the reader's conviction that s/he has witnessed the key moments or been privy to the primary aspects of a given character's life and can deduce the rest—that is, the reader responds appropriately to the metonymy of a life exposed largely in metaphorical terms. By exploding a standard unfolding of time and space, Tolstaya abstracts the enormous gaps in the narrative of that biography and merely provides several highly charged details from which to extrapolate and fill in the spaces. Since intensity of impact must compensate for lack of exhaustive documentation, those details tend toward dramatic contrasts, establishing poles between which our input may range. That polarization explains why quite a few of Tolstaya's portraits smack of caricature if divorced from the metaphors where the revelatory nuances lie. Tolstaya's metaphors, then, decelerate the metonymical narrative momentum. Yet, paradoxically, by yielding insights carefully distributed throughout the narrative, they render the forward movement necessary and meaningful and so in a sense vindicate verticality even as they assimilate into metonymy along the horizontal axis. Its efficiency notwithstanding, metonymy is not a trope that captivates readers or reveals what is unique about a given writer. Metaphors, by contrast, tend to make indelible impressions through their unexpectedness, daring, revelatory capacity, or sheer cleverness. As Wayne Booth's example of students' responses to a metaphor-glutted passage from Norman Mailer's *Armies of the Night* illustrates (56–58), far from all metaphors elicit unanimous reactions. Few would dispute, however, that the abundance of striking and original metaphors in Tolstaya's prose, as in Mailer's, constitutes one of its major and immediate seductive appeals. Nietzsche conceived of metaphor as an imperialistic principle that is identical to the principle of life because it is "a proof of the strength of spirit, to be able to leap over what lies before our feet and grasp after what lies far away" (Cantor, 75). Indeed, perhaps Tolstaya's mastery of metaphor accounts in large measure for the vitality, zest, and receptivity to life's pulsations that her prose emanates. During an interview several years ago, Tolstaya asserted: "Language exists prior to us; we are born into language. Language is cleverer than we are" ("Iazyk ran'she nas sushchestvuet; my rozhdaemsia v iazyk. Iazyk umnee nas"

[Barta, 5–6]). That view, alongside Tolstaya's express desire to exploit maximally the full range of possibilities within Russian, enjoins the reader to revise Fazil' Iskander's tentative ascription of a compensatory function to Tolstaya's jeweled language. Whereas Iskander speculates that the extraordinary lavishness of Tolstaya's linguistic span may be an unconscious gift from the author to the "poor losers" she portrays ("bessoznatel'nyi dar khudozhnika svoim bednym neudachnikam" [5]), I would contend that the rhetoric of Tolstaya's fiction initiates the *reader* into the plenitude of life that her prose celebrates.

Postscript

Admirers of Tolstaya's prose have voiced disappointment at her apparent abandonment of fiction after the publication of "Plot" ("Siuzhet"). Indeed, since 1990 and her continued residence in the United States, Tolstaya has transferred her authorial hand to book reviews and opinion pieces for a number of such well-known journals and newspapers as *The New Republic*, *The Wilson Quarterly*, and *The New York Review of Books*.

Her fictional silence has witnessed Tolstaya's rise as a public persona in the United States—one who not only regularly teaches at Skidmore College but also participates in Slavic, writers', and women's conferences, gives lectures and interviews, and frequently writes book reviews and articles. Perhaps the most striking feature of Tolstaya as speaker/critic/journalist is the degree to which her interviews and nonfictional prose overlap with her stories. In other words, she has merely smuggled her signature fictional devices into the other genres in which she now exclusively operates. Those key Tolstayan traits include wicked humor, grotesquerie, vivid characterization, and narrative momentum.

Virtually every interview, review, and article contains memorable personae briefly etched with sardonic bite: for example, the hapless Russian militiamen "lying in wait for helpless women shoppers" so as "to snatch their change" ("The Nation Needs Hard Currency")[1] and the roster of idiosyncratic Americans who in 1989 impressed Tolstaya by their childlike naïveté and escapism from unpleasantness of any sort ("Discovering America").[2] As depicted by Tolstaya, the pathetically risible characteristics of Aleksandr Solzhenitsyn as denunciatory host of his now-defunct biweekly program on Russian television (he "fumes for fifteen minutes twice a month")[3] and as demagogic author of *"The Russian Question" at the End of the Twentieth Century* ("if they'd listened to him everything would have been different") recall such fictional Tolstayan *rarae aves* as Peters, Shura, and Zhenechka.

One of her most beguiling parodies, "I Cannot Keep Silent" ("Ne mogu molchat'"), hilariously satirizes the anti-Semitism of Russia's nationalist writers, particularly its rural contingent. Her accelerated survey of Russian "classics"—from Pushkin to prominent figures among the contemporary anti-Semitic Village Prosaists themselves—"unmasks" the supposed Jew-ishness and "Russophobia" of the entire Russian literary tradition.[4]

Embedded plots of potential fictional dramas and linguistically lush re-creations of ways of life, larded with stunning lists, likewise find their way into Tolstaya's journalism. "Notes from Underground," her polemical, blinkered review of Francine du Plessix Gray's *Soviet Women: Walking the Tightrope*,[5] affords ample illustration of the first (see the minifarce of the male domestic volunteer [3]). The second emerges most visibly in her re-views of Robert Conquest's *The Great Terror: A Reassessment*, 1991,[6] and especially of Joyce Toomre's impressive translation of Elena Molokho-vets's epic cookbook, *A Gift to Young Housewives*.[7]

In like fashion, one encounters here the interrogative, vocative, and ex-clamatory intrusion of an irreverent narrator familiar from Tolstaya's debut story to her last—a narrator quick with her rapier thrusts and low-placed kicks in the midst of humor and seemingly reasoned assessment: of Toomre, "her conscientious, highly qualified work deserves endless respect. She killed with love" ("The Age of Innocence," 26); of Gail Sheehy, "you have to be quite fearless, an adventurer, extraordinarily self-assured, to offer American readers a book about a country that you yourself do not understand. Gail Sheehy possesses all these qualities in abundance" ("Presi-dent Potemkin," 27).

Those detractors of Tolstaya who waxed indignant at her endorsement of Gray's popularizing collage of impressions from her Soviet trip and who also resented her grudging, double-edged praise for aspects of Toomre's mammoth achievement approached Tolstaya's "reviews" as precisely that: unalloyed exercises in that well-established, highly conventionalized genre. For Tolstaya, however, reviews sooner present an opportunity to improvise and narrativize. They allow her imagination, humor, and rhetorical inven-tiveness play, often with scant regard for the accuracy of an allegedly re-ported or recalled event. And, as she once observed, "A negative stance allows more room for interesting writing" (telephone conversation in 1993).

If her last two stories, "Limpopo" and "Plot," suddenly incorporated elements of a type of sociohistorical satire almost wholly absent from her earlier fiction, her so-called journalism has always demonstrated a recep-tivity to devices normally confined to fiction. While Tolstaya's articles by no means compare with her fiction, they reflect, however faintly, some of the seductive magic that emanates from that world wrought in words.

Notes

Introduction

1. Two collections of Petrushevskaia's dramas appeared in 1988 and 1989, respectively titled *Songs of the XX Century (Pesni XX veka,* Moscow) and *Three Girls in Blue (Tri devushki v golubom,* Moscow). The first collection of her prose, *Along Eros Way (Po doroge boga Erosa,* Moscow), was published in 1993. Only the British have undertaken substantial translations of her fiction: the long novella *The Time: Night (Vremia noch')* trans. Sally Laird (London: Virago Press, 1994) and the anthology *Immortal Love (Bessmertnaia liubov'),* trans. Sally Laird (London: Virago, 1995), as well as of her plays: *Cinzano,* trans. & intro. by Stephen Mulrine (London: Nick Hern Books, 1991).

2. The technique, traceable to Nikolai Gogol, was revived by Andrei Bely and, subsequently, by Vladimir Nabokov, who have disquieted the "gentle reader" by their "coldness" combined with paronomasia, as has Tolstaya.

3. Much of the discomfort and disapproval among critics commenting on her prose in the late 1980s was prompted by her colorful sassiness and her boldly imaginative use of language. Deemed a verbal spendthrift by those weaned on the impoverished Soviet norms of linguistic economy, she became the target of *class* resentment: in conversations and articles her detractors resentfully noted that she belonged, after all, to the "privileged" family of Tolstoys and had inherited their notorious "arrogance."

Chapter 1

1. Tolstaya's twenty-one stories, in the sequence of their publication, are: " 'Na zolotom kryl'tse sideli . . . ,' " *Avrora* 8 (1983): 94–101; "Svidanie s ptitsei," *Oktiabr'* 12 (1983): 52–57; "Sonia," *Avrora* 10 (1984): 76–83; "Chistyi list," *Neva* 12 (1984): 116–26; "Reka Okkervil'," *Avrora* 3 (1985): 137–46; "Milaia Shura" and "Okhota na mamonta," *Oktiabr'* 12 (1985): 113–17 and 117–21; "Peters," *Novyi mir* 1 (1986): 123–31; "Spi spokoino, synok," *Avrora* 4 (1986): 94–101; "Ogon' i pyl' " and "Samaia liubimaia," *Avrora* 10 (1986): 82–91 and 92–110; "Poet i muza," "Fakir," and "Serafim," *Novyi mir* 12 (1986): 113–19, 119–30, 130–33; "Vyshel mesiats iz tumana," *Krest'ianka* 4 (1987): 32–35; "Krug"—collective title for three stories: "Liubish'—ne liubish'," "Noch'," and "Krug," *Oktiabr'* 4 (1987): 89–95, 95–99, 99–104; "Plamen' nebesnyi," *Avrora* 11 (1987): 130–39; "Somnambula v tumane," *Novyi mir* 7 (1988): 8–26; and "Limpopo," *Sintaksis* 27 (1990): 75–121; and *Znamia* 11 (1991): 45–70. Only by stretching genre boundaries could one call her latest "narrative" a story. Titled "Siuzhet," it appeared in *Sintaksis* 31 (1991): 100–9. The collection *"Na zolotom kryl'tse sideli . . . "* (1987) omitted "Samaia liubimaia," "Poet i muza," "Serafim," and "Noch'." In view of the unsolicited editorial changes in the original journal versions, where possible, all passages cited from Tolstaya's works refer to the anthology and are identified by page number in parentheses within the body of the text.

2. Bouis renders the title as "Date with a Bird" (116–30), which to a British ear conjures up macho Cockney speech of the 1960s.

3. For example, see Vysotskaia.

4. Tolstaya, "Ten' na zakate," 7.

5. Comparable misalliances recur in "Sonia," "The Poet and the Muse," "Peters," and "Fire and Dust," among others.

6. On the matrix metaphor in Tolstaya's prose, see Goscilo, "Tat'iana Tolstaia's 'Dome of Many-Coloured Glass.' " Tolstaya's and Evgenii Zamiatin's matrix metaphors resemble the "root metaphor" as described by Victor Turner: a basic analogy on a comprehensive level that automatically generates a network of subsidiary metaphors. It provides a means of talking about entire systems of thought. Robert Nisbet likewise acknowledges the enabling function of tropological formulations (e.g., in Freudianism) when he maintains that "complex philosophical systems can proceed from metaphorical premises." See Nisbet, 5; Turner, 24–30.

7. Raine, 7. For more on this aspect of childhood, see Coe, 41–75. On largely mythologized re-creations of childhood, see Wachtel.

8. In Zamiatin's dystopia, which relies heavily on the *topos* of Eden, the decisive moment of the protagonist's plunge into knowledge, through disobedience and sexual intercourse, necessitates his transfer to the Ancient House, which he reaches by aero: "Vot uzhe vidny izdali mutno-zelenye piatna—tam, za Stenoiu. Zatem, legkoe, nevol'noe zamiranie serdtsa—*vniz, vniz, vniz*—kak s krutoi gory—i my u Drevnego Doma." Zamiatin, 25 (emphasis added).

9. The egg, which carries crucial significance in Tolstaya's second story, has a rich and varied symbolism in the folklore of most nations. Many prehistorical tombs in Russia and Sweden have revealed clay eggs that had been left there as emblems of immortality, an identification manifestly confirmed by Easter rituals. In various cultures the egg, unsurprisingly, represents the mystery of life or potentiality. On these and other of its properties, see the sources cited in Cirlot, 90.

10. On the highly evocative possibilities of solar symbolism, see Cirlot, 302–5. Bulgakov's novel *Master and Margarita*, following Goethe's example in *Faust*, likewise erects a complex system of interrelated celestial symbols. On the incorruptibility and immortality associated with gold, see von Franz, 60.

11. This passage evokes specifically Bulgakov's loving Margarita, Pilate's faithful canine companion, Banga, and the direct ascent to the heavens via an illuminated path: "Priamo k etomu sadu protianulas' dolgozhdannaia prokuratorom lunnaia doroga, i pervym po nei kinulsia bezhat' ostroukhii pes. [. . .] vsled za svoim vernym strazhem po lunnoi doroge stremitel'no pobezhal i on [Pilate]." Bulgakov, 379. More generally, the two works share a preoccupation with time, mortality, materialism, and transcendence.

12. Analogous deaths occur in a number of Tolstaya's stories, notably "Sonia," "Sweet Shura," and "The Poet and the Muse."

13. In terms of plot, he presumably is cremated, but Tolstaya collapses time by omitting all mention of the process and referring only to the metal can filled with his ashes (50).

14. As von Franz notes, antiquity regarded the dog as a guarantor of eternal life, as attested by Cerberus in Hades and the images of dogs on antique Roman graves (von Franz, 95).

15. Marks, 206. The English prose translation reads: "Milky Way, O luminous sister of the white streams of Canaan and of the white bodies of women in love, shall we, dead swimmers, panting follow your course toward other nebulae?" (206–7).

16. Having imbibed many of his uncle's unorthodox ideas, young Iurii Zhivago encourages the bed-ridden Anna Ivanovna not to fear death, for "Chelovek v drugikh

liudiakh i est' dusha cheloveka [. . .] . V drugikh vy byli, v drugikh i ostanetes'. I kakaia vam raznitsa, chto potom eto budet nazyvat'sia pamiat'iu. Eto budete vy, voshedshaia v sostav budushchego." Pasternak, 68.

17. The same web of elements plays a major role in such Tolstayan works as "The Circle," "Sweet Shura," "Most Beloved," "Okkervil River," and "Sonia."

18. Bergson distinguishes between time as an abstraction that can affect nothing, and duration, which is a felt reality, experienced with particular vividness, for example, during waiting. See Bergson, *Evolution créatrice,* passim. In Ian Alexander's lucid summary of Bergson's distinction between *durée réelle* and scientific time, "the latter consists of discrete points juxtaposed in a homogeneous medium, which has all the chracteristics of space, [whereas] the former is a *duration,* a fusion of heterogeneous instants, an indivisible flux and becoming; the one is quantitative, numerical relation, the other qualitative, internal relation." Alexander, 8. Furthermore, Bergson in *Matière et mémoire* (1896) argues that memory is the source of conservation of the aggregate of instantaneous images that constitute matter.

19. The process has a certain affinity with that implied by William Wordsworth's definition of the origin of poetry as "emotion recollected in tranquillity," the famous equation formulated in a letter to Lady Beaumont. It also recalls Andrei Bitov's contention that Pushkin's contemporaries were perhaps less capable of presenting him "accurately" than the myths and anecdotes of subsequent generations. See Bitov, 227–28. Czeslaw Milosz similarly perceives the role of time and memory in the creative act of re-creation: "Memory was once regarded the mother of the Muses: *Mnemosyne mater musarum.* I can testify that it is really so, that when perfection summons, it is untrappable except as the detail recalled. [. . .] And if distance is the essence of beauty [. . .] then there is also a distance to be gained by bodying forth the world in recollection." Milosz, 10–11. Along the same lines, see Brodsky's lecture to the British Academy: Brodsky, 1150 and 1160.

20. Andrei Bely in his autobiographical *Kotik Letaev* also elaborates on the visual permutations enabled by a lamp that seems to stimulate both *trompes l'oeil* and the imagination. Objects such as crystals, lanterns, kaleidoscopes, and so forth, evoke not only the multihued potential of changed perception, but the magic and mystery with which children invest concrete objects. See Coe, 205–11.

21. Tolstoya, "Ten' na zakate," 7.

22. See Pushkin, vol. 6 (1974–78), xxxvii. On the role of perspectivism in *Eugene Onegin,* see Goscilo, "Multiple Texts in *Eugene Onegin.*"

23. Several of Carol Ueland's observations in an unpublished paper devoted to the same story ("An Auspicious Literary Debut: Tolstaia's 'Na zolotom kryl'tse sideli . . . ' ") accord with mine.

24. Uncle Boria's efforts to hide his and Tamila's feet echo Adam's attempt to cover his body, of which his newborn knowledge makes him aware. For Biblical parallels drawn between genitals and feet, see Exodus 4:25 and Isaiah 7:20. Many of Pushkin's famous references to women's feet (*nozhki*) rely on such association and may be of Biblical origin. See Goscilo, "Feet Pushkin Scanned, or Seeming *Idée Fixe* as Implied Aesthetic Credo."

25. Tolstaya invests the egg with a wealth of significance. Within the diegesis of the story, Alkonost's egg may be read as representative of the rites of passage undergone by the soul of every human who attains *conscious* knowledge of sin and mortality. Lenechka's as yet unawakened soul is thus portrayed as a sealed egg, smooth and impervious to the world's forces, while Petia's soul loses transparency and independence from the surrounding world when it spills, clots, and grows opaque, like cooked egg white (130; 123). The interplay between these personalized

images and Alkonost's egg illuminates Petia's acquisition of the egg as a decisive stage in his spiritual development.

26. In this context, see especially the Revelation to John, particularly 18, 21, and 22: "The city was pure gold, clear as glass," "the street of the city was pure gold, transparent as glass," "the river of the water of life, bright as crystal," "its radiance like a most rare jewel, like a jasper, clear as crystal." *The Holy Bible*, 241–42.

27. From among the many related concepts in the widespread symbolism of the dragon, Tolstaya selects its associations with the Serpent (see Revelation), the number seven, power, matter, and dissolution. For the fascinating permutations prevailing among various cultures, see Cirlot, 81–85.

28. The antithesis of the frog, which connotes fertility, creation, and resurrection (and of the cold-blooded animals most anticipates Man), the toad suggests sterility and destruction. In the traditional language of esoteric thought, the toad and the basilisk are "animals whose mission it is to break up the astral light by a process of absorption peculiar to them." See Cirlot, 109 and 326. In von Franz's Jungian reading of fairy tales, those identifications are implicitly reversed: "In general, the frog in mythology is often a masculine object, whereas the toad is feminine. [. . .] In our civilization, the toad has always been associated with the earth-mother, especially in her function of helping at child-birth." She proceeds to discuss the toad as a representation of the maternal womb (von Franz, 53). Her various examples, curiously, suggest that the tangible images of the toad throughout Europe are part of a ritual supplication intended to ensure fertility, doubtless initiated by those who are or fear being infertile.

29. Attached to these numbers are diverse principles of a primary ontological nature, with the ternary representing the spiritual or intellectual order, and the septenary the planetary or moral order (Cirlot, 220–27). In Revelation, the dragon is fairly consistently linked to the number seven.

30. The four birds of paradise are Finist (Phoenix), Sirin, Aklonost, and the least known, Gamaiun. See Kiparsky. My gratitude to Felix J. Oinas for acquainting me with this source.

According to Dal', Alkonost is a "fantastic/fairy-tale bird of paradise with a human face, depicted on *lubok* images," and Sirin, likewise a bird of paradise, also appears on *lubok* illustrations, sometimes paired with Alkonost. The expression "halcyon days" derives from Alkonost, the bird that ancient Greek legend identified with the king-fisher, reputed to nest at sea about the time of the winter solstice and to calm the waves during incubation. Traditionally considered an owl, Sirin has a nocturnal identity that meshes nicely with the imagery of Tolstaya's story, for it reinforces the "dark death" function that the story assigns him. See Dal', I, 11 and IV, 188. In Russian sacred verse, Sirin descends to earth from paradise, bewitching people with its singing, whereas in West European legends Sirin incarnates an unhappy soul. See *Mify narodov mira*, II, 438. According to other sources, Sirin appears as either a red-haired man or a dark-haired woman, the former also known as the Soulbird, and the latter evolving into mermaids. For confirmation of the above details, plus additional information, see Kiparsky.

31. See the fairy tale "Peryshko Finista iasna sokola," catalogued in two variants as Nos. 234 and 235 in Afanas'ev, II, 236–46. In both versions Finist serves as the occasion and the prize for a contest between two "maidens," contrastingly motivated by spiritual and material impulses. Finist (also known as Finiks) is a variant of the Phoenix, the fabulous bird sacred to the Egyptians that arises, reborn, from its own ashes and functions as a symbol of the sun. Resurrection has particular relevance for Tolstaya's story, of course. See *Encyclopedia Brittanica*, vol. 21, 457–58. The Russian fairy tale surfaces, in less developed fashion, in other Tolstaya stories, notably "The Poet and the

Muse" and "The Moon Came Out." Kiparsky notes that in *Golubinaia kniga* the phoenix appears as the mother of all birds ("als 'Mutter aller Vogel' "). Kiparsky, 5.

32. As in her first story, Tolstaya generalizes mortality as the universal condition through the symbolism of the mythical birds, the mythical death by water (rusalka-siren-Sirin?) of the supposed daughter of the gray-haired lady who constantly asks what time it is, and the literal death of Grandfather and the bird that Petia circumnavigates en route to the store. In "Rendezvous with a Bird," Tolstaya introduces the concept of resurrection through mention of Finist, but she withholds specific intimations of its promise of rebirth by excluding Finist from the story's diegesis through Tamila's claimed contretemps with him and his subsequent (and consequent?) withdrawal.

33. In addition, Uncle Boria has wolf's teeth, which indicate his rapaciousness and sexuality (Cirlot, 313–14). Tolstaya makes much more extensive and imaginative use of the connection between teeth and sexuality in her later story, "Fire and Dust" (see Chapter 5).

34. The compatibility of Biblical myth with a host of pagan legends need not be belabored. In this instance, emergent Christianity willingly accepted and interpreted the Phoenix myth, which probably originated in the Orient and later penetrated Egyptian sun worship by the priests of Heliopolis, as an allegory of resurrection and life after death. If one sums up the lapsarian myth as humankind's transgressive desire for knowledge at the price of suffering and mortality, then its trajectory may be traced in the Alkonost legend, in which humans irrationally seek its mysterious egg: "Kto naidet, na vsiu zhizn' zatoskuet. A vse ravno ishchut, vse ravno khochetsia." Tolstaya, 116.

35. Her last two narratives, "Limpopo" and "Plot," are the sole exceptions to this rule and signal a new direction in Tolstaya's fiction.

36. Jameson, 50. For a view of postmodernism as continuous with modernism, see Hutcheon, *A Poetics of Postmodernism*, xiii. Andreas Huyssen trenchantly summarizes the terms of the conflicting positions when he observes: "Either it is said that postmodernism is continuous with modernism, in which case the whole debate opposing the two is specious; or it is claimed that there is a radical rupture, a break with modernism, which is then evaluated in either positive or negative terms." Huyssen, 9–10.

37. See Erlich.

38. Barta, 267.

39. Grekova, "Anketa 'LR' "; Voznesenskii, 4. Both single out Tolstaya's prose as one of the most exciting literary events of 1986 and 1987, respectively.

40. See Vysotskaia. Russian critics seem discomfited by the stylistic opulence of Tolstaya's prose, especially in light of what they label her "cruelty" and "coldness." As much may be deduced from reviews such as those by the Soviet Zolotonosov, "Mechty i fantomy," and the émigré Raisa Shishkova, "Nich'i babushki na zolotom kryl'tse." Why Tolstaya's "attitude toward her characters" has become a *topos* in Tolstaya criticism was analyzed in Konstantin Kustanovich's unpublished paper at the Tolstaya Seminar (October 29, 1988) organized by Uliana Gabara in Richmond, VA, where Tolstaya was writer in residence during three months of 1988.

41. Tolstaya's use of rhetorical devices is the subject of Chapter 9.

42. The uncommonly multivoiced nature of Tolstaya's narrative also receives brief but intelligent commentary in Condee, 18; Nevzgliadova, 111–13. See also Goscilo, "Tolstaia's 'Dome,' " 283–84. For further elaboration on the topic, see the analysis of Tolstaya's treatment of time in Chapter 8.

43. As this study was going to press, an article that offers a Freudian reading in a Kleinian key of " 'On the Golden Porch' " appeared, emphasizing (excessively, in my view) the sadism of the story. See Rancour-Laferrière et al.

Chapter 2

1. Although "Night" contains no children in the literal sense, Tolstaya clearly equates the mental and emotional level of its mentally handicapped protagonist with that of a child: throughout, his mother appears as Mamochka, Tolstaya adverts repeatedly to his status as a "late-born child" ("pozdnii rebenok" [95]), and his conduct and perceptions generally resemble those of children portrayed in Tolstaya's other stories. Originally, "Night" followed "Loves Me—Loves Me Not" in the trio of stories published under the collective title taken from the last of the three, "The Circle" ("Krug").

2. Peter Marinelli, in his examination of the pastoral as a literary mode, draws an eloquent connection between the decline of the pastoral at the end of the eighteenth century and the simultaneous rise of childhood autobiography. As parallels between the two genres, he cites the ubiquity of the garden image, the myth of an original innocence destroyed by the Fall into adolescence, the discovery of sexuality, and the author's tendency to distance herself from the earlier vision. See Marinelli. The alleged innocence and hence separateness of children that Peter Brooks and others have remarked irresistibly evoke the Garden of Eden as a natural setting for their activities. See Brooks, "Toward Supreme Fiction," 11.

3. As Richard Coe notes in his survey of childhood autobiographies, the child's world is a small one, usually confined to a limited space charted by certain favorite landmarks, beyond which stretches the great and potentially ominous Unknown. Coe, 127–28. The gradual expansion of the child's geographical domain—from the womb, to a single room, to the house, the local streets, and so on, all the way, potentially, to the entire universe—furnishes an index in spatial terms of her or his spiritual, emotional, and intellectual growth. That enlargement emerges clearly in Andrei Bely's autobiographical *Kotik Letaev* (1915), which shares with Tolstaya's childhood stories a reliance on the Edenic myth, a principle of expansion and contraction to signal the child's relationship to the world around her/him and (in Bely) the evolution in the child's linguistic processes, an empathetic nurse who communicates wordlessly with the child, and a series of objects imbued with special significance in the child's developing consciousness.

4. True to folklore beliefs, Marivanna's possessions function as an extension of her and thus arouse revulsion in the little girl, who cannot tolerate her.

5. Nanny Grusha's loving understanding makes apposite the quote from Pushkin's "Podruga dnei moikh surovykh," which pays tribute to his nurse's selfless solicitude:

> Podruga dnei moikh surovykh,
> Golubka driakhlaia moia,
> Odna v glushi lesov sosnovykh
> Davno, davno ty zhdesh' menia.

6. For the lampshade as an image of Marivanna's past and future fate, see Chapter 8.

7. The generalizing tendency of the statement signals a change of voice, for the philosophical nature of such an observation is utterly alien to a child.

8. Kornei Chukovskii's classic text (1970) finds particular delight in the liberties children nonchalantly take with prefixes, among them the negative "ne," to derive neologisms. See the section entitled "L'zia i nel'zia" in Chukovskii, I, 371–73, also 368–71. Chukovskii's observations about a child's cognitive and verbal skills coincide with Tolstaya's assumptions about children's relationship to the world around them. For instance, in a section signally entitled "Protiv metafor," Chukovskii declares, "my, vzroslye [. . .] myslim slovami, slovesnymi formulami, a malen'kie deti—veshchami, predmetami predmetnogo mira. Ikh mysl' na pervykh porakh sviazana tol'ko s konkretnymi obrazami. Potomu-to oni tak goriacho vozrazhaiut protiv nashikh allegorii i

metafor" (388). That opposition captures perfectly a fundamental aspect of the incommunicability dividing Marivanna and her five-year-old pupil.

Tolstaya's treatment of children's perceptions and discursive habits shows that at some stage she must have been an attentive reader of such Chukovskii works as *Ot dvukh do piati* and *Aibolit*, the tale in verse about an animal healer Aibolit (Ouch-it-hurts), which supplies the title of her tale "Limpopo."

9. A similar dispensation from taboos marks the parodic dialogues created by the protagonist and her sister. Like the linguistic negation of single words, these exchanges reverse on the conceptual level the "norms" of Marivanna's syrupy conversations with Katia. For example: "'Doesh' cherviakov do kontsa, dorogaia Katiusha!' 'S udovol'stviem, nenagliadnaia Mar'ivanna!'" "'Skushai marinovannuiu liagushky, detochka!'" (4). For the role of reversal in children's nonsense, see Flescher, 128–44.

10. Marivanna is completely deaf to the irony of the parallel that implicitly indicts her conduct vis-à-vis her charge. In her capacity as governess, she substitutes for a parent, just as in Georges's/Tolstaya's lyric a nanny substitutes for Goethe's parent figure.

11. For samples of children's reactions to death, see Chukovskii's *Ot dvukh do piati* in I, 484–93. See also Piaget, *The Language and Thought of the Child.*

12. Coe, 199–204, especially 203.

13. Chukovskii, I., 484–86.

14. During the single outing that brings the little girl enjoyment, Marivanna is conspicuously absent. Even that pleasure, however, cedes to revulsion as it merges with the feverish apparitions in one of Tolstaya's temporal dissolves. See a parallel passage in the first chapter of Bely's *Kotik Letaev*, where the boy also succumbs to the delirious imaginings in which eyes, snakes, oceans, and so forth, assail his senses.

On children's animistic beliefs, see Piaget, *Plays, Dreams, and Imitation in Childhood*, 250–55.

15. Culler, *Framing the Sign*, 204; Genette, *Narrative Discourse*, 189–94.

16. Composed on his twenty-ninth birthday (May 26, 1828), Pushkin's lyric through a series of rhetorical questions implicitly indicts the divinity for having implanted in him desires and doubts that are a source of torment in a life shackled by pointlessness and tedium, and doomed to extinction. Tolstaya's lines echo the second stanza:

> Kto menia vrazhdebnoi vlast'iu
> Iz nichtozhestva vozzval,
> Dushu mne napolnil strast'iu,
> Um somnen'em vzvolnoval?

Pushkin, I, 506.

17. That is why some critics view children as arch-solipsists, immured in their own world of absolute egotism. See Coe, 51–63, especially 58, and Porter.

18. Here also the narrative voice undergoes change, gradually branching out from the confiding concreteness of the little girl's perspective to the broader, more principle-oriented generalization of the adult.

19. The distinction resembles Bakhtin's contrast between centripetal and centrifugal linguistic forces, where the former represent homogenizing, hierarchicizing, normative tendencies, while the latter are dispersive in their individualizing, disruptive orientation. For an admirably lucid exposition of the distinction between the two, see Morson and Emerson, 30–35.

20. That device is used elsewhere to convey how adult ideas in general strike a child as peculiar, for example, when the five-year-old directly reports in quotation marks an adult's description of someone's fiddling with the fringe of a lampshade: "tam p'iut chai, zagorelsia oranzhevyi abazhur, i kto-nibud' iz starshikh uzhe pletet iz ego bakhromy nedozvolennye kosichki—'portit veshch'' " (6).

21. The opening of the story, in fact, smacks of Mozart's opera *Der Zauberflote*, with its Queen of the Night, monster, and forces of darkness and light.

22. As Piaget has argued, "absence of individual identity and of general class" are two traits intrinsic to a child's perception of the objects in the surrounding world. See Piaget, *Plays*, 226.

23. Piaget maintains that in handling space, children start "by egocentric assimilation that reduces the data of distant space and time to those of the child's own immediate activity." Piaget, *Plays*, 270.

24. Fantastic alterations in dimension are endemic to various childhood texts, for example, Bely's *Kotik Letaev*, where Kotik himself and everything around him constantly diminish drastically or swell into gigantic, overwhelming proportions. See, for example, "Jack and the Beanstalk" or Alice's sudden dwarfing in the rabbit-hole and just as startling elongation in the pool of tears. Carroll, 30, 33.

Small figures, such as Tom Thumb, dwarves, and so forth, proliferate in children's material as images of the Self awaiting development and suggest the helplessness, the fragility children feel in an environment that seems limitless and arbitrary—beyond their powers of assimilation and control.

25. Fairy tales from Russia, Germany, England, and elsewhere corroborate that what Marc Soriano and Paul Delarue claim for French tradition is, in fact, diffused across Western cultures in general, namely: " 'There is really only one monster which has remained traditionally the same for centuries and centuries: the wolf, terror of adults and children alike, the wolf who has in fact carried off and devoured so many children.' " Cited in Soriano, 28. Alice in Lewis Carroll's *Through the Looking Glass*, fascinatingly, equates entering a wood with a loss of naming powers; language and reference break down completely. On this, see Flescher, 135.

26. According to folklore accounts, walking backward can protect one from various spirits, for example, the forest "king" (*leshii*). The direction also recalls the pleasure Aleksei derives from Pushkin's poem "Devils" ("Besy") because the words move forward, then backward ("slova do kontsa doidut—i nazad povorachivaiut, snova doidut—i snova povorachivaiut" [97]). Such a reversal of normal direction is characteristic of nonsense literature, presumably geared toward children, in which "[r]unning backwards is a reversal of conventional order, legalized by the mirror." Flescher, 128.

27. The unprecedented power of Pushkin's metonymical role in Russian literature finds ample illustration in the fiction of writers like Dostoevsky, Turgenev, Zamiatin, Zoshchenko, Bulgakov, Solzhenitsyn, Iskander, Bitov, Narbikova, and countless other worshipers, who continue to enrich the signified behind the signifier "Pushkin."

28. Unveiled in 1880, to the accompaniment of Dostoevsky's idiosyncratic paean.

29. In Bulgakov's works, this lyric, curiously enough, is regularly singled out as the exemplar of Pushkin's talent. On Pushkin's role in Bulgakov's writings, see Goscilo, "His Master's Voice," 54–66.

Chapter 3

1. A native of Leningrad who resided in Moscow for many years, Tolstaya set four of her most affective stories in the "European" city built by Peter the Great. Three are analyzed here; the fourth is "Okkervil River" ("Reka Okkervil' ").

2. Romantic failures are the norm rather than the exception in Tolstaya's fiction. See, for example, "Hunting the Wooly Mammoth," "The Poet and the Muse," "Sonia," "The Circle." Page numbers in the body of the text identifying passages from the three stories refer to the following English translations: Bouis for "Sonia" and "Peters";

Gambrell for "The Moon Came Out." For the Russian originals of "Sonia" and "Peters," see Tolstaia, *"Na zolotom kryl'tse sideli . . . "*, 136–46 and 169–86, respectively; "Vyshel mesiats iz tumana" in *Krest'ianka* 4 (1987): 32–35.

3. I. Grekova, in her review of Tolstaya's collection, *"Na zolotom kryl'tse sideli . . . "* (1987), maintains that "zhalost' k svoim geroiam—odna iz otlichitel'nykh chert tvorchestva T. Tolstoi. [. . .] Zhalost' [. . .] odin iz glavnykh dvigatelei tvorchestva T. Tolstoi." Grekova, "Rastochitel'nost' talanta," 255. That opinion directly challenges Zolotonosov's (among others'), who descries in Tolstaya's prose "Neobychnoe sochetanie bezzhalostnosti, pugaiushchego vsevedeniia o geroe s kakoi-to literaturnoi 'igroi,' sochetanie ot kotorogo my otvykli." Zolotonosov, 58. Another reviewer notes, "V etikh rasskazakh ves'ma slozhnaia igra, sputano miloserdie i besposhchadnost'." Shishkova, 401. For dissenting and percipient reviews of Tolstaya's stories, see Vasilevskii and Bakhnov.

4. Not only Tolstaya's multifaceted, seemingly contradictory presentation of her personae, but the verbal pyrotechnics of her colorfully stylized narrators also recall Gogol. "Peters" and "Okkervil River" especially evoke Gogol's Petersburg tales, mainly because in the narrative the city's anatomy, its personality, becomes part of the protagonist's identity and the texture of his everyday life.

5. In a letter, Tolstaya revealed that in the plot of "Sonia" she transformed a story told by a relative. Tolstaya intended to portray her protagonist as stupid and nasty (*zlaia*), but failed in the latter, as Tolstaya herself acknowledges. Private correspondence of October 1990.

6. It would be difficult to find a feminine name in Russian more redolent of spiritual qualities than Sonia. Russian culture boasts Dostoevsky's Sonia Marmeladova, Tolstoy's self-abnegating Sonia in *War and Peace*, Bely's idiosyncratic Sonia Likhutina in *Petersburg*, Iurii Trifonov's Sonia in *House on the Embankment*, and Liudmila Ulitskaia's in *Sonechka*. To varying degrees, these draw on the Orthodox associations with Sofia as Divine Wisdom. First found in late Judaism, this concept of a personalized Divine Wisdom posited a feminine form as mediator, both of the work of creation and of God's knowledge of man. In Russian iconography, Divine Wisdom is customarily represented together with her three daughters, Faith, Love, and Hope (Sonia's chief attributes in Tolstaya's text). Although traditionalist Orthodox theologians strongly opposed the elaborate Sofiology developed by Vladimir Solov'ev, Pavel Florenskii, V.N. Il'in, and Sergei Bulgakov, Russian literature has proved more receptive to the notion of Sofia as a kind of entelechy of the universe, "comprehending the whole world in her ideal form and beauty." Benz, 63. For Tolstaya's repeated denial of selecting names for the sake of their denotative significance, see her comments at the conference in Lubbock, Texas, in October 1990 and her personal correspondence, also of October 1990.

7. So Platonic, in fact, that its "reality" exists only on the plane of the ideal.

8. According to Slavic belief, at death the soul turns into a dove. That the dove is symbolic of souls in the majority of cultures is confirmed by its function as a motif in Visigothic and Romanesque, as well as most Christian, art, the last being inspired by the Scriptures, which visually equate the dove with the religious concept of the Holy Ghost. Cirlot, 81. In many fairy tales, the white dove signifies a loving woman. On this, see von Franz, 30.

9. The ancients and modern literature (the Symbolists, Joseph Conrad, Nabokov) conceive of the butterfly as an emblem of the soul and of unconscious attraction toward the light, while psychoanalysis regards it as a symbol of rebirth (Cirlot, 33–34). Jung explicitly speaks of the soul (anima/psyche) as a butterfly. See Jung, "The Phenomenology of the Spirit in Fairy Tales," 66.

10. Since Sonia's function is emblematic, she is depicted externally; by contrast,

Peters's psychology has primacy in the later story, hence his perception of events shapes the narrative.

11. See Freud's claim: "as well as Eros there was an instinct of death. The phenomena of life could be explained from the concurrent or mutually opposing action of these two instincts. [. . .] the meaning of the evolution of civilization is no longer obscure to us. It must present the struggle between Eros and Death, between the instinct of life and the instinct of destruction, as it works itself out in the human species." Freud, 66, 69.

12. She represents Jung's negative engulfing mother. Jung, *Symbols of Transformation*, 328.

13. See the major argument of *Civilization and Its Discontents*, which turns on "the eternal struggle between Eros and the instinct of destruction or death" (Freud, 79). "If civilization imposes such great sacrifices not only on man's sexuality but on his aggressivity, we can understand better why it is hard for him to be happy in that civilization" (Freud, 52).

14. Peters thus becomes his grandmother's substitute son/husband, shuttling between the two poles of Eros/Thanatos.

15. Russian literature has rendered both names virtually synonymous with inaccessible feminine desirability: Faina in the verses of Blok and in Andrei Bitov's *Pushkin House*, and athletic, youthful Valia in Olesha's *Envy*. The peri recalls Bely's description of Nikolai Apollonovich Ableukhov's Sonia Likhutina in *Petersburg*.

16. Marcuse, 27, 29.

17. Whereas Grekova, who judges the story ultimately flawed, singles out the conclusion as the *pièce de résistance* not only of "Peters" but of Tolstaya's entire collection ("No vse iskupaet zamechatel'naia kontsovka—eiu venchaet ne tol'ko rasskaz 'Peters,' no i vsia kniga" ["Rastochitel'nost . . ." 25]), Zolotonosov, perhaps less attuned to Tolstaya's methods, finds the ending unconvincing and tacked on (Zolotonosov, 58). A more penetrating, if fleeting, glance at the story's ending is provided by Spivak, 202.

18. Peters's symbolic act of allowing life from the outside to enter his death-sanctuary resolves the dilemma of two insupportable alternatives that have gripped Peters up to this point. Here he sheds his psychological baggage and embarks on what could be a fresh, independent path to self-fulfillment. The notion, advanced by Galya Diment and noncommittally raised by John Givens, that the story's closing scene depicts Peters's suicide through defenestration ignores the tone of the conclusion and its transformation of earlier dark elements into positive signs (sun, spring, smiles, youth, birds in flight, gratitude). See Givens, 269.

19. Tolstaya appropriated the title, like that of her first story, from a children's counting rhyme.

20. The passage indicates that, despite Tolstaya's disclaimers, she recognizes that names trail associations behind them and in that sense are susceptible to interpretation. If the name Natasha evokes lyrical associations, they are above all due to Natasha Rostova, the young heroine of Tolstoy's *War and Peace*.

21. Vasilevskii draws an astute and essential distinction in his review of Tolstaya's fiction between Tolstaya's awareness of life's sorrows and banalities, on the one hand, and the narrative zest and imaginative originality in her depiction of them (Vasilevskii, 256–57).

22. As in her first two published stories, " 'On the Golden Porch' " and "Rendezvous with a Bird," Tolstaya conceives of childhood as a primal, enriching perspective on the world that time inevitably impoverishes or shatters (see Chapter 1). Here, as in " 'On the Golden Porch,' " Tolstaya invokes the suggestive image of the kaleidoscope:

> And then something broke, something went wrong. The kaleidoscope—and everything in it—shattered: a handful of dull glass shards, bits of cardboard, and stripe of

fiery, crimson-backed mirror. The world began to dwindle and wither, the grass receded, the ceiling lowered, borders started to show through, the delightful games were forgotten. (55)

A potom chto-to slomalos', chto-to poshlo ne tak; kaleidoskop razbilsia, a v nem vsego-to: gorst' tusklykh stekliashek, karton da ognennye s iznanki poloski zerkal. Mir nachal s''ezhivat'sia v razmerakh i chakhnut', trava poshla na ubyl', potolok opustilsia vniz, prostupili granitsy, schastlivye igry zabylis'. (34)

23. Of the two available models for her old age, Natasha characteristically yearns for the visually comforting, idealized variant of women reared in gracious, privileged surroundings:

On the summer boulevards sat old women who had known a better life: gilded cups, the frosty flora of lace hems, the tiny antlike facets of foreign fragrance vials, and perhaps—indeed, most likely—secret lovers; they sat with one leg crossed over the other, their gaze lifted to where the heavenly evening theaters silently lavished burning crimsons, golden treasures; and the loving western light crowned the blue hair of these former women with tea roses. (61)

Na letnikh bul'varakh starukhi, znavshie lushchuiu zhizn'—pozolochennye chashki, moroznuiu floru kruzhevnykh podolov, melkuiu murav'inuiu gran' zamorskikh tsilindrikov s aromatami, a mozhet byt'—i dazhe navernoe,—tainykh vozliublennykh, sideli noga na nogu, podniav vzory vverkh, gde vechernii nebesnyi teatr bezmolvno rastochal goriashchie alye, zolotye sokrovishcha i laskovyi zapadnyi svet venchal chainymi rozami golubye volosy byvshikh zhenshchin. (35)

In keeping with the overall pattern of her fate, however, the alternative she dreads and rejects is what awaits her:

But nearby, heavily spreading their swollen legs, with drooping hands and drooping heads wrapped in dotted kerchiefs, flames all snuffed out, *like dead swans* sat those who had lived for years in brown communal kitchens, in dim corridors, those who had slept on iron frame beds next to deep-set windows, where beyond the speckled blue casserole, beyond the heavy smell of fermentation, beyond the tearstained glass, another person's wall darkens and swells with autumn anguish. (61, emphasis added)

A riadom, tiazhelo rasstaviv opukhshie nogi, opustiv ruki, opustiv golovy v krapchatykh platkakh, pogasiv vse ogni, *mertvymi lebediami* sideli te, chto prozhili gody v korichnevykh obshchikh kukhniakh, v tusklykh koridorakh, na zheleznykh krovatiakh, u gluboko prorublennykh okon, gde za sinei riabovatoi kastriul'koi, za tiazhelym dukhom kvashen'ia, za zaplakannym steklom temneet i nabukhaet osennei toskoi chuzhaia stena. (35)

24. See, for instance, "solntse [. . .] drozhit v vysote," "solntse polzet vverkh," "na samom verkhu," "vzory vverkh," "vospominaniia ob [. . .] ukhodiashchikh vvys' kupolakh potolkov," "nado vsem v vyshine prostiralsia mir vzroslykh—shumiashchikh, gudiashchikh vysoko vverkhu."

25. Bakhnov, in a short but for the most part discerning review of Tolstaya's collection, recognizes her concern with "eternal," "big" questions. Bakhnov, 226–28.

Chapter 4

1. For Tynianov's concept of parody as a catalyst to literary evolution, see Tynianov, "Dostoevskii i Gogol'. K teorii parodii" (Petrograd, 1921), reprinted in *Arkhaisty i novatory*, 412–55, and in *Poetika*, 198–226. See also Iurii Tynianov, "O parodii," in *Poetika*, 284–309.

2. Hutcheon, "Modern Parody and Bakhtin," 87, 93–94, 98. For a more extensive survey of parody, see Hutcheon's *A Theory of Parody*.

3. Tolstaya draws most liberally on Russian literature, folklore, and music, but also makes use of West European literature (especially French) and universal myths. On this, see Chapter 1.

4. Whether Tolstaya "likes" or "pities" her protagonists seems to have inordinately preoccupied both Soviet and émigré commentators, among them I. Grekova, F. Iskander, and Petr Vail' and Aleksandr Genis (who see her stories as "zhestoki, dazhe bezzhalostny k tem, kto ne zhelaet podchiniat'sia skazochnym poriadkam," in "Popytka k begstvu," 400).

5. The issue of intertextuality is a controversial one, especially among literary theorists. Roland Barthes, for instance, conceives of intertextuality as a phenomenon that by definition cannot be intentional. Harold Bloom, on the contrary, advances a "genetic theory" that describes the act of origination, positing intertextuality as a writer's conscious struggle with a dominant predecessor. A clear and balanced discussion of the two antithetical concepts and their influential exponents form a chapter entitled "Presuppositions and Intertextuality" in Culler, *The Pursuit of Signs*, 110–18. Common sense, I believe, dictates a synthetic notion of intertextuality, whereby writers consciously introduce some intertexts, while others seep unobtrusively into writings without their authors' awareness, simply because writers' creative selves are incubated in an environment of prior texts.

6. "Reka Okkervil'" first appeared in *Avrora* 3 (1985): 137–46, "Krug" in *Oktiabr'* 4 (1987): 99–104. Citations in Russian refer to the later collection, *"Na zolotom kryl'tse sideli. . . ."*

7. On the subject of minimalized plots in Tolstaya, see Chapter 1.

8. Cirlot, 262.

9. The apple, being also spherical in shape, signifies totality. Its role in the lapsarian myth has added temptation and desire to its connotations. The circle traditionally has been associated with perfection and eternity. Cirlot, 14 and 45.

10. Most Western cultures identify chrysanthemums with autumn, especially October. Because in Russia they are usually sold outside cemeteries, there they have associations with death. See Champion, 45.

11. At this point in the narrative the journal version of the story differs from the one in the anthology. Whereas originally the text read "I on snova, snova i snova ustanavlival iglu" (138)("Again, again, and again he'd stop the stylus"), in the later version Tolstaya prolongs the metonymical equation between record and woman: "I, perevernuv ee na spinu, ustanavlival iglu" (18) ("Turning her/it on her/its back, he'd stop the stylus). The change carries strong sexual overtones and more vividly, if comically, communicates the erotic aspect of Simeonov's obsession.

12. Lermontov, I (1964), 126. All further citations from Lermontov within this chapter refer to this edition and will be identified by volume and page numbers in the body of the text.

13. Several Soviet scholars have hypothesized that Lermontov's lyric refers to his distant relative Ekaterina Bykhovets, who reminded the poet of Varvara Lopukhina, an earlier "amour" who married another. Lermontov, I, 597.

14. Weldon, 119.

15. The pattern of a dreamer's flight to a familiar but undesired woman after rejection by his unattainable ideal recalls Kavalerov's retreat to Annechka's bed after Valia is lost to him forever at the conclusion of Iurii Olesha's *Envy* (Zavist').

16. Any reader of Gogol will detect the parallel between Simeonov's condition and that of Piskarev, the young idealist in "Nevsky Avenue" ("Nevskii Prospekt"), who

chooses to sink into drug-induced dreams of the Ideal Woman when confronted with the reality of a Petersburg prostitute onto whom he projects his yearnings for the unattainable sublime. A version of the same syndrome may be found in E.T.A. Hoffmann's "Der goldene Topf."

17. On Mann's handling of the myth, see Lindenberger, 188–91, and especially the references listed in n. 56 (189).

18. For a brief survey of the versions and an extensive discussion of Wagner's opera, see the study by one of the foremost American authorities on Wagner, Newman, 169–73, 173–278.

Wagner's operas, perhaps on account of the high identifiability of their code, have attracted many parodists (e.g., the British Anna Russell's humorous rendition of *The Ring*), while *Tristan and Isolde* was parodied by *Tristanderl uns Sussholde* before it even appeared on the stage (Hutcheon, "Modern Parody and Bakhtin," 101). Jean Cocteau's film *The Eternal Return* (1943) reworks the Tristan legend unparodically.

19. In Wagner, only one such meeting occurs, whereas in other versions (e.g., Thomas), they occur regularly.

20. Quoted in Singer, II, 474.

21. For instance, Singer, II, 477. The *Liebestod* section of Wagner's opera is so sensual that listeners could be forgiven for hearing in it a musical rendition of indefinitely protracted sexual union rather than spiritual purification, whereby Tristan and Isolde "turn their instinctual freedom to a chaste moral separateness, disdaining mere physical consummation." Conrad, 156.

22. On *Sehnsucht*, see Singer II, 472, and Newman, 269.

23. On Wagner's original treatment of night and day, see Newman, 254, and Singer, II, 472.

24. Quoted in Singer, II, 474.

25. It is surely not fortuitous that his two mistresses apart from Izolda have the eloquent names of Klara (*klar* in German means "clear" or "lit") and Svetlana (*svet* in Russian means "light"). On the question of Tolstayan names, see Chapter 3.

26. On the briars in the myth, see Newman, 181–82.

27. To register Vasilii Mikhailovich's lack of growth, Tolstaya at several junctures blurs the temporal boundaries of her narrative. For example, the reader has no idea of Vasilii Mikhailovich's age during his affairs with Klara and Svetlana or of exactly how long he stays with Izolda. General statements about his moods and states of mind likewise lack temporal markers and so could easily apply to him at twenty, forty, or sixty.

28. Given the story's use of German materials, Tolstaya, in associating Izolda with the color blue (face, arms, fence along which she walks) may be evoking the famous blue flower of Novalis's *Heinrich von Ofterdingen*.

Chapter 5

Adapted from "Monsters . . . Gender Stereotypes," by Helena Goscilo, in *Sexuality and the Body in Russian Culture*, edited by Jane T. Costlow, Stephanie Sandler, and Judith Vowles, with permission of the publishers, Stanford University Press. Original version © 1993 by the Board of Trustees of the Leland Stanford Junior University.

1. On the grotesque in Tolstaya's fiction, see Goscilo, "Tat'iana Tolstaia's 'Dome of Many-Coloured Glass.' " On externally grotesque couplings, see Chapter 3.

2. Such carnivalized pairings, of course, destabilize dogmatic distinctions and institutionalized hierarchies.

3. All passages from "Poet i Muza," which was not reprinted in the volume, refer to the original journal publication, *Novyi mir* 12 (1986): 113–19.

4. Zoia's motivation and her perception of the "love object" recall A. Terts's *The Trial Begins* (Sud Idet, 1956), wherein Karlinskii similarly equates Marina with his Purpose.

5. "Zoia worked in a hospital, in the information bureau, and she wore a white coat and thereby belonged a bit to that amazing, white, starched world [. . .]. And the king of this world is the surgeon" (52–53). In an interview with me in Moscow (May 31, 1988), Tolstaya acknowledged her animus against the medical profession, particularly its personal, intimate invasion of the body for impersonal reasons. That sense of violation by doctors communicates itself also in "The Poet and the Muse" and "A Clean Sheet" ("Chistyi list," first published in *Neva* 12 [1984]: 116–26), in *On the Golden Porch*, 77–99.

6. The *topos* of love as hunt may be traced to antiquity, when it enjoyed widespread use in the poetry of Ovid, Horace, and Virgil.

7. Feminist film theory first elaborated the notion that women frequently function as passive objects of male voyeuristic desire/possession within the subjective narrative of patriarchal (mis)representation in artistic form. The pioneering piece on the topic, which since has been superseded by somewhat subtler analyses in a more discriminating vein, is the article by the British feminist filmmaker and theorist Laura Mulvey, "Visual Pleasure and Narrative Cinema." For subsequent refinements of Mulvey's central thesis, see Kaplan, especially the section entitled "Is the Gaze Male?" 23–35; also Modleski, especially 13–14. Mulvey herself has been revising her original insight: see Mulvey, "Afterthoughts on 'Visual Pleasure and Narrative Cinema,' " 15, and "Changes: Thoughts of Myth, Narrative, and Historical Experience."

8. On the implications of the mirror as a traditional image of *vanitas*, see Berger, 51.

9. Zoia represents a prime instance of the conventional female vicious cycle whereby "women are accustomed to seeing themselves being seen, to valuing themselves according to others' evaluations of their appearance, and then to being devalued for this 'narcissism.' " Gardiner, 128.

10. In this orgy of vulgar pleasure one recognizes the "mercantile psychology" of which Tolstaya spoke in an interview, deploring the addiction to brand names and fancy goods that she considers a hallmark of "feminine prose," which, she notes, "is mostly written by men." Tolstaya, "A Little Man Is a Normal Man," 10.

11. In his trenchant examination of the politics of style in contemporary culture, Stuart Ewen restates the Marxist position via Georg Lukacs's *History and Class Consciousness* (1971), noting: "As relations among people are drawn, more and more, into a web of commodity exchange, 'the reduction of all objects for the gratification of human needs to commodities' takes on a 'ghostly objectivity,' establishing a common discourse for survival, and for aspiration." Ewen, 156.

12. Kappeler, 79.

13. That slogan is inscribed, for instance, in Elena Makarova's novella *To Bring to Term* (Na sokhranenii), where the hospital patient satirized as a typical "norm" of aggressive womanhood playing by Soviet society's rules (and clichés) pronounces: "Ona sumela sebia postavit'. Dokazat', chto ona tozhe chelovek i *imeet pravo na schast'e.*" Makarova, 82 (emphasis added).

14. Compare the passage with Flaubert's catalogue of ingredients in the romances that exerted a fatal formative influence on Emma Bovary's impressionable and undisciplined imagination: "Ce n'étaient qu'amours, amants, amantes, dames persecutées s'évanouissant dans des pavillons solitaires, postillons qu'on tue à tous les relais, chevaux qu'on crève à toutes les pages, forêts sombres, troubles du coeur, serments,

sanglots, larmes et baisers, nacelles au clair de lune, rossignols dans les bosquets, *messieurs* braves comme des lions, doux comme des agneaux, vertueux comme on ne l'est pas, toujours bien mis, et qui pleurent commes des urnes." Flaubert, *Madame Bovary*, 1957, 39. In translation, the passage reads: "They were all love, lovers, sweethearts, persecuted ladies fainting in lonely pavilions, postilions killed at every stage, horses ridden to death on every page, sombre forests, heart-aches, vows, sobs, tears and kisses, little skiffs by moonlight, nightingales in shady groves, 'gentlemen' brave as lions, gentle as lambs, virtuous as no one ever was, always well dressed, and weeping like fountains." Flaubert, *Madame Bovary* (1940), 42.

15. Tolstaya returns to the fairy tale for ironic comparison of motives when Nina starts hounding Lizaveta so as to eradicate her from Grisha's life. Compare Tolstaya's text, "Seven pairs of iron boots had Nina worn out tramping across passport desks and through police stations, seven iron staffs had she broken on Lizaveta's back, seven kilos of iron gingerbread had she devoured in the hated custodian's lodge: it was time for the wedding" (126), with that of "The Feather of Finist, the Bright Falcon": "Three cast-iron staffs have I broken, three pairs of iron slippers have I worn out, three stone communion breads have I devoured, all in my constant search for you, beloved!" ("Tri chugunnykh posokha izlomala, tri pary zheleznykh bashmachkov istoptala, tri kamennykh prosviry izglodala—vse tebia, milogo, iskala!"). Afanas'ev, II, 239. Finist, one of the four birds of paradise in Slavic folklore, is a variant of the Phoenix, the fabulous bird sacred to the Egyptians that arises, reborn, from its own ashes and functions as a symbol of the sun. The Russian fairy tale conflates the myth of rebirth with the myth of Cupid and Psyche, which narrates the synthesis of the body (material) and the spirit (transcendent). The latter myth, found in Apuleius's *Golden Ass*, La Fontaine's *Psyche*, I. Bogdanovich's *Dushen'ka*, and put to evocative use by Leo Tolstoy in *Anna Karenina* and Andrei Platonov's "Fro," follows the folktale pattern of "the search for the lost husband" (No. 425 according to Stith Thompson's classification). Thompson, 98.

On Platonov's reliance on the myth, see Zholkovsky, 270–96.

16. In this double-layered discourse, the style of the idealistic 1840s seems grafted onto the utilitarian values of the 1860s, creating an inner tension that evokes the clashing worlds of the fathers and sons captured in Turgenev's and Dostoevsky's generational novels, *Fathers and Sons* and *The Possessed*.

17. Dijkstra's compellingly argued thesis that fin-de-siècle culture entertained erotic fantasies of feminine evil is richly supported by the plethora of reproductions in the volume, which diagnoses, inter alia, the period's inordinate fascination with prostrate women who are sleeping or merely sprawling languidly in poses calculated to stimulate libidinous thoughts in the viewer. In some cases, sickness, of which there was an unprecedented cult at the time, accounted for the women's lying in bed. Frailty and consumptiveness were deemed desirable in women as evidence of their purity, whereas health and vigor, as masculine traits, compromised the "feminine essence." Dijkstra, especially 25–63. For additional insight into the cult of invalidism, see the chapter entitled "The Sexual Politics of Sickness," in Ehrenreich and English, 101–40.

18. Tolstoy's *Anna Karenina*, which studies, inter alia, sexuality and possession of diverse sorts, synthesizes the two in the powerful scene in which Anna gazes avidly at the sleeping Vronskii, whom she views as lover, enemy, and victimizer even as she herself victimizes him:

> To escape from her fears, she hastily went to him in his study. He was sound asleep. She went up to him, and *holding the lighted candle over his face*, stood a long time looking at him. Now, when he was asleep, she loved him so much that she could not

restrain tears of tenderness at the sight of him; but she knew that were he to wake up, he would look at her coldly, conscious of his own rightness. (Tolstoy, 744)

. . . chtoby spastis' ot svoego strakha, ona pospeshno poshla v kabinet k nemu. On spal v kabinete krepkim snom. Ona podoshla k nemu i, *sverkhu osveshchaia ego litso,* dolgo smotrela na nego. Teper', kogda on spal, ona liubila ego tak, chto pri vide ego ne mogla uderzhat' slez nezhnosti; no ona znala, chto esli b on prosnulsia, to on posmotrel by na nee kholodnym, soznaiushchim svoiu pravotu vzgliadom. (Tolstoi, vol. XIX, 331–32)

A reading of *Anna Karenina* from the standpoint of folk myth and psychology has also noticed the Cupid/Psyche analogy here. See Mandelker, 63–64.

19. The Russian text in *Novyi mir* omits this sentence, translated by Jamey Gambrell in the English version from Tolstaya's manuscript (*Sleepwalker in a Fog,* 129).

20. The motif of fatality that accompanies their misunion is introduced at the very outset and repeats itself throughout the narrative: "Grisha beat his porcelain brow against the wall and cried out that fine, all right, he was prepared to die, but after his death—you'll see—he'd come back to his friends and never be parted from them again" (127); "Only he was a frail thing: he cried a lot and didn't want to eat, [. . .] whimpered and made up poems that offended Nina, about how motherwort had sprouted in his heart, his garden had gone to seed, the forests had burned to the ground, and some sort of crow was plucking, so to speak, the last star from the now-silent horizon, and how he, Grishunia, seemed to be inside some hut, pushing and pushing at the frozen door, but there was no way out" (128); "He roamed the apartment and muttered—muttered that he would soon die, and the earth would be heaped over him" (129).

21. See also the passage: "Oh, to wrest Grisha from that noxious milieu! To scrape away the extraneous women who'd stuck to him like barnacles to the bottom of a boat; to pull him from the stormy sea, turn him upside down, tar and caulk him and set him in dry dock in some calm, quiet place!" (124–25).

22. Douglas, 47–48. See also Culler, "Rubbish Theory," in *Framing the Sign,* 168–82.

23. The startling capacity to add a human being to one's collection of objects, which Marxist feminists view as inherent in bourgeois patriarchy, likewise defines the character of the duke in Robert Browning's *My Last Duchess* and Gilbert Osmond in Henry James's *Portrait of a Lady.*

24. Here, as elsewhere, Tolstaya refracts an admirable character through the distorting lens of a less than reliable narrating persona with a vested interest in presenting the other, her polar opposite, in a negative light. All of Tolstaya's likable personae are presented from without, whereas Tolstaya tends to reveal the inner workings of her shabbier or self-deluded individuals via quasi-direct discourse. As Tolstaya once remarked during a telephone conversatin, "negation is easier and, for a writer, more interesting" (1994).

25. See also: "There they supposedly ravished her, knocked out half her teeth, and abandoned her, naked, on the seashore in a puddle of oil" (103); "Still completely naked, she and the ethnographer, who called her Svetka-Pipetka [. . .], holed up in an abandoned watchtower dating back to Shamil's time" (103).

26. It is possible that Tolstaya is familiar with the tradition, dating at least from Chaucer's time, of associating gaps in teeth with sexuality. See, for instance, the following lines from Chaucer's "Wife of Bath," which find a clear resonance in the specifics of Pipka's fate: "She knew all about wandering—and straying:/For she was gap-toothed, if you take my meaning," which, as Walter Skeat observes, equates "gap-toothed" with lascivious. Chaucer, 44. That opinion is echoed by John H. Fisher, who agrees that physiognomists interpreted gaps between teeth in a woman as indicating "a bold, lascivious nature." Fisher, 18.

27. If Peter Brooks's thesis is correct that narrative momentum and desire are intertwined, inasmuch as "plot is the internal logic of the discourse of mortality," then Pipka's exuberant accounts of her exploits conflate narrative drive and sexual energy in the teeth of temporality. See Brooks, *Reading for the Plot*, 22.

28. Pipka's final disappearance, for example, is surrounded by dramatic ambiguity:

> Some were certain that she'd married a blind storyteller [Homer's shade! —H.G.] and had taken off for Australia—to flash her new white teeth among the eucalyptus trees and duck-billed platypuses above the coral reefs, but others crossed their hearts and swore that she'd been in a crash and burned in a taxi on the Yaroslavl Highway one rainy, slippery night, and that the flames were visible from afar, a pillar reaching to the skies. (115)

29. The imagery of sirens, which James Joyce used analogously in *Ulysses* and T.S. Eliot in *The Love Song of J. Alfred Prufrock*, has a venerable tradition stretching back at least as far as Homer. Throughout the story, as in Byron's poetry and elsewhere, dust carries the rich connotation of mutability, reminding one of human mortality ("from dust to dust") and thereby lending a certain urgency to the issue of how one should spend the limited time at one's disposal. Rimma and Svetlana embody the quintessential Tolstayan contrast of matter/impermanence and spirit/transcendence, also elaborated in "Sonia," "Okkervil River," "The Heavenly Flame," and other narratives. On this, see Chapter 3.

30. In keeping with age-old prejudices and actual conditions in Russia in the nineteenth century, numerous novels of the age set on gentry estates use the arrival of the male protagonist on the scene as a catalyst to action and narrative momentum. In the majority of cases he departs (through travel or death), while the heroine in whose life he has caused untold upheaval remains as part and parcel of the stable environment. See, for instance, *Eugene Onegin*, sections of *Hero of Our Time*, *Dead Souls*, *Rudin*, and *A Common Story*, to name but a few.

31. Tolstaya's namesake Leo Tolstoy authored the classic nineteenth-century Russian fictional manual for woman's "natural self-fulfillment." Total immersion in her uxorial and particularly maternal duties, Tolstoy contended, are what bring a woman "Family Happiness" (Semeinoe schast'e, 1859). As in other spheres, Soviet ideology trod in Tolstoy's footsteps, championing family structures and rewarding prodigious feats of reproduction by monetary aid and decorations.

Nina Katerli's fine novella "Polina" depicts a parallel situation, with a comparable pair of female friends and a similar conclusion. See Katerli, 96–181, first published in *Neva* 1 (1984): 11–60.

32. The most lush sequences in the narrative tend to occur in summaries of Pipka's fabled adventures and in descriptions of Rimma's daydreams, both of which affirm the vividness of a varied, intensely felt life.

33. See, for instance, Remnick, especially p. B6, col. 6; Tolstaya, "A Little Man Is a Normal Man," 10; and, more recently, "In a Land of Conquered Men," 13: "I take a special interest in one type of Russian woman whom I constantly come across: a miserable, unenlightened tyrant craving power and happiness. 'Happiness' is one of the key words in Russian cultural mythology." During interviews Tolstaya emerges as a vociferous opponent of feminism, yet when, in a talk entitled "Tolstaya's Women" at a conference on contemporary women's fiction, I maintained that she, like most Russians, has a poor grasp of what constitutes feminism in the West, Tolstaya readily conceded that she has no familiarity with feminist scholarship (Conference on Soviet Women Writers, coordinated by Anthony Vanchu, University of Texas at Austin, November 1989).

34. Jacobus, 138.

35. Tolstaya was then unaware of the opening in 1990 of the Center of Gender Studies at the Academy of Sciences and knows little about Tat'iana Mamonova, Iuliia

Voznesenskaia, and the other feminists who in 1980 fell afoul of the government and were expelled from the Soviet Union. She has not heard of such current activists as Anastasiia Posadskaia, former director of Moscow's Gender Center, Ol'ga Lipovskaia, former editor of the unofficial women's publication *Zhenskoe chtenie*, Ol'ga Voronina, and other Russian intellectuals committed to the feminist cause.

36. Tolstaya's outspokenness regarding Belov doubtless swayed the vote against her when her name first came up for membership in the Writers' Union, dominated by the notoriously conservative contingent of literati. The organization finally admitted her in October 1988.

37. Tolstaya, "Notes from Underground."

38. For a sobering summary of Soviet misconceptions about feminism, see Belyaeva.

39. Ebeling, 9.

40. Ebeling's measuring stick for failure and success would be anathema to Tolstaya, who in a 1987 interview voiced her disgust with what she called writers' "mercantile psychology." Among various symptoms, she cited the irresistible compulsion to identify brands of goods because of a vulgar respect for prestigious trademarks. Tolstaya, "A Little Man Is a Normal Man," 10.

41. See n. 27.

42. *Wall Street Journal* (Thursday, May 11, 1989).

43. *Moscow News* 8 (1987): 10.

44. Conference on Contemporary Soviet–Russian Literature, Texas Technical University, Lubbock, Texas, October 4–6, 1990.

45. During a private conversation after the conference.

46. Ransel, 2.

47. As Nelly Furman has argued, "from a feminist viewpoint the question [for the textual reader] is not whether a literary work has been written by a woman and reflects her experience of life, or how it compares to other works by women, but rather how it lends itself to be read from a feminist position." Furman, 69.

I share Peter Brooks's nicely phrased conviction that "Most viable works of literature tell us something about how they are to be read, guide us toward the conditions of their interpretations" (Brooks, *Reading for the Plot*, xii). Yet I readily acknowledge that my reading of Tolstaya's textual "triptych" by no means excludes the possibility of other readings that I find less satisfying because they fail to account for many passages. For example, the notorious regimentation of literature in the Soviet Union might encourage readers to interpret the story as an indictment of official repression of authentic talent. At a conference sponsored by the Canadian Association of Slavists (Quebec, June 1989), where I delivered a paper that contained this chapter in embryo, a male colleague favored precisely such a "classically political" interpretation, finding a feminist approach "original and fascinating" but "far-fetched." My response that we were focusing on different aspects of the same phenomenon—political coercion—only served to confuse him.

Chapter 6

1. Whereas Hegel tends to concentrate on the pictorial arts, from which he draws the majority of his examples, my more comprehensive usage encompasses music, literature, and sculpture as well as painting.

2. The absence of a Renaissance in Russia strengthened its medieval tendencies in the modern era, hence the dogmatism and overt politicization in all of its arts that persisted until very recently.

3. Although Tolstaya vigorously denies assigning her characters eloquent names, the literal meaning of the Russian *filin* makes her choice of name here at the very least a happy accident. An eagle owl is a decoy bird in hunting. Galia comes to the conclusion that Filin, too, is an imposter, once his deceptive resemblance to the "genuine article" is unmasked as fraudulent.

4. Mephistopheles in Goethe's *Faust* as well as in other literary and operatic versions of the Faust myth entertains an audience in the Ratskeller with dazzling acts of transformation (black magic).

5. One of the ways in which Filin ensures that his Alisa, or Alice in Wonderland, is enshrouded in mystery is to prevent her from completing the tale of her mother's brooch. She embarks on that story three times, only to be interrupted each time by Filin, whose intervention is calculated to withhold the narrative from the reader. In fact, the reader learns nothing substantive about Alisa, other than the noncommittal information with which the story opens: that she is Filin's latest "passion"—on exhibit to Galia and Iura ("invited us over: to have a look at his new passion" [155]/"priglasil v gosti: posmotret' na ego novuiu passiiu" [147]), although the text does not explain whether the passion is for Alisa or for a recently acquired bibelot.

6. From Bulat Okudzhava's "Midnight Trolley" ("Polnochnyi trolleibus"). Okudzhava, 219–20.

7. From Pushkin's poem "The Stormcloud" ("Tucha" [1835]).

8. Like Filin, the improviser in Pushkin's unfinished narrative is unprepossessing and even suspect outside his role as artist. Once launched on an inspired improvisation, however, he seems transformed into a "higher category" of being.

9. An analogous distinction in the pictorial arts is wittily made by Magritte, particularly in his famous painting entitled "Ceci n'est pas une pipe," which has become "a condensed manifesto about language and the way meaning is conveyed, or blocked, by symbols." As Robert Hughes puts it, "No painter had ever made the point that 'A painting is not what it represents' with such epigrammatic clarity before. Corbusier's pipe, as redone by Magritte, was the hole in the mirror of illusion, a passage into a quite different world where things lose their names or, keeping them, change their meanings." Hughes, 244.

10. If the notion that any object transplanted from its context of utility into a showcase potentially qualifies as art has any merit, it carries weighty implications for the nonutilitarian nature of art itself.

11. The nonsensical verbal units sufficiently approximate bona fide words to create the illusion of language. The "poem's" veneer of authenticity is a clever achievement in a work that exposes brilliantly the arbitrariness of the signifier.

12. Tolstaya's use of this famous high-rise apartment building, located in Insurrection Square, has been analyzed by Natal'ia Ivanova, "Bakhtin's Concept of the Grotesque and the Art of Petrushevskaia and Tolstaia," in Goscilo, *Fruits of Her Plume*, 21–32.

13. A classic poetic formulation of the artist's solipsistic recoil from society into the hermeticism of a "pure art," Alfred Tennyson's "Palace of Art" also dramatizes the dire consequences of a flight from living life. The dilemma of art's social engagement versus its independence from all but formal constraints runs throughout the poetry of such English Romantics as Keats and Shelley, French Romantics like Huge and de Musset, and Russian Romantics—Marlinskii, Ryleev, and, of course, Pushkin.

14. Regardless of his own finesse and the rarefied atmosphere of the apartment, Filin extends his hospitality to a wide array of types, many of them conspicuously lacking refinement and education. In that sense, Filin is a true democrat.

15. Tolstaya's wolf contrasts dramatically with the most famous wolf in Russian literature, that in chapter 4 of Pushkin's *Eugene Onegin*, in the lines that all Russian

schoolchildren memorize: "Vstaet zaria vo mgle kholodnoi;/Na nivakh shum rabot umolk;/
S svoei volchikhoiu golodnoi/Vykhodit na dorogu volk" (IV, 41). Pushkin, 1937, 90.

16. Thomas Hobbes's *Leviathan* immortalized the cheerless apothegm, originating
in Plautus's *The Comedy of Asses* (Asinaria, line 495): "lupus est homo homini" (man is
wolf to man). The complete thought, however, is: "lupus est homo homini, non homo,
quom qualis sit non novit," rendered by P. Nixon, the volume's translator in the Loeb
edition, as "Man is no man, but a wolf, to a stranger" (more accurately, "to someone he
doesn't know"), which minimally refines the generalization. Plautus, 176.

17. Culture here is understood as the cultivation (L. *cultura*) of values.

18. It is surely no coincidence that, as Karsten Harries points out, the institution of
museums emerged in the first half of the nineteenth century—precisely when art became the
object of "almost religious reverence and respect," while losing its status as an integral part of
mass life (Harries, "Hegel on the Future of Art," 677). The recent self-conscious division of
culture into "high" and "popular," with "high" by definition denoting distance from the vast
majority of the populace, explicitly reflects the conviction that what the West has historically
labeled "culture" is located on a lofty, remote perch in a (real or imaginary) social hierarchy.
Both Pushkin's and Lermontov's lyrics, as well as the entire Symbolist repertoire, pro-
claimed in tragic or denunciatory tones the impassable divide separating the poet from the
"herd." Galia's deification of Filin as one of the elect continues that trend.

19. The visual metaphor parallels the focal one in Stanislaw Lem's *Solaris*, where
the space station suspended over the mysterious ocean symbolizes the stratification of
consciousness and unconsciousness, respectively.

20. Translated into practical terms, in the Soviet Union, art's elevation guaranteed
artists a much higher standard of living, owing to special food privileges, housing
opportunities, vacation packages, and similar perquisites.

21. The poet's two contrasting identities—a divinely inspired creator, on the one
hand, and an unremarkable human being, on the other—find eloquent expression in
Pushkin's lyric "The Poet" (1827), recast in stronger terms in Baudelaire's "Albatross."

22. Any ritual, of course, requires a willingness to subscribe to the conventions that
regulate its structure and system of beliefs, whether it be a church service (also derided
by Tolstoy in *Voskresenie*), consumption of meals, or any of the countless ceremonies in
which we engage daily without much reflection.

23. The term "willing suspension of disbelief" is Coleridge's.

24. Although the pithy statement is Tolstaya's, it echoes the Lermontov lyric that
Tolstaya's line turns on its head:

> Rasstalis' my; no tvoi portret
> Ia na grudi moei khraniu:
> Kak blednyi prizrak luchshikh let,
> On dushu raduet moiu.
>
> I novym predannyi strastiam,
> Ia razliubit' ego ne mog:
> *Tak khram ostavlennyi—vse khram,*
> *Kumir poverzhennyi—vse bog!*

> (Lermontov, I, 382, 1964, emphasis added.)

25. Such an innocent approach to art has helped to create mythologies around Pus-
kin, Blok, and countless other poets. Since writers were figures of incalculable moral
authority in both tsarist and Soviet Russia, Russians have tended to canonize them, even
when that process has necessitated its own form of censorship: glaring omissions and
alteration of recorded facts. Pushkin, above all, has attained the status of a near-divinity
and in that capacity appears in numerous contemporary works as a metonymy for Art

(see, for instance, Bulgakov's *Master and Margarita*, Zamiatin's *We* [My], Solzhenitsyn's *First Circle* [V kruge pervom], and Bitov's *Pushkin House* [Pushkinskii Dom]). Tolstaya's most recent publication, "Plot" ("Siuzhet"), makes ironic use of Pushkin as a cultural matrix.

For a more complex and thought-provoking concept of authorship, see Foucault's essay, "What Is an Author?" which maintains that the author "is the principle of thrift in the proliferation of meaning [. . .] he is a certain functional principle by which, in our culture, one limits, excludes, and chooses: in short, by which one impedes the free circulation, the free manipulation, the free composition, decomposition, and recomposition of fiction" (Foucault, 118–19). The essay originally appeared in English translation in *Textual Strategies: Perspectives in Post-Structuralist Criticism*, ed. Josue V. Harari (Ithaca: Cornell University Press, 1979), 141–60.

26. See the closing line of the "little tragedy," in which Salieri asserts: "Genii i zlodeistvo/Dve veshchi nesovmestnye." Pushkin, III, 300, 1974–78.

27. The opening of Virgil's *Aeneid* cited here takes its cue, of course, from the original models of oral epic, Homer's *Iliad* and *Odyssey*, which were actually chanted (see Lord, *The Singer of Tales*). Since "to sing" thereafter meant "to compose epics," the various divisions of that genre, even in its written variant, were labeled cantos (*cantare*), as in Byron's mock-epic *Don Juan*. Pushkin's *Eugene Onegin* parodies the conventional epic exordium in the last stanza of its penultimate chapter.

28. For a relatively up-to-date bibliography of narratology, topically arranged, see Wallace Martin, 212–38.

29. See also the recent monograph by Sandra Nadaff, indebted to Brooks, Tsvetan Todorov, and Gilles Deleuze, which analyzes the nature of repetition in the construction of the text of *The Thousand and One Nights* and its contribution to "arabesque," or nonrepresentational, structure.

30. Pipka, whose desire is reflected in her evocative name, her nakedness, her sexual exploits, and her *vagina dentata* mouth, is an ambulatory storehouse of narratives. With her disappearance, the narrative momentum grinds to a near-halt, and with her purported death, ceases altogether. Tolstaya repeatedly associates narrative energy with the life force.

31. That paradoxical impulse finds lyrical expression in Goethe's "Dauer im Wechsel."

32. Following Brooks, Miller identifies the two primary elements motivating the narratable as "the drift of desire, continually wandering in a suggestible state of mediation, and the drift of the sign, producing other signs as it moves toward—or away from—a full and settled meaning." Miller denies closure "the totalizing powers of organization" and its corollary of resolved meaning that critics like Jean-Paul Sartre, Roland Barthes, and Charles Grivel have claimed for it. Although I share Miller's discomfort with the enshrinement of closure as "an all-embracing cause in which the elements of a narrative find their ultimate justification," my objection to Miller's own argument is that a bona fide closure *makes possible* (but not inescapable) a "totally coherent" reading of the text in which questions may not be fully answered, yet are effectively silenced or laid to rest. Suppression *is* an authorial solution, though it obviously should not be mistaken for a satisfactory resolution. If Miller equates authentic closure, as he seems to, with a harmonious settling of every issue, however minor, explicitly or implicitly raised by a narrative, then, indeed, given the nature of language, closure can never be complete and airtight. But surely that kind of maximalism trivializes the issue. See Miller, xi–xiii.

Curiously, although Miller refers to Bakhtin at one juncture, he makes no mention of Bakhtin's concept of the novel as the quintessentially open-ended form, with which Miller's own ideas accord to an extent. Where Miller's understanding of openness diverges from Bakhtin's is that, whereas for the latter it means an author's systematic exploitation through dialogized heteroglossia of a potential inherent in the genre per se and made manifest throughout the narrative, Miller's focus falls on a narrower unit—the novelistic ending—which he relates to the narrative preceding it, without, however, surrendering the priority of the ending in his thesis.

33. With the exception of her first story, " 'On the Golden Porch' " (" 'Na zolotom kryl'tse sideli . . . ' "), and "Peters," both of which stress origins, Tolstaya's stories favor openings *in medias res*, whether they be a line of dialogue ("Loves Me—Loves Me Not"/"Liubish'—ne liubish'!"), a rhetorical question ("Fire and Dust"/"Ogon' i pyl' "), or a provocative, named statement of fact devoid of all context ("Sweet Dreams, Son"/"Spi spokoino, synok" and "A Clean Sheet"/"Chistyi list").

34. For an elegant, insightful investigation into the nature of beginnings, see Said.

35. Since I discuss "Okkervil River" at some length in Chapter 4 as a parody of the myth of the Eternal Feminine and since Chapter 9 examines its exfoliation of metaphors, I shall limit my commentary here to those aspects of the story salient when juxtaposed with "Fakir."

36. Whereas it would be impossible not to detect instantly Pushkin's and Gogol's presence in Tolstaya's text, the latter's links with Dostoevsky's and Bely's novels operate more subtly and covertly. For instance, Simeonov parallels Raskolnikov in that he also lives alone in a dingy apartment, translating, but above all dreaming in solitude, while pestered by a "domestic" woman. Once his private fantasies are taken outdoors and confront "living life," they prove untenable and result in death—metaphorical in Tolstaya's scenario, as opposed to literal in Dostoevsky's. The connection with Bely primarily consists of treating mental activities and categories as landmarks in the city's topography.

37. On the role of Anna Akhmatova in Vera Vasilevna's portrait, see Chapter 9, devoted to Tolstaya's tropes.

38. The moral aspect of Peter's watershed enterprise enters Tolstaya's text via Pushkin's narrative poem, which characteristically poses the paradox that Bely subsequently explored in his apocalyptic *Petersburg*: every act of creation entails an element of destruction. Tolstaya introduces *The Bronze Horseman* through the motifs of history, flooding, white bones, and the death of hopes and illusions.

39. For an analysis of how women's clothes, bodies, individual bodily parts, and movements have been fetishized into erotic commodities for (mental or physical) male consumption, see Brownmiller. Brownmiller singles out several motifs on which Tolstaya's Simeonov dwells: the "staccato clickety-click of the heels" (Brownmiller, 70) and the wobbly walk owing to exaggeratedly high heels (183–87), and the veil as "a worldwide symbol of mysterious female sexuality" (96). The act of sheathing one's arms in long black gloves and then stripping them off is, of course, patently sexual, as corroborated by numerous strip shows in which elbow-length gloves are frequently worn by women clad only in tassels and a G-string.

40. That confrontation with Vera Vasilevna in the flesh signals the demise of Simeonov's envisioned ideal is conveyed through death imagery: white bones, chrysanthemums (Russian cemetery flowers), autumn. See Chapter 4 on the parodic use of intertexts in the story.

41. The title of Roland Barthes's account (London, 1976).

Chapter 7

1. See Sloan.

2. That association recalls the connection between life and narrative instantiated in Shahrazad's *A Thousand and One Nights* and elaborated in Peter Brooks's Freud-indebted study *Reading for the Plot*.

3. White, "The Value of Narrativity."

4. The atmosphere of the story recalls works such as *Rudin* and *Smoke*.

5. Walter Benjamin in his essay "The Storyteller" likewise has recourse to the metaphor of flame in characterizing the storyteller as "the man who could let the wick of his life be consumed completely by the gentle flame of his story." See Benjamin.

6. Throughout, I cite both from the original and from the English version of Jamey Gambrell, 77–90.

7. The process recalls a technique used by Tolstoy in both *War and Peace* and *Anna Karenina* to discredit totalization. For instance, in the latter novel, when Levin shifts from exaltation to sullenness, he interprets everything around him according to the pendular swings in his mood, as does Anna. The device enables the reader to detect the error of sweeping generalization, undifferentiated summary, and similar unprosaic neglect of shades and details.

8. An extreme version of this idea is J. Hillis Miller's contention that "reading [and listening?] involves a universal necessity to lie." On this, see Scholes.

9. Among other motivations, of course, is the desire to supply readers with the pleasures of vicarious experience, but my major concern in this chapter is with questions of veracity.

10. What self-interest does exist to a large extent stems from both parties' sub- or unconscious desire for legitimation of a worldview that is, of course, inseparable from the self. Neither writer nor reader approaches a text innocently, for, as Scholes remarks, "we are never outside the whole web of textuality in which we hold our cultural being and in which every text awakens echoes and harmonies" (Scholes, 6).

11. This is what Roland Barthes had in mind when he asserted that reading/listening means "rewriting the text of the work within the text of our lives."

12. Eliot, *Middlemarch*, 255.

13. Although Dostoevsky in his *Notes from Underground* pioneered the accusation masquerading as confession, the Soviet period was especially rich in such two-faced genres: Olesha's *Envy*, Zamiatin's *We*, Bulgakov's *Master and Margarita*, and Siniavskii's signally titled *The Trial Begins*.

Chapter 8

1. "Time Is an Understanding," 143. Further citations from Trifonov refer to this source and hereafter will be identified by page numbers in parentheses in the body of the text.

2. Ricoeur, *Time and Narrative*. For Ricoeur, monumental time, "of which chronological time is but the audible expression," results from "all the complicities between clock time and figures of authority," of official tabulation (II, 106 and 112). In his massive study, he takes considerable pains to distinguish between Bergson's spatialized time and his concept of monumental time (II, 190, n. 23).

3. Henri Bergson made the subjective notion of duration (*durée*) central in his philosophy. He postulated physical time as something spatialized and intellectualized (measurable only through its "strange and incomprehensible contamination by space," to cite Ricoeur [*Time and Narrative*, III, 12]), whereas intuition (inner experience) teaches us that "pure time" or real duration, in the form of directly experienced change, is the "real" phenomenon of time. Bergson, *Essai sur les donnés immédiates* and *Matière et mémoire*.

4. In his late period, Mikhail Bakhtin equated "great time" with entire lifetimes, with "the sense that past events, as they become congealed in institutions, languages of heteroglossia, and genres, pose specific problems and offer specific resources for each

present moment that follows." Morson and Emerson, 414. To grasp the inner connectedness of past, present, and future means to understand "the fullness of time," with which Bakhtin credits Goethe. See Bakhtin, *"Bildungsroman,"* 10–59.

5. See Ricoeur's discussion of Husserl versus Kant, *Time and Narrative,* III, 46–47.

6. Ricoeur appropriately stresses the importance for a theory of narrative that both approaches to the problem of time remain open, "by way of the mind as well as by way of the world. The aporia of temporality, to which the narrative operation replies in a variety of ways, lies precisely in the difficulty in holding on to both ends of this chain, the time of the soul and that of the world." Ricoeur, *Time and Narrative* III, 14. Tolstaya's concept of time and its narrative articulation acknowledge both ends but valorize the "soul." Her orientation on first glance seems to ally her, unsurprisingly, with Augustine and his refutation of the cosmological thesis, until a close reading of her texts reveals the extent to which Tolstaya realizes that world time cannot be simply peeled away from soul time but interacts with it (if, most often, conflictively).

Unlike Ricoeur, Kermode contrasts "soul" time with "simple chronicity" or "humanly uninteresting successiveness." Kermode, 46.

7. Folkloric elements appear in most Tolstayan stories that re-create childhood: "'On the Golden Porch,'" "Rendezvous with a Bird," "The Moon Came Out," and "Most Beloved." "Most Beloved," for instance, shifts into a fairy-tale mode when it introduces the childhood motif: "Davnym-davno, po tu storonu snov, na zemle stoialo detstvo." Tat'iana Tolstaia, "Samaia liubimaia," *Avrora* 10 (1986): 93. All citations from the Russian text hereafter will be identified by page numbers in parentheses within the text.

8. On the garden topos in autobiography, see Lifson. On the portrayal of childhood in Russian literature, see Wachtel.

9. That inability to discriminate between generations is perhaps best illustrated by the classic child's avowed intention of marrying her/his parent, interpolated in "Rendezvous with a Bird," where Petia decides to marry the "seven-thousand-year-old" Tamila instead of his mother, as he originally planned: "Earlier he'd planned to marry his mother, but now that he had promised Tamila" (122) ("Ran'she on sobiralsia zhenit'sia na mame, no raz uzh on obeshchal Tamile" [116]). An index of Peters's infantilism is his regressive fantasy of retreat into marriage with his grandmother: "he should have married his own grandmother and quietly melted away in the warm room to the ticking of the clock" (191) ("nado bylo emu v svoe vremia zhenit'sia na sobstvennoi babushke i tikho tlet' v teploi komnate pod tikan'e chasov" [179]). On the Freudian implications of this, see Chapter 3.

Nabokov notes: "the inner knowledge that I was I and that my parents were my parents seems to have been established only later, when it was associated with my discovering their age in relation to mine" (14).

10. For a more thorough analysis of the lapsarian myth in Tolstaya's early stories, see Chapter 1.

11. For Aristotle's treatise on time, see *Physics,* Books III–IV.

12. Augustine's ruminations on temporality are contained in his *Confessions,* especially Book XI. As Ricoeur notes, for Augustine, "the before-and-after—that is, the relation of succession—is foreign to the notions of present, past, and future, and hence to the dialectic of intention and distension that is grafted to these notions." Ricoeur, *Time and Narrative,* III, 19. Augustine's predilection for the inward and Aristotle's for the scientifically verifiable (largely external) justify Ricoeur's respective labels for their theories of "time of the soul" and "time of physics."

13. Ricoeur, *Time and Narrative,* III, 16 and 18. Tolstaya's adult "now" occurs at the moment a child acquires knowledge of mortality (and sexuality). The break is definitive in one sense, for, as Dostoevsky rightly argued, (self-)consciousness, once

attained, cannot be voluntarily abrogated. Yet lapping against the watershed of this "now" (as opposed to the child's perpetual "now," to which Aristotle's formula is irrelevant) are memories of irrevocable bliss, for which adults yearn and which therefore inform post-"now" experience. So the break in Tolstaya's world is final insofar as childhood resists recapturing, yet paradoxically illusory because the impulse to regain that state persists throughout adulthood.

14. See Genette, *Narrative Discourse*, 35–40.

15. See, for instance, François Villon's "Où sont les neiges d'antan?" and Lenskii's lament, overpopularized by the tenor's aria from Tchaikovsky's opera, "Kuda, kuda, kuda vy udalilis'?"

16. The distinction, codified by Genette, is between *narrated*, or *story*, and *narrative*. What Tolstaya capitalizes on is not only the discrepancy between story time (*erzählte Zeit*) and narrative time (*Erzählzeit*) but the implications of spatial proximity on the printed page. Genette, *Narrative Discourse*, 33–34. This dualism resulting from retrospection is nicely encapsulated in Freud's notion of Nachträglichkeit.

17. On this, see, respectively, Ricoeur, *Time and Narrative*, passim, and White, *Metahistory* and *Tropics of Discourse*.

18. Compare these passages with Nabokov's "walls of time separating me and my bruised fists from the free world of timelessness," and his "prison of time" (14) with Tolstaya's "tugie zakony prostranstva i vremeni" (in "Sonia," 136).

19. On "multitemporality" or heterochrony (*raznovremennost'*), see Bakhtin, "*Bildungsroman*," especially 26, 32–42, and Morson and Emerson, 368, 424, 426.

20. To cite one of numerous instances, in *Dead Souls* [Mertvye dushi] Gogol describes the paper wrapped around a chicken carried by a passerby who pops up, never to reappear, and whose sole function is that of irrelevance.

21. The very issue of Zhenechka's death, however, is less clear-cut than one might suppose, for in a passage that seems to reflect or register the "now" of writing, Tolstaya's narrator muses: "Perhaps she actually is somewhere around here right now, only we can't see her" (92) ("Mozhet byt' ona gde-to est' i seichas, gde-to tut, prosto my ee ne vidim" [93]).

22. Through that strategy she forces the reader to share the narrator's obsession with the past and her a posteriori reassessment of Zhenechka's role in her life.

23. The first line of Fedor Tiutchev's lyric to autumnal passions, commemorating in poetic form his middle-aged love for the young I. Deniseva.

24. But not the items it would be most natural to omit. See Lodge, 75–76; Jakobson, 90–96.

25. Whatever their antithetical traits, the two axes obviously share the characteristic of selection.

26. Bakhtin, *Dialogic Imagination*, 155–57.

27. Tolstaya's depiction of Simeonov's "imagined" world carries so much aesthetic seductiveness and emotional conviction that the hermeneutically inclined critic is practically forced to read it not as an individual's fantasy but as a penetration into a transcendent realm accessible only to the elect—an "extratemporal otherworldly ideal," in Bakhtin's words (*Dialogic Imagination*, 158). Those two options recall E.T.A. Hoffmann, of course, above all such works as "Der Sandmann." A tropological solution to ontological and metaphysical issues such as Tolstaya's has come under criticism most notably by Paul de Man. See de Man, "Impasse de la critique formaliste."

28. The terms "tenor" and "vehicle" coined by I.A. Richards to designate the two components of a metaphor (or simile) tacitly assume that maintaining distance between the two elements under comparison is crucial. A "holds firm" (tenor), as one "travels"

(vehicle) to B. Tolstaya's frequent tendency is to stay with the vehicle instead of the tenor so as to make unexpected transitions the abruptness of which is disguised by the sheer lyrical power of the richly embroidered vehicle.

29. Heidegger in *Sein und Zeit* (1927) usefully observes that things or entities ("stuff"—*Zeug*) for "use" (*Gebrauch*) that are at hand or "ready-to-hand" (*zuhanden*) articulate their identities in the process of unreflecting usage and unobtrusively tend to comprise the part of our environment that we take for granted. When the "unusability" of equipment is discovered, it becomes "conspicuous" (*auffälig*) and present-at-hand (*vorhanden*) as well as potentially un-ready-to-hand (*unzuhanden*). See Heidegger, 95–107.

Karsten Harries, in comparing the contemporary museal attitude to art with Hegel's thesis on the future of art, echoes Heidegger in the insight that "What needs preserving does so precisely because it has lost its place in our world and must therefore be given a special place—often at great expense." Harries, "Hegel on the Future of Art," 678.

30. Passages such as these spotlight the nature of several generalizations made by two well-known and talented émigré commentators, Aleksandr Genis and Petr Vail´, here, specifically, their palpably inaccurate claim that "Things in Tolstaya generally fare better than people—they don't change the way people do" ("Veshchi u Tolstoi voobshche schastlivee liudei—oni ne meniaiutsia, kak liudi"). See Vail´ and Genis, 129.

31. The identical idea finds voice, in a less condensed mode, in Irina Polianskaia's novella *Mitigating Circumstances* [Predlagaemye obstoiatel´stva], 163.

32. Culler, *Framing the Sign*, 170–72.

33. On Solzhenitsyn and Shalamov in this connection, see Oja, 62.

34. Shishkova, 399. Genis and Vail´ conceive of time's passage as Tolstaya's greatest enemy, but rather fancifully ascribe what they call her enmity toward the relentless flow of time to her refusal to grow up: "In short, the author is a person who refuses to grow up. That's precisely why her main enemy is the relentless flow of time" ("Koroche, avtor—chelovek, kotoryi otkazyvaetsia vyrasti. Imenno poetomu ee glavnyi vrag—neostanovimyi beg vremeni"). Vail´ and Genis, 126.

35. In this context, see Walter Benjamin's conviction that "to articulate the past historically does not mean to recognize it 'the way it really was' (Ranke). It means to seize hold of a memory as it flashes up at a moment of danger"; "The past can be seized only as an image which flashes up at the instant when it can be recognized and is never seen again." Benjamin, 255. See also Wolf, "Reading and Writing" and *The Quest for Christa T.*

36. Cited in Cassirer, 72. See also Ricoeur's comments regarding the constructions of history (as reconstuctions answering to the need for a *Gegenuber*) on the "relation of indebtedness which assigns to the people of the present the task of repaying their due to people of the past—to the dead." Ricoeur, *Time and Narrative*, III, 157.

37. Operating, as Jakobson noted, on the principle of contiguity. Jakobson, 90–96. The essay in question is entitled "The Metaphoric and Metonymic Poles" and is part of a larger study, "Two Aspects of Language and Two Types of Aphasic Disturbances."

38. Cassirer, 72. The appraisal that for Tolstaya is crucial Cassirer explicitly rejects, confining the process to recognition and identification.

39. Tat´iana Tolstaia, "Somnambula v tumane," *Novyi mir* 7 (1988): 8–26. All citations from the story refer to this edition and hereafter will be identified by page numbers in parentheses in the body of the text.

40. In the English translation by Jamey Gambrell, the compact (*pudrenitsa*) becomes a perfume flacon (13).

Chapter 9

1. One of the strikingly few handbooks of rhetoric published in recent decades acknowledges that "rhetorical theory has [. . .] often, in its history, overlapped poetics" (Lanham, 87).

2. Cato, famous for his oratory skills, defined an orator as "vir bonus, dicendi peritus" (a good man skilled in speaking), and Cicero maintained that the orator's functions consisted of teaching, pleasing, and moving his audience (Lanham, 87–88).

For Quintilian, virtue was the primary quality needed by a master of rhetoric: "Oratorem autem instituimus illum perfectum, qui esse nisi vir bonus non potest; ideoque non dicendi modo eximiam in eo facultatem sed omnes animi virtutes exigimus" (The first essential for such a one is that he should be a good man, and consequently we demand of him not merely the possession of exceptional gifts of speech, but of all the excellences of character as well). Quintilian specifically refutes Plato by insisting that the principles of "upright and honorable living" are not a province exclusive to philosophy (Quintilian, 9–11).

3. In *Gorgias* and the *Phaedrus*, Plato contrasted rhetoric not with poetics but with philosophy. See Lanham, 88, and Ricoeur, *Rule of Metaphor*, 11. Recent debates on metaphor, however, have emphasized the tropological cast of philosophical discourse. See, for instance, Paul de Man's argument that "philosophy either has to give up its own constitutive claim to rigor in order to come to terms with the figurality of its own language or [. . .] it has to free itself from figuration altogether." De Man, "Epistemology of Metaphor," 11. Commentators have remarked also on the figurative infusion in scientific and biblical discourse and psychological investigation. See, respectively, Rorty ("the language of theoretical science is irreducibly metaphorical and unformalizable"), 33–34; Tracy, 89; Roger Tourangeau, "Metaphor and Cognitive Structure," *Metaphor: Problems and Perspectives*, 14–15; Kenneth Burke, *The Rhetoric of Religion: Studies in Logology* (Boston: Beacon Press, 1961); and Chapters 3 and 5 in *Metaphor and Thought*, 150–253 and 356–437.

4. Ricoeur, *The Rule of Metaphor*, 11.

5. De Man, "Rhetoric of Temporality," 187–88.

6. Because the epithet "ornamental" connotes embellishment, an afterthought superimposed for decoration, it, too, is not a completely satisfactory term but at least has the advantage of not relying on poetry to characterize prose.

7. See Kenneth Burke, *Philosophy of Literary Form: Studies in Symbolic Action* (Baton Rouge: Louisiana State University, 1941); *A Rhetoric of Motives*; Richards, *The Philosophy of Rhetoric*; Wayne Booth, *The Rhetoric of Fiction* (Chicago: University of Chicago Press, 1961/1983) (see especially the Preface to the first edition); de Man, *Allegories of Reading, Blindness and Insight*, and *Rhetoric of Romanticism* (New York: Columbia University Press, 1984).

Two Soviet critics have astutely noted Tolstaya's ironic stylizations of Symbolist poetry and prose. Their eloquent juxtaposition of a passage from "Peters" with fragments from Andrei Bely's *Simfoniia* spotlights the stylistic kinship of the two. Piskunova and Piskunov, 196.

8. When Jonathan Culler states, "Rhetoric, once rumored to have died in the nineteenth century, is once again a flourishing discipline, or at least a very active field," he inexplicably fails to note that although rhetoric as an independent discipline virtually vanished in the course of the preceding century, study of rhetorical devices never abated. It was pursued, however, under the aegis of poetics, notably formalism, and so forth. Culler, *Pursuit of Signs*, 188. The turnabout in literary theory and criticism starting in the 1970s has resulted in a changed terminology. Old labels have been replaced by new

ones (most in either category bearing overt or covert value judgments) that reflect the reconceptualizations: "literature" with "texts," "language" with "discourse," "quotation" with "intertexts," "coherent" or "consistent" with "totalizing," "poetics" with "rhetoric," and so forth. John Ellis turns his skeptical attention to this phenomenon in his rigorously argued polemic *Against Deconstruction*.

Paul Ricoeur's study of metaphor (*The Rule of Metaphor*) reviews, in characteristically painstaking detail, the fate of rhetoric from Aristotle to the present day. No existent volume devoted to metaphor can pretend to a comparable range and exhaustiveness, and I have relied prodigiously on his impressive, nuanced survey.

9. Passages from Tolstaya's fiction cited in Russian refer to the only volume of her prose published in Russian for all stories except those not included in that collection (see Chapter 1, n. 1).

10. Through juxtaposition, " 'On the Golden Porch' " dazzlingly exploits the potential of *accumulatio* as a device for communicating both plenitude and moribundness (R45, 47–48). In many cases, Tolstaya hitches *accumulatio* to anaphora in order to condense the disparate elements of an entire life into a suggestive summary, as in the first paragraph of "Sleepwalker in a Fog," which maps out much of the remainder of the narrative (R8).

11. Similes such as the following from "Peters" (contained within a personifying metaphor, incidentally) are infrequent in her texts: "Zhizn' proshumela, obognula ego i uneslas', kak ogibaet stremitel'nyi potok tiazheluiu, lezhachuiu grudu kamnei" (180).

12. For example, "I v skladkakh ee plat'ia, na grudi, solov'em nachinaet strekotat' slukhovoi apparat" (94).

13. In other words, Stein Olsen has compelling reason for calling a summarizing metaphor (both cognitive and decorative) "an economising device." Olsen, 40.

14. Quintilian, Book VIII, vi, 4–5.

15. For a meticulous analysis of Aristotle's concept of metaphor as formalized in his two treatises, see Ricoeur, *The Rule of Metaphor*. There and in his contribution to the conference and volume *On Metaphor*, Ricoeur assigns an ontological function to metaphor. He defines the latter as "an act of *predication* rather than of denomination," with a "new congruence" emerging at the predicative level. Essential to the notion of metaphorical sense, according to Ricoeur, is an awareness of the "*split reference* [cf. R. Jakobson] which is specific to poetic discourse," in which both feeling and imagination play a role. Ricoeur, "Metaphorical Process," 156. Although my understanding of the function of metaphor in Tolstaya's work differs somewhat from Ricoeur's presentation of the trope, both his erudite study and his complex essay have been useful for this chapter.

16. For instance, whereas Max Black, Ricoeur, and John Searle argue for metaphor's cognitive properties, L. Jonathan Cohen and Donald Davidson (in *On Metaphor*) account for metaphor in purely semantic terms. See especially *Metaphor and Thought*.

17. Cohen, 3.

18. To cite but a few, the Conference on Metaphor and Thought at the University of Illinois (September 1977); the Symposium on Metaphor at the University of Chicago (February 1978), which yielded the volume *On Metaphor*, ed. Sheldon Sacks; the Interdisciplinary Conference on Metaphor at the University of California at Davis (April 1978); the Conference on Philosophy and Metaphor at the University of Geneva (June 1978); *New Literary History* 6, 1 (1974); *Critical Inquiry* 5, 1 (1978); Ricoeur, *Rule of Metaphor*; *Metaphor: Problems and Perspectives*, ed. David S. Miall; Lakoff and Turner, *More than Cool Reason: A Field Guide to Poetic Metaphor*; and *Metaphor and Thought*, ed. Andrew Ortony.

19. That metaphor is a constitutive part of language, or, as Richards phrases it, its "omnipresent principle" (92), has been regularly acknowledged by some, while ignored

by others, for centuries. See, for example, Shelley's acute observation: "Language is vitally metaphorical; that is, it marks the unapprehended relations of things and perpetuates their apprehension, until words, which represent them, become[,] through time, signs for portions or classes of thought instead of pictures of integral thought: and then, if no new poets should arise to create afresh the associations which have been thus disorganised, language will be dead to all the purposes of human discourse." Percy Bysshe Shelley, "Defence of Poetry," quoted in Richards, 90–91.

Paul de Man posits the inescapably metaphorical quality of all human discourse.

20. On the matrix metaphor in Tolstaya's prose, see Goscilo, "Tat′iana Tolstaia's 'Dome,' " especially 287–88.

21. Debates about the cognitive properties of metaphor have persisted to this day and continue to vex such commentators as Ricoeur, de Man, and Max Black. See *On Metaphor* and *Metaphor and Thought*. Black first made the case for the cognitive status of metaphor in his watershed article "Metaphor."

22. The recent reinstatement of the name Petersburg to the city of Leningrad, which signaled an attempt to recuperate the concomitant cultural baggage, pays homage to the significance of words and the symbolic importance of naming.

23. I am indebted to Alexander Zholkovsky for first alerting me to the Akhmatovian elements in Vera Vasilevna's depiction. Notorious for her seductive appeal in her youth, Akhmatova during her autumnal years grew large, heavy, and torpid, suffered from ill health, and relied on the ministrations of younger men, who tended to her practical daily needs. According to Tolstaya herself, she heard a version of this story about Anna Akhmatova from the poet A. Kushner. Letter (at Chapel Hill) received from Tolstaya (Lubbock), October 20, 1990.

24. Pushkin often used the verb "to translate" metaphorically, to characterize the process of "transferring" reality into an artistic medium. See, for instance, *Eugene Onegin*, Chapter III, xxi.

25. See Richards, 47–66; J. Martin and R. Harre reprise Richards's emphasis on metaphor as an interaction of thought. See Martin and Harre, 89–105.

26. The paradox of Tolstaya's adamant assertion that she dislikes and avoids "tag names" pointing to a given persona's inner qualities when so many of her fictional names (Vera here, Svetlana/Pipka and Rimma in "Fire and Dust," Izolda in "The Circle," etc.) reflect character tendencies raises the intriguing and insoluble question of the subconscious element in creativity. See Tolstaya's closing remarks during the Conference on Contemporary Soviet–Russian Literature organized by Peter Barta at Texas Technical University, Lubbock, Texas, October 4–6, 1990, and her personal correspondence (letter of October 29, 1990).

27. The behavior of the poet Afanasii Fet offers a sterling, if perhaps extreme, instance of the discontinuity between an artist's work and his biography.

28. See especially Aleksandr Blok's poem "A Girl Sang in a Chorus" ("Devushka pela v khore" [1905]). The (often singing) voice as a transcendent sign recurs repeatedly in Blok's lyrics throughout his career. See, for example, "Ia shel k blazhenstvu. Put′ blestel . . . " (1899); "Lenivo i tiazhko plyvut oblaka" (1900); "Ona zhdala i bilas′ v smertnoi muke" (1902). Many metapoetic texts rely on the trope of the "divine voice" speaking through the poet (e.g., Pushkin's "Prophet" ["Prorok"]). As Joseph Brodsky notes in a rather quirky article, in antiquity the only way the (impalpable) Muse would reveal herself to a mortal was through her voice, by dictating a line of a poet's verse. Brodsky, 1150.

Widespread wings over a "lesser" landscape likewise play a key role in such Blok lyrics as "Kryl′ia" (1907), "I ia provel bezumnyi god" (1907), and countless other poems.

29. Mikhail Zolotonosov has voiced de Manian qualms about what he views as Tolstaya's attempts to resolve life's dilemmas through exclusively literary (chiefly

tropologial) means. See Zolotonosov, especially 59. In a predominantly enthusiastic review, the writer Fazil' Iskander has also remarked that Tolstaya's reliance on metaphor may be excessive. "Metaforicheskii les Tat'iany Tolstoi inogda kazhetsia chereschur obil'nym i zakoliuchennym." Iskander, 5.

30. The substantial article (pp. 3–45) offers an acute, nuanced survey, with the aid of such Bakhtinian concepts as dialogism and the chronotope, of what has been labeled contemporary "alternative prose." Lipovetskii, 14.

31. On these, see Chapter 1. In an unpublished paper, John Givens has neatly pinpointed the relevance of Ecclesiastes to Tolstaya's story "The Circle."

32. Although metaphor itself is frequently conceived of as deviant or improper denomination (see Harries, "Metaphor and Transcendence," 72; Moore, 2–7), it is nonetheless governed by certain general laws of propriety, violation of which results in catachresis (abuse through extravagance, misapplication, etc.). Probably the most common form of catachresis in modern usage is the mixed metaphor. See Lanham, 21.

Doubts regarding Tolstaya's handling of metaphor find expression in one reviewer's own rather belabored trope: "Metaphor hasn't quite run amok here, but it's been exercising and it's breathing hard" (Peter S. Prescott, *Newsweek*, May 15, 1989, 80); in Iskander's opinion, cited in note 29; in one critic's complicitous report: "T. Tolstuiu uprekaiut v islishestvakh stilia, perebore po chasti metafor i t.d. Vrode by verno" (Vysotskaia); and in Zolotonosov's impression that in the overly literary world of Tolstaya's fiction the tropes stifle her characters: "obilie metafor, metonimii, sravnenii [*sic*] sozdaet oshchushchenie nepronitsaemosti, plotnosti, dukhoty" (Zolotonosov, "Mechty i fantomy," 59; in expanded form, reprinted as Mikhail Zolotonosov, "Tat'ianin den'," *Molodye o molodykh* [Moscow: Molodaia gvardiia, 1988], 105–18). Zolotonosov's observation that her tropes lend her fictional world "corporality" is sound.

33. See *Webster's Seventh New Collegiate Dictionary* (Springfield, MA: G & C Merriam Co., 1963).

34. In his *Reflections on Poetry* (1735), the German Baumgarten analogizes the ordered world of God with the domain of a poem overseen by the poet as divine creator (63).

35. I.A. Richards, who instituted the terminology of tenor and vehicle (Richards, 96), early observed that

> with different metaphors the relative importance of the contributions of vehicle and tenor to this resultant meaning varies immensely. At one extreme the vehicle may become almost a mere decoration or coloring of the tenor, at the other extreme, the tenor may become almost a mere excuse for the introduction of the vehicle, and so no longer be "the principal subject." And the degree to which the tenor is imagined "to be that very thing which it only resembles" also varies immensely. (100–1)

36. Harries, "Metaphor and Transcendence," 81.

37. Genette, "Métonymie chez Proust," 42–43; de Man, *Allegories of Reading*, 65–67. Culler discusses the two positions in "The Turns of Metaphor," 192–99.

38. On this topic, see, for example, Culler, "The Turns of Metaphor," 194–98.

39. Jakobson, 90–96; Lodge, 73–93. My cursory synopsis of the two tropes relies on Lodge's excellent statement of the issues involved.

40. Peter Brooks has written eloquently on the inseparability of metaphor and metonymy in narrative, particularly in his analysis of Sir Arthur Conan Doyle's "The Musgrave Ritual," where, Brooks claims, "The metaphoric work of eventual totalization determines the meaning and status of the metonymic work of sequence—though it must be claimed that the metonymies of the middle produced, gave birth to, the final metaphor. The contradiction may be in the very nature of narrative, which not only uses but *is* a double logic." Brooks, *Reading for the Plot*, 29.

41. Johnson, 157. The volume is dedicated to the memory of de Man and Linda Miller. The essay in question, "Metaphor, Metonymy, and Voice in *Their Eyes Were Watching God*," originally appeared in *Black Literature and Literary Theory*, ed. Henry Louis Gates, Jr. (New York: Methuen, 1984).

Conclusion

1. *Moscow News* 11 (March 25–April 1, 1990): 14.
2. *London Review of Books* (June 1989): 23.
3. "Russian Lessons," *The New York Review of Books* (October 19, 1996): 7.
4. *Ogonek* (March 14, 1990): 31.
5. *The New York Review of Books* (May 31, 1990): 3–7.
6. "In Cannibalistic Times," *The New York Review of Books* (April 11, 1991): 3–6.
7. "The Age of Innocence," *The New York Review of Books* (October 21, 1990): 24–26.
8. "President Potemkin," *The New Republic* (May 27, 1991): 27–35.

Works Cited

Afanas'ev, A.N., ed. *Narodnye russkie skazki*. 3 vols. Moscow: Gosizkhudlit, 1958.

Alexander, Ian. *Bergson. Philosopher of Reflection*. New York: Hillary House, 1957.

Bakhnov, Leonid. "Chelovek so storony." *Znamia* 7 (1988): 226–28.

Bakhtin, Mikhail. "The *Bildungsroman* and Its Significance in the History of Realism (Toward a Typology of the Novel)." In *Speech Genres and Other Late Essays*, ed. Caryl Emerson and Michael Holquist. Austin: University of Texas Press, 1986.

———. *The Dialogic Imagination*, ed. Michael Holquist, trans. Caryl Emerson and Michael Holquist. Austin: University of Texas Press, 1981.

Barta, Peter I. "The Author, the Cultural Tradition and Glasnost: An Interview with Tatyana Tolstaya." *Russian Language Journal* 147–149 (1990): 268.

Barthes, Roland. *The Pleasure of the Text*. New York: Hill and Wang, 1975.

Baumgarten, Alexander Gottlieb. *Reflections on Poetry*, trans. Karl Aschenbrenner and William B. Holther. Berkeley and Los Angeles: University of California Press, 1954.

Belyaeva, Nina. "Feminism in the USSR." *Canadian Woman Studies* 10, 4 (Winter 1989): 17–19.

Benjamin, Walter. *Illuminations*. New York: Schocken Books, 1969.

Benz, Ernst. *The Eastern Orthodox Church*. New York: Anchor/Doubleday and Co., 1963.

Berger, John. *Ways of Seeing*. Harmondsworth: Penguin Books, 1972.

Bergson, Henri. *Essai sur les donnés immédiates de la conscience* (1889).

———. *Evolution créatrice*. Paris, 1907.

———. *Matière et mémoire* (1896).

Bitov, Andrei. *Stat'i iz romana*. Moscow: Sovetskii pisatel', 1986.

Black, Max. "Metaphor." In *Proceedings of the Aristotelian Society* 55 (1954–55): 273–94.

Bloom, Harold. *Poetry and Repression*. New Haven: Yale University Press, 1976.

Booth, Wayne C. "Metaphors as Rhetoric: The Problem of Evaluation." In *On Metaphor*, ed. Sheldon Sacks, 47–70.

Brodsky, Joseph. "The Poet, the Loved One and the Muse." *Times Literary Supplement* (October 26–November 1, 1980): 1150, 1160.

Brooks, Peter. *Reading for the Plot: Design and Intention in Narrative*. New York: Alfred A. Knopf, 1984.

———. "Toward Supreme Fiction." In *The Child's Part*, ed. Peter Brooks. Boston: Beacon Press, 1969/1972, 5–14.

Brownmiller, Susan. *Femininity*. New York: Fawcett Columbine, 1984.

Bulgakov, Mikhail. *Sobranie sochinenii*. Vol. 8. Ann Arbor: Ardis, 1988.

Burke, Kenneth. *A Rhetoric of Motives*. Berkeley: University of California Press, 1950/1969.

Cantor, Paul. "Friedrich Nietzsche: The Use and Abuse of Metaphor." In *Metaphor: Problems and Perspectives*, ed. David S. Miall.

Carroll, Lewis. *Alice's Adventures in Wonderland. Through the Looking Glass*. Harmondsworth/Baltimore/Victoria: Puffin Books, 1948/1968.

Cassirer, Ernst. *An Essay on Man: An Introduction to a Philosophy of Human Culture.* Garden City, New York: Doubleday and Co., 1944.

Champion, Marie-Hélène, ed. *Les Secrets du language des fleurs d'après G. Dugaston.* Paris: Editions Albin Michel, 1974.

Chaucer, Geoffrey. *The Complete Works of Geoffrey Chaucer,* ed. Walter Skeat. Oxford: Clarendon Press, 1894.

The Child's Part. Peter Brooks, ed. Boston: Beacon Press, 1969/1972.

Chukovskii, Kornei. *Sobranie sochinenii.* 6 vols. Moscow: Khudlit, 1965–69.

Cirlot, J.E. *A Dictionary of Symbols.* New York: The Philosophical Library, 1962.

Coe, Richard N. *When the Grass Was Taller: Autobiography and the Experience of Childhood.* New Haven: Yale University Press, 1984.

Cohen, Ted. "Metaphor and the Cultivation of Intimacy." In *On Metaphor,* ed. Sheldon Sacks, 1–10.

Condee, Nancy. *Newsletter,* Institute of Current World Affairs, 17 (1986): 8–9.

Conrad, Peter. *Romantic Opera and Literary Form.* Berkeley: University of California Press, 1977.

Cuddon, J.A. *A Dictionary of Literary Terms.* Garden City, N.Y.: Doubleday and Co., 1976.

Culler, Jonathan. *Framing the Sign.* Norman and London: University of Oklahoma Press, 1988.

———. *The Pursuit of Signs.* Ithaca: Cornell University Press, 1981.

———. "The Turns of Metaphor." In *The Pursuit of Signs,* 188–209.

Dal', Vladimir. *Tolkovyi slovar' zhivogo velikorusskogo iazyka.* 4 vols. Moscow: Russkii iazyk, 1978.

de Man, Paul. *Allegories of Reading.* New Haven: Yale University Press, 1979.

———. *Critical Writings, 1953–1978.* Minneapolis: University of Minnesota Press, 1989.

———. "The Epistemology of Metaphor." In *On Metaphor,* ed. Sheldon Sacks, 11–28.

———. "Impasse de la critique formaliste." In *Blindness and Insight,* ed. Wlad Godzich. Minneapolis: University of Minnesota Press, 1971/1983.

———. "The Rhetoric of Temporality." In *Blindness and Insight,* ed. Wlad Godzich. Minneapolis: University of Minnesota Press, 1971/1983.

Dijkstra, Bram. *Idols of Perversity.* Oxford and New York: Oxford University Press, 1986.

Douglas, Mary. *Purity and Danger: An Analysis of Concepts of Pollution and Taboo.* Harmondsworth: Penguin, 1970.

Eagleton, Terry. *Literary Theory.* Minneapolis: University of Minnesota Press, 1983.

Ebeling, Kay. "The Failure of Feminism." *Newsweek* (November 19, 1990): 9.

Ehrenreich, Barbara, and Deirdre English. *For Her Own Good.* New York: Anchor/ Doubleday and Co., 1978.

Ellis, John. *Against Deconstruction.* Princeton: Princeton University Press, 1989.

Eliot, George. *Middlemarch.* New York: Houghton Mifflin, 1956.

Encyclopedia Brittanica. New York: The Encyclopedia Brittanica Society, 11th ed., 1910–11.

Erlich, Victor. "The Maker and the Seer." In *The Verbal Icon,* ed. William S. Wimsatt. Lexington: University of Kentucky Press, 1954.

Ewen, Stuart. *All Consuming Images.* New York: Basic Books, 1988.

Fisher, John H., ed. *Complete Poetry and Prose of Geoffrey Chaucer.* New York: Holt, Rinehart, Winston, 1977.

Flaubert, Gustave. *Madame Bovary.* Paris: Librairie Armand Colin, 1957.

———. *Madame Bovary,* trans. Eleanor Marx Aveling. New York: Modern Library, 1940.

Flescher, Jacqueline. "The Language of Nonsense in *Alice*." In *The Child's Part*, ed. Peter Brooks, 128–44.

Foucault, Michel. *The Foucault Reader*, ed. Paul Rabinow. New York: Pantheon Books, 1984.

Freud, Sigmund. *Civilization and Its Discontents*. New York and London: W.W. Norton and Co., 1961.

Furman, Nelly. "The Politics of Language: Beyond the Gender Principle?" In *Making a Difference: Feminist Literary Criticism,* ed. Gayle Greene and Coppelia Kahn. London and New York: Methuen, 1985/1986, 59–79.

Gardiner, Judith Kegan. "Mind Mother: Psychoanalysis and Feminism." In *Making a Difference: Feminist Literary Criticism*, ed. Gayle Greene and Coppelia Kahn. London and New York: Methuen, 1985, 113–45.

Genette, Gerard. *Narrative Discourse*. Ithaca: Cornell University Press, 1980/1987.

———. "Métonymie chez Proust." In *Figures III*. Paris: Seuil, 1972.

Givens, John. "Reflections, Crooked Mirrors, Magic Theaters. Tat'iana Tolstaia's 'Peters.' " In *Fruits of Her Plume: Essays on Contemporary Russian Women's Culture*, ed. Helena Goscilo. Armonk, N.Y.: M.E. Sharpe, 1993, 251–70.

Goscilo, Helena. "Feet Pushkin Scanned, or Seeming *Idée Fixe* as Implied Aesthetic Credo." *Slavic and East European Journal* 32, 4 (1988): 562–73.

———. "His Master's Voice: Pushkin *Chez* Bulgakov." In *James Daniel Armstrong. In Memoriam*. Columbus, Ohio: Slavica Publisher, 1993, 54–66.

———. "Multiple Texts in *Eugene Onegin*: A Preliminary Examination." *Russian Literature Triquarterly* 23 (1990): 271–85.

———. "Tat'iana Tolstaia's 'Dome of Many-Coloured Glass': The World Refracted through Multiple Perspective." *Slavic Review* 47, 2 (Summer 1988): 280–90.

Goscilo, Helena, ed. *Fruits of Her Plume: Essays in Contemporary Russian Women's Culture*. Armonk, N.Y.: M.E. Sharpe, 1993.

Greenwood, E.B. "Critical Forum." *Essays in Criticism* (July 1962).

Grekova, I. "Rastochitel'nost' talanta." *Novyi mir* 1 (1988): 252–56.

———. "Anketa 'LR': Mezhdu proshlym i budushchim." *Literaturnaia Rossiia* 1 (January 2, 1987).

Harries, Kirsten. "Hegel on the Future of Art." *Review of Metaphysics* 27 (1974): 677–96.

———. "Metaphor and Transcendence." In *On Metaphor*, ed. Sheldon Sacks, 71–88.

Heidegger, Martin. *Being and Time*, trans. John Macquarrie and Edward Robinson. New York: Harper and Row, 1962.

Holy Bible. Revised Standard Version. New York and Scarborough: New American Library, 1962.

Hughes, Robert. *The Shock of the New*. New York: Alfred A. Knopf, 1981.

Hutcheon, Linda. *A Poetics of Postmodernism: History, Theory, Fiction*. New York: Routledge, 1988.

———. "Modern Parody and Bakhtin." In *Rethinking Bakhtin*, ed. Gary Saul Morson and Caryl Emerson. Evanston: Northwestern University Press, 1989.

———. *A Theory of Parody*. New York: Methuen, 1985.

Huyssen, Andreas. "Mapping the Postmodern." *New German Critique* 33 (Fall 1984): 5–52.

Iskander, Fazil'. "Poeziia grusti." *Literaturnaia gazeta* (August 26, 1987): 5.

Jacobus, Mary. "Is There a Woman In This Text?" *New Literary History* 14 (Autumn 1982): 117–41.

Jakobson, Roman. *Fundamentals of Language*. The Hague and Paris: Mouton, 1975.

Jameson, Fredric. "The Politics of Theory: Ideological Positions in the Postmodern Debate." *New German Critique* 33 (Fall 1984): 53–66.

Johnson, Barbara. *A World of Difference*. Baltimore: Johns Hopkins University Press, 1987.

Jung, C.J. "The Phenomenology of the Spirit in Fairy Tales." *Psyche and Symbol*. Garden City, N.Y.: Anchor/Doubleday and Co., 1958.

———. *Symbols of Transformation*. Princeton: Princeton University Press, 1976.

Kaledin, Sergei, ed. *Poslednii etazh*. Moscow: Knizhnaia palata, 1989.

Kaplan, E. Ann. *Women and Film: Both Sides of the Camera*. New York: Methuen, 1983.

Kappeler, Susanne. *The Pornography of Representation*. Minneapolis: University of Minnesota Press, 1986.

Katerli, Nina. *Tsvetnye otkrytki*. Leningrad: Sovetskii pisatel', 1986.

Kermode, Frank. *The Sense of an Ending: Studies in the Theory of Fiction*. New York: Oxford University Press, 1967.

Kiparsky, V. *Paradiesvogel im russischen Schrifttum*. Helsingfors: Societas Scientiarum Fennica Arsbok—Vuosikirja, 29, 2 (1960).

Lakoff, George, and Mark Turner. *More Than Cool Reason: A Field Guide to Poetic Metaphor*. Chicago: University of Chicago Press, 1989.

Lanham, Richard A. *A Handlist of Rhetorical Terms*. Berkeley/Los Angeles/London: University of California Press, 1968/1969.

Leitch, Vincent B. *Deconstructive Criticism*. New York: Columbia University Press, 1983.

Lermontov, M. Iu. *Sobranie sochinenii*. 4 vols. Moscow, 1964.

———. *Sobranie sochinenii*. 4 vols. Leningrad: Nauka, 1979.

Lifson, Martha Ronk. "The Myth of the Fall: A Description of Autobiography." *Genre* 12 (Spring 1979): 45–67.

Lindenberger, Herbert. *Opera: The Extravagant Art*. Ithaca: Cornell University Press, 1984.

Lipovetskii, Mark. " 'Svobody chernaia rabota' [Ob 'artisticheskoi proze' novogo pokoleniia]." *Voprosy literatury* 9 (1989).

Lodge, David. *The Modes of Modern Writing*. Ithaca: Cornell University Press, 1980.

Lord, Albert B. *The Singer of Tales*. New York: Atheneum, 1965.

Marcuse, Herbert. *Eros and Civilization: A Philosophical Inquiry into Freud*. Boston: Beacon Press, 1955/1966.

Makarova, Elena. *Otkrytyi final*. Moscow: Sovetskii pisatel', 1989.

Mandelker, Amy. "Woman with a Shadow: Fables of Demon and Psyche in *Anna Karenina*." *Novel: A Forum on Fiction* 24, 1 (Fall 1990): 48–68.

Marinelli, Peter. *The Pastoral*. London: Methuen, 1971.

Marks, Elaine, ed. *French Poetry from Baudelaire to the Present*. New York: Laurel/Dell Publishing Co., 1962.

Martin, J., and R. Harre. "Metaphor in Science." In *Metaphor: Problems and Perspectives*, ed. David S. Miall, 89–105.

Martin, Wallace. *Recent Theories of Narrative*. Ithaca: Cornell University Press, 1986.

Metaphor and Thought. Andrew Ortony, ed. Cambridge: Cambridge University Press, 1979.

Metaphor: Problems and Perspectives. David S. Miall, ed. Atlantic Highlands, N.J.: Humanities Press, 1982.

Mify narodov mira. Entsiklopediia. 2 vols. Moscow: Sovetskaia entsiklopediia, 1980.

Miller, D.A. *Narrative and Its Discontents*. Princeton: Princeton University Press, 1981.

Milosz, Czeslaw. *The Land of Ulro*, trans. Louis Iribarne. New York: Farrar, Strauss, Giroux, 1984.

Modleski, Tania. *The Women Who Knew Too Much: Hitchcock and Feminist Theory*. New York and London: Methuen, 1988.

Moore, F.C.T. "On Taking Metaphor Literally." In *Metaphor: Problems and Perspectives*, ed. David S. Miall, 2–7.

Morson, Gary Saul, and Caryl Emerson. *Mikhail Bakhtin: Creation of a Prosaics*. Stanford: Stanford University Press, 1990.

Muir, Edwin. *An Autobiography*. New York: W. Sloane Associates, 1954.

Mulvey, Laura. "Afterthoughts on 'Visual Pleasure and Narrative Cinema' Inspired by *Duel in the Sun*." *Framework* 15–17 (1981): 12–15.

―――. "Changes: Thoughts of Myth, Narrative, and Historical Experience." *History Workshop Journal* 23 (Spring 1987): 1–19.

―――. "Visual Pleasure and Narrative Cinema." *Screen* 16, 3 (1975): 6–18.

Nabokov, Vladimir. *Speak, Memory*. New York: Pyramid Books, 1947/1968.

Nadaff, Sandra. *Arabesque: Narrative Structure and the Aesthetics of Repetition in "The Thousand and One Nights"*. Evanston: Northwestern University Press, 1991.

Nevzgliadova, Elena. "Eta prekrasnaia zhizn'." *Avrora* 10 (1986): 111–13.

Newman, Ernest. *The Wagner Operas*. New York: Alfred A. Knopf, 1949.

Nisbet, Robert A. *Social Change and History*. New York: Oxford University Press, 1969.

Oja, Matt F. "Shalamov, Solzhenitsyn, and the Mission of Memory." *Survey* 29, 2 (Summer 1985): 62–69.

Okudzhava, Bulat. *Proza i poeziia*. Frankfurt/Main: Posev, 1968.

Olsen, Stein Haugom. "Understanding Literary Metaphor." In *Metaphor: Problems and Perspectives*, ed. David S. Miall.

On Metaphor. Sheldon Sacks, ed. London and Chicago: University of Chicago Press, 1978/1979.

Ortega y Gasset, José. *The Dehumanization of Art* and *Notes on the Novel*. Princeton: Princeton University Press, 1948.

Pasternak, Boris. *Doktor Zhivago*. Ann Arbor: University of Michigan Press, 1958.

Piaget, Jean. *The Language and Thought of the Child*. Cleveland and New York: World Pub./Meridian Books, 1955/1969.

―――. *Plays, Dreams, and Imitation in Childhood*. New York and London: W.W. Norton, 1962.

Piskunova, S., and S. Piskunov. "Uroki sozerkal'ia." *Oktiabr'* 8 (1988): 188–98.

Plautus. *Works*. London and Cambridge, Mass.: Harvard University Press, 1979.

Polianskaia, Irina. *Predlagaemye obstoiatel'stva*. Moscow: Molodaia gvardiia, 1988.

Porter, Hal. *The Watcher on the Cast-Iron Balcony*. London, 1963.

Prescott, Peter S. "Extravagant Imaginings." *Newsweek* (May 15, 1989): 80.

Pushkin, Aleksandr. *Polnoe sobranie sochinenii*, Vol. 6. Moscow: Akademiia, 1937.

―――. *Sobranie sochinenii*. 10 vols. Moscow: Khudlit, 1974–78.

Quintilian. *Institutio Oratoria*, trans. J.E. Butler. Loeb ed. Cambridge, Mass.: Harvard University Press, 1st ed. 1920; repr. 1980.

Raine, Kathleen, *Farewell Happy Fields*. London: Hamish Hamilton, 1973.

Rancour-Laferrière, Daniel; Vera Loseva; and Aleksej Lunkov. "Violence in the Garden: A Work by Tolstaja in Kleinian Perspective." *Slavic and East European Journal* 39 (Winter 1995): 524–34.

Ransel, David. *Women's Studies in Indiana* 15, 3 (1990): 1–3.

Remnick, David. "The Literary Limits of Glasnost." *Washington Post* (April 18, 1988): B6.

Richards, I.A. *The Philosophy of Rhetoric*. Oxford: Oxford University Press, 1936/1971.

Ricoeur, Paul. "The Metaphorical Process of Cognition, Imagination, and Feeling." In *On Metaphor*, ed. Sheldon Sacks, 141–57.

―――. *The Rule of Metaphor*. Toronto and Buffalo: University of Toronto Press, 1977.

————. *Time and Narrative*. 3 vols. Chicago and London: University of Chicago Press, 1983–85.

Rorty, Richard. "Habermas and Lyotard on Postmodernity." In *Praxis International* 4 (April 1984): 32–44.

Said, Edward. *Beginnings: Intention and Method*. New York: Columbia University Press, 1985.

Scholes, Robert. *Protocols of Reading*. New Haven: Yale University Press, 1989. Repr. New York: Alfred H. Knopf, 1991.

Shishkova, Raisa. "Nich'i babushki na zolotom kryl'tse." *Kontinent* 56 (1988): 398–402.

Singer, Irving. *The Nature of Love*. Chicago and London: University of Chicago Press, 1984.

Sloan, James Park. "Kosinski's War." *The New Yorker* (October 10, 1994): 46–53.

Soriano, Marc. "From Tales of Warning to Formulettes." In *The Child's Part*, ed. Peter Brooks, 24–43.

Spivak, P. "Vo sne i naiavu." *Oktiabr'* 2 (1988): 201–3.

Steiner, Wendy. *The Colors of Rhetoric*. Chicago: University of Chicago Press, 1982.

Thompson, Stith. *The Folktale*. Berkeley and Los Angeles: University of California Press, 1977.

Tolstaia, Tat'iana. "Limpopo." *Znamia* 11 (1991): 45–70.

————. *"Na zolotom kryl'tse sideli . . . "*. Moscow: Molodaia gvardiia, 1987.

————. "Ne mogu molchat'." *Ogonek* (March 14, 1990): 31.

————. "Noch'." *Oktiabr'* 4 (1987): 89–95.

————. "Plamen' nebesnyi." *Avrora* 11 (1987): 131–38.

————. "Poet i muza." *Novyi mir* 12 (1986): 113–19.

————. "Samaia liubimaia." *Avrora* 10 (1986): 92–110.

————. "Serafim." *Novyi mir* 12 (1986): 130–33.

————. "Siuzhet." *Sintaksis* 31 (1991): 100–9.

————. "Somnambula v tumane." *Novyi mir* 7 (1988): 8–26.

————. "Ten' na zakate." *Literaturnaia gazeta* 30 (July 23, 1986): 7.

————. "Vyshel mesiats iz tumana." *Krest'ianka* 4 (1987): 32–35.

Tolstaya, Tatyana. *On the Golden Porch*, trans. Antonina Bouis. New York: Alfred A. Knopf, 1989.

————. *Sleepwalker in a Fog*, trans. Jamey Gambrell. New York: Alfred A. Knopf, 1991.

————. "The Age of Innocence." *The New York Review of Books* (October 21, 1990): 24–26.

————. "A Little Man Is a Normal Man." *Moscow News* 8 (1987): 10.

————. "Discovering America." *London Review of Books* (June 1989): 23.

————. "In a Land of Conquered Men." *Moscow News* (September 24–October 1, 1989): 13.

————. "In Cannibalistic Times." *The New York Review of Books* (April 11, 1991): 3–6.

————. "The Nation Needs Hard Currency." *Moscow News* 11 (March 25–April 1, 1990): 14.

————. "Notes from Underground." *The New York Review of Books* (May 31, 1990): 3–7.

————. "President Potemkin." *The New Republic* (May 27, 1991): 27–35.

————. "Russian Lessons." *The New York Review of Books* (October 19, 1996): 7.

Tolstoi, L.N. *Polnoe sobranie sochinenii*. Vol. 19. Moscow: Khudlit., 1935.

Tolstoy, Leo. *Anna Karenina*, trans. David Magarshack. New York: Signet/New American Library, 1961.

Tracy, David. "Metaphor and Religion: The Test Case of Christian Texts." In *On Metaphor*, ed. Sheldon Sacks, 89–104.

Trifonov, Yuri. "Time Is an Understanding." *Soviet Literature* 1 (1990).

Turner, Victor. *Dramas, Fields, and Metaphors: Symbolic Action in Human Society.* Ithaca: Cornell University Press, 1974.

Tynianov, Iurii. *Arkhaisty i novatory.* Leningrad, 1928.

———. *Poetika.* Moscow: Nauka, 1977, 198–226 and 284–309.

Vail', Petr, and Aleksandr Genis. "Popytka k begstvu: II: Gorodok v Tabakerke—Proza Tat'iany Tolstoi." *Sintaksis* 24 (1988): 116–31.

Vasilevskii, Andrei. "Nochi kholodny." *Druzhba narodov* 7 (1988): 256–58.

von Franz, Marie Louise. *Interpretation of Fairy Tales.* Dallas: Spring Publications, 1987.

Voznesenskii, Andrei. "Anketa 'LR': Mezhdu proshlym i budushchim." *Literaturnaia Rossiia* (January 1, 1988): 4.

Vysotskaia, Natal'ia. "Obretenie novogo dykhaniia." *Literaturnaia Rossiia* 9 (February 27, 1987).

Wachtel, Andrew Baruch. *The Battle for Childhood.* Stanford: Stanford University Press, 1990.

Waters, Lindsay. "Introduction. Paul de Man: Life and Works." In de Man, *Critical Writings, 1953–1978.*

Weldon, Fay. *Letters to Alice: On First Reading Austen.* London: Hodder and Stoughton, 1984.

White, Hayden. *Metahistory: The Historical Imagination in Nineteenth-Century Europe.* Baltimore: Johns Hopkins University Press, 1973.

———. *The Tropics of Discourse.* Baltimore: Johns Hopkins University Press, 1978.

———. "The Value of Narrativity in the Representation of Reality." *Critical Inquiry* 7 (1980): 5–27.

Wolf, Christa. *The Quest for Christa T.,* trans. Christopher Middleton. New York: Farrar, Strauss, Giroux, 1970.

———. "Reading and Writing." In Wolf, *The Writer's Dimensions. Selected Essays,* ed. Alexander Stephan. London: Virago, 1993, 20–48.

Zamiatin, Evgenii. *My.* New York: Inter-Language Literary Associates, 1967.

Zholkovsky, Alexander. *Text Counter Text: Readings in Russian Literary History.* Stanford: Stanford University Press, 1994.

Zolotonosov, Mikhail. "Mechty i fantomy." *Literaturnoe obozrenie* 4 (1987): 58–61.

Index

About the Author

Currently the Chairwoman of the Slavic Department at the University of Pittsburgh, Helena Goscilo specializes in Romanticism, contemporary Russian literature and culture, and Slavic women's writing. Her publications include articles on Pushkin, Lermontov, Tolstoi, and Bulgakov, and, in the last four years, the following volumes: *Skirted Issues: The Discreteness and Indiscretions of Russian Women's Prose* (Russian Studies in Literature, M.E. Sharpe, 1993); *Fruits of Her Plume: Essays on Contemporary Women's Culture* (M.E. Sharpe, 1993); *Lives in Transit* (Ardis, 1993); *Dehexing Sex: Womanhood Before and After Glasnost* (University of Michigan Press, 1996); and *Russia*Women*Culture*, co-edited with Beth Holmgren (Indiana University Press, 1996). Her works in progress are a monograph on Liudmila Petrushevskaia, a cultural study of the New Russians (co-written with Nadezhda Azhgikina), and a collection of essays on Russian women as products and producers of Russian culture.